Perspectives
on Pastoral Ministry

Perspectives on Pastoral Ministry

EDITED BY
*Maurice Elliott and
Patrick G. McGlinchey*

WIPF & STOCK · Eugene, Oregon

PERSPECTIVES ON PASTORAL MINISTRY

Copyright © 2026 Wipf and Stock Publishers. All rights reserved. Except for brief quotations in critical publications or reviews, no part of this book may be reproduced in any manner without prior written permission from the publisher. Write: Permissions, Wipf and Stock Publishers, 199 W. 8th Ave., Suite 3, Eugene, OR 97401.

Wipf & Stock
An Imprint of Wipf and Stock Publishers
199 W. 8th Ave., Suite 3
Eugene, OR 97401

www.wipfandstock.com

PAPERBACK ISBN: 978-1-6667-8976-8
HARDCOVER ISBN: 978-1-6667-8977-5
EBOOK ISBN: 978-1-6667-8978-2

Material from *The Book of Common Prayer* copyright © RCB 2004 with permission.
Scripture quotations marked NIV taken from The Holy Bible, New International Version®, NIV®. Copyright © 1973, 1978, 1984, 2011 by Biblica, Inc. Used with permission of Zondervan. All rights reserved worldwide. zondervan.com.
Scripture quotations marked NRSV taken from New Revised Standard Version Bible, copyright © 1989 National Council of the Churches of Christ in the United States of America. Used by permission. All rights reserved worldwide.
Scripture quotations marked (KJV) are taken from the King James Version, public domain.
Scripture quotations marked ESV are taken from are from The ESV® Bible (The Holy Bible, English Standard Version®), © 2001 by Crossway, a publishing ministry of Good News Publishers. Used by permission. All rights reserved.

Contents

Contributors | vii
Acknowledgements | ix
Abbreviations | x

Introduction | Maurice Elliott | 1

BIBLICAL AND THEOLOGICAL PRINCIPLES

1 Pastoral Care in the Christian Tradition |
Cynthia Bennett Brown | 15

2 Love and Pastoral Ministry: A Case Study of Paul the Pastor |
Patrick Mitchel | 32

3 Christian Maturity as the Goal of Pastoral Ministry |
Patrick McGlinchey | 51

ANGLICAN PERSPECTIVES

4 The Bible and Pastoral Ministry: "Two Facets of One Reality" |
William Olhausen | 73

5 Pastoral Care in the Anglican Ordinal | Harold Miller | 92

6 Discovering Resilience Within Pastoral Ministry |
Maurice Elliott | 114

7 "Pastor pastorum": The Responsibility of a Bishop |
Patricia Storey | 135

PASTORAL SKILLS

8 "Rejoice with Those Who Rejoice, Weep with Those Who Weep": Reflections on Pastoral Visiting | ROBIN STOCKITT | 151

9 Pastoral Care in Christian Marriage | DREW GIBSON | 168

10 "With Hearts That See": Ministry in a Healthcare Setting | COLUMBA TOMAN, OP | 187

11 Bereavement Care: Pastoral Presence and Meaningful Hope | DANIEL NUZUM | 201

12 Establishing Collaborative Pastoral Ministry | JOHN ALDERDICE | 212

13 Ministering Cross-Culturally to Those on the Margins | LAURENCE GRAHAM | 232

14 The Role of Mentoring in Pastoral Development | CHRISTINA BAXTER | 252

Conclusion | PATRICK MCGLINCHEY | 273

Bibliography | 283
Name Index | 299
Subject Index | 302

Contributors

John Alderdice is currently the Northeastern District Superintendent of the Methodist Church in Ireland, and a former President. He has a deep concern for ministry and leadership development as a means of advancing God's mission in the world today.

Christina Baxter is a former Principal of Saint John's College, Nottingham. She served on the Archbishop's Council and as chair of the House of Laity of the Church of England. She regularly leads training sessions on aspects of ministry and discipleship.

Cynthia Bennett Brown is Director of the MA in Theology and Ministry at Cranmer Hall, Durham. She teaches and supervises in Christian doctrine, theological reflection, and church ministries, disciplines that both inform and are informed by Christian pastoral care.

Maurice Elliott is Director of the Church of Ireland Theological Institute and lecturer in homiletics and church leadership. His publications include volumes on *Perspectives on Preaching* (2016) and *Perspectives on Prayer and Spirituality* (2021).

Drew Gibson is Professor Emeritus of Practical Theology at Union Theological College, Belfast (UTC). After ordination and six years in pastoral ministry, he served for six years in East Africa, before returning to teach at Belfast Bible College, then fifteen years at UTC.

Laurence Graham has been a Methodist Minister for almost three decades and currently serves in Dublin Central Mission, which includes a congregation representing at least twenty nations. He is also the general secretary of Irish Methodist World Mission Partnership.

Patrick McGlinchey is lecturer in missiology and pastoral studies in the Church of Ireland Theological Institute. His publications include *Atonement as Gift* (2014) and *Ratzinger's Augustinianism and Evangelicalism* (2017).

Harold Miller is the retired Bishop of the Diocese of Down and Dromore in the Church of Ireland. Earlier in his career he taught liturgy at St. John's College, Nottingham.

Patrick Mitchel is Director of Learning and Senior Lecturer in Theology at the Irish Bible Institute in Dublin where he has worked for thirty years. He is author of numerous publications, particularly related to Christianity in Ireland as well as New Testament studies.

Daniel Nuzum is a healthcare chaplain and CPE supervisor based in Cork. He also serves as an adjunct lecturer at the College of Medicine and Health in University College, Cork, and is a senior researcher in spiritual care at the European Research Institute for Chaplains in Healthcare based at KU Leuven.

William Olhausen is a Church of Ireland parish minister in the Diocese of Cork, Cloyne, and Ross, where he also serves as an examining chaplain to the Anglican bishop. He is an adjunct lecturer at Trinity College Dublin for the Church of Ireland Theological Institute.

Robin Stockitt was for several years the minister of the Anglican church in Freiburg, Germany, followed by seven years of rural ministry in Northern Ireland. He has studied theology at Ridley Hall, Cambridge, St. Andrews, and Tübingen University.

Patricia Storey is the Church of Ireland Bishop of Meath and Kildare. Within the central church she focuses on care for clergy, leads a mental health project, and chairs the Church of Ireland Youth Department and Central Communications Board.

Columba Toman OP is a Catholic priest and a member of the Dominican Order. He is currently the program leader of undergraduate theological studies in the Priory Institute, Tallaght, and lectures in The Dominican Studium, Dublin.

Acknowledgments

We wish to thank each of the contributors for their generous gifts of time, effort, and expertise. Each have shed fresh light on what it means to exercise pastoral ministry well.

We are also grateful to Wipf and Stock for enabling what began as a seed idea to develop into an exciting final product, which we hope will be of benefit to the wider church. Special thanks are due to Matt Wimer and George Callihan who have been supportive editorial guides on the journey to publication. Finally, we thank the Representative Church Body for the generous subvention towards publishing costs.

Abbreviations

- AMICUM — Anglican Methodist International Commission for Unity in Mission
- BCP 1662 — Church of England. *The Book of Common Prayer*. Cambridge: John Baskerville, 1662.
- BCP 2004 — Church of Ireland. *The Book of Common Prayer*. Dublin: Representative Body of the Church of Ireland, 2004.
- BRF — Bible Reading Fellowship
- CME — Continuing Ministerial Education
- CPE — Clinical Pastoral Education
- ESV — English Standard Version
- KJV — King James Version
- NRSV — New Revised Standard Version
- NIV — New International Version
- OP — Order of Preachers
- PGD — Prolonged Grief Disorder
- RCN — Royal College of Nursing
- REB — Revised English Bible

The translations used in the various biblical citations have been left to the individual author's discretion.

Introduction

Maurice Elliott

Setting a Context

Given that the ministry of Jesus was causing such a stir among the Jewish religious authorities, it was no surprise that on one occasion, somewhere in and around the temple courts in Jerusalem, a teacher of the law quizzed him as to what was the greatest commandment. In reply Jesus reached immediately for the *Shema Israel* of Deuteronomy—"Hear O Israel, The Lord our God, the Lord is one. Love the Lord your God with all your heart and with all your soul and with all your strength" (6:4–5)—and he then added, "And the second is like it: 'Love your neighbor as yourself.'"[1] Inasmuch as these two commands capture the essence of faithful Christian discipleship, it seems appropriate that a consideration of pastoral care should take its lead from such a template. As neatly summarized by Alastair Campbell, pastoral ministry is about "enabling people and communities to love God and each other better."[2] In what follows, therefore, our hope as editors is that readers will be inspired towards this grand and overarching purpose.

Whereas these twin dimensions of the pastor's duty may sound lofty and even desirable, in truth the multifaceted nature of the pastoral task renders it both blessed and burdensome. The pastoral role involves acting as an under-shepherd, and undoubtedly pastors are bound to their flocks in a close and loving relationship. All the evidence suggests that for the most part those in pastoral office do genuinely flourish in their ministry.

---

1. Matt 22:39. All Scripture quotations in the introduction are taken from the NIV.
2. Campbell, *Pastoral Care*, 188.

Yet even the very metaphor "shepherd" serves as a reminder that "the sheep" in question, just like real sheep, can be stubborn, unruly, wayward, irritable, and beset with all kinds of needs. Moreover, even as they seek to serve the well-being of their congregants, pastors themselves remain "sheep"—in other words, they, too, must continue to live as disciples of Christ—and a significant aspect of the challenge that their role presents lies in balancing care for their own needs against being so continually focused on the needs of others.

In his exploration of *The Clergy's Experience of Pastoral Care*, Sean Cathie notes that in the contemporary context such tensions within the pastoral office have become more accentuated, and that those who serve as pastors nowadays feel under real pressure. Drawing on six identified sources of occupational stress—volume overload, lack of control, absence of appropriate support, relationships at work, role-based stress, and changes in the job and the organization—Cathie suggests that virtually all of these can be applied to the pastorate. Pastors experience significant "volume overload" when the competing demands of too much to do and too few resources with which to do it become unsustainable. This can result in feeling overwhelmed, and invariably it leads to a deeper sense of feeling unsupported, even within the normal networks of family and friends. Or again, many pastors see themselves as having been let down by their church hierarchy, citing a lack of clarity concerning their role and an ever-increasing level of expectation. Just ask those who serve about how conflicted they feel when torn between caring for others, taking charge of administrative systems, and having responsibility for statutory compliance, with such "role conflict"[3] then resulting in job dissatisfaction, lower self-confidence, reduced self-esteem, and diminished levels of motivation. Cathie further observes that such difficulties are compounded by the "accumulated disruption to the ecology of relations between Church and society."[4] Certainly in the West the church has lost its cultural prominence, and, while there may be vestiges of former glory, such as fine buildings, church schools, and certain university foundations, any prestige that being a pastor may have previously carried has effectively disappeared. Simply put, while it is accurate to suggest that being a pastor can be rightly considered the highest of all callings, the ministry to which it brings those who answer that call is perhaps the hardest work of all.

---

3. Cathie, *Clergy's Experience*, 11.
4. Cathie, *Clergy's Experience*, 8.

A Blend of Call, Character and Competence

Even a glance at the contents of this book will indicate that those who serve as pastors are expected to be multitaskers, with an ability to live among complex and often fast-moving sets of coordinates. Yet underlying the role in its entirety, there remain the fundamental requirements of call, character, and competence.[5]

In relation to the matter of "call," it is vital for pastors to cling persistently to the fact that theirs is not a job but a vocation. Since the pastoral journey invariably brings with it both good days and difficult days, sometimes the only thing that pastors may have to fall back upon is that inner conviction that stems from an affirmation deep within their hearts that they have been chosen by God to carry out this role. Like Paul in 2 Corinthians, even though the "thorn" cannot be removed, the assurance of God's sufficient grace remains.[6] In the sixteenth century, Martin Luther was known to be fond of wordplays, and one of these to which he often returned, as a kind of ministerial mantra, had to do with the German term *Aufgabe*, meaning "a task." What intrigued Luther was that the etymology of *Aufgabe* could be linked directly to *Gabe*, the corresponding word for "a gift." Hence, he would declare that, where God had called someone into a particular task—an *Aufgabe*—God would also provide the necessary equipping—the *Gabe*—for that task to be completed. On many occasions it is precisely that quiet sense of personal calling that alone enables pastors to disentangle some of the frustrations with which they struggle.

Secondly, there is an absolute imperative of godly character. Writing to Timothy as one charged with pastoring a group of churches around Ephesus, Paul advised, "Do not let anyone look down on you because you are young, but set an example for the believers in speech, in life, in love, in faith, and in purity."[7] Each of these attributes is a manifestation of Christlike character, and to display them consistently is part of the challenge that every pastor must face. Likewise, when giving his apostolic advice concerning the selection of elders and deacons, it is striking that Paul's major emphasis is again on character ahead of function. In fact, whereas in 1 Tim 3 he lists as many as eleven vital personal qualities for

---

5. Lawrence, *Growing Leaders*, 7.
6. 2 Cor 12:7–10.
7. 1 Tim 4:12.

eldership, the only functional requirement is an ability to teach.[8] This is not to suggest that those who serve are to be paragons of perfection—even at the height of his powers John Wesley, for instance, knew that he was deeply flawed and once reportedly admitted, "Worst of all my foes I fear the enemy within"—however, it is to insist that those who are charged with pastoral leadership must live up to certain standards, and that their own walk with God should set an example to those under their authority. In the words of Doug Gay, albeit that he speaks primarily about the enterprise of preaching, those in pastoral ministry ought to be able to say, "Look at me when I am talking to you."[9]

Lastly, in order to be effective there is a need for pastors to be competent. A number of years ago I recall talking to a young mum at our church toddler group and I was convinced that she had told me her husband was a pastor. Not surprisingly my interest was piqued. A few moments later, however, it transpired that I had completely misheard her, and that her husband was in fact a plasterer—so much for my sense of hearing! And yet, perhaps there is something worth following in this unintended analogy. To be a reputable plasterer requires years of training; there is an apprenticeship to serve; there are skills to acquire; there is a sense of pride in the quality of one's workmanship; and when the craft is put to good use, there is usually an outcome that brings satisfaction to the customer, smoothing over the cracks and creating a better finish. Likewise, those in pastoral ministry must learn requisite skills. They, too, can be fulfilled as they are privileged to see what God is doing through their ministry. While there may not be quick fixes to some of the problems that they encounter, over the long haul they, too, can be confident that their work is making a difference that can result in transformation to the quality of people's lives and will ultimately lead towards a better "finish" eternally.

In their recently published volume, *On Being a Pastor: Understanding Our Calling and Our Work*, Derek Prime and Alastair Begg consider a number of essential competencies: disciplines such as prayer and devotional life; a commitment to study, preaching, and the care of others; the practicalities of conducting worship; the responsibility to lead and delegate; and the ability to manage family life and leisure time. Their final chapter, "Perils Tempered by Privileges," in many ways once again captures the kind of ambivalence that underlies the pastoral office. The

---

8. 1 Tim 3:1–7.
9. Gay, *God be in my Mouth*, 115.

authors discuss social and moral issues; opposition and the spiritual battle; laziness, discouragement, and vulnerability to criticism; overinvolvement in people's problems; stress; escapism; and pride. Such a list could be extended, and for all such challenges of the ministerial role there are essential skills that need to be honed.

As the editors of this volume, we would draw the attention of readers to our own priorities here. This book forms volume 3 of a trilogy, and we make no apology for emphasizing that arguably what matters most for pastoral effectiveness should align itself with the two earlier titles in this series, namely "preaching" and "prayer."[10] This in turn conforms to the portrayal of pastoral ministry as depicted in the New Testament. In Acts, the reason for establishing the order of deacons was so that the apostles might devote themselves to "prayer and the ministry of the word" (6:4) and in a similar vein, within the list of word ministries put forward by Paul in Ephesians, it is clearly indicated that the gift of being a "pastor and [a] teacher" is necessarily unified (4:11).

Chapter Overview

So, what then do the various chapters that follow offer the thoughtful reader? The book is divided into three broad sections, the first of which brings together three essays exploring "Biblical and Theological Principles" of Christian pastoral care. The discussion begins with an overview of "Pastoral Care in the Christian Tradition," in which Cindy Bennett Brown synthesizes more than two thousand years of theological heritage. Bennett Brown differentiates between generic pastoral care within wider society and that which is demonstrably Christian—she rightly insists that the latter must be "an expression of, and response to, the good news of divine mercy," and that true "soul care" must deal with spiritual realities, not solely the felt-needs of recipients. In keeping with the witness of the early church, Brown notes that pastoral ministry must be grounded in the Christian virtues of humility, empathy, and non-condemnation, that it ought to "prepare believers for the future life which Christ has promised," and ultimately, that it should draw others more fully into the life of the church.

---

10. See Elliott and McGlinchey, *Perspectives on Preaching*; and Elliott and McGlinchey, *Perspectives on Prayer and Spirituality*.

Following this, Patrick Mitchel takes up the theme of Pauline theology in relation to pastoral care. Mitchel foregrounds his discussion against the concepts of "love" and "Christoformity," positing that, insofar as Paul's primary goal was to ensure that Christian believers might enjoy healthy relationality and be found "blameless" at the coming of Christ, all his theology was essentially pastoral. Mitchell draws attention to Paul's method of framing his apostolic counsel within both past and future points of reference. Hence, for example, because of what Christ had already accomplished, evil was defeated; and on account of what he would bring in the future, bodily purity and living up to certain standards of behavior did matter. Mitchel emphasizes important Pauline motifs such as anxiety on the part of the pastor, collegiality, and the need for dedicated prayer, and, as with Bennett Brown, he insists that authentic pastoral ministry can only be animated by the Spirit.

Finally in this first section, Patrick McGlinchey unpacks the topic of "Christian Maturity as the Goal of Pastoral Ministry." McGlinchey notes the famous expression of C. S. Lewis concerning the need for Christian disciples to become like "little Christs," and, contrary to what he sees as a prevailing mood of pessimism in both church and society, he argues that real change can happen. McGlinchey's assertion is that for this to take place there must be an inner working of the Spirit and a strong commitment on the part of the Christ-follower to the practices of self-discipline, matched by the indispensable support of the church community. He speaks openly of his own journey in discipleship, and he offers a suite of indicators against which progress towards spiritual maturity might be gauged—these include cherishing what it means to belong to others, the capacity to love, a self-giving pattern of life, a passion for unity, and an attitude of joy.

Given that the majority of the contributors to this collection are members of the Church of Ireland, the second section moves to an excursus on "Anglican Perspectives." To begin with, William Olhausen presents a fascinating overview of the place of the Bible within pastoral ministry, suggesting as per Michael Ramsey, that these are essentially "two facets of one reality." If pastors are to be effective, then a robust grounding in Scripture is *sine qua non*, and Olhausen notes the symbolism of the Anglican rite of ordination according to which each candidate is presented with a Bible—the tools of the trade, as it were. Olhausen discusses how the pastor-teacher's role must be textured with love for God and love for people; in willingness to bear a cost; and through cherishing the "Tradition," and he helpfully addresses the need for critical awareness in the task of interpreting the Bible without diminishing its authority. His piece ends with a heart-warming reminder that biblical proclamation is the primary means by which people are led to Christ-crucified, and hence that pastoral ministry cannot forsake its rootedness in what Olhausen portrays as "this diagram of love."

Harold Miller's chapter takes the reader into a discussion of "Pastoral Care in the Anglican Ordinal." Miller's contention is simple—from beginning to end, the Ordinal is all about pastoral ministry—and he develops this thesis under ten headings. According to the Anglican rite, those who serve, whether as presbyters or bishops, are enjoined to prayerfulness, to acting diligently as shepherds and teachers, and to being an example for the flock. Moreover, because this "cure of souls" involves such a weighty responsibility, it warrants thorough screening and careful preparation—in Miller's view the existence of self-styled pastors is not something with which Anglicans are likely to feel comfortable. In his final sections, Miller surveys pastoral care in the Anglican tradition as a ministry of "presence," "protection," and "outreach," before ending with a sober reminder that one day it is also "a ministry which God will judge."

Maurice Elliott's chapter introduces a vital question—how might pastors find greater resilience in light of the challenges that they face? Given the way in which ministerial experience often oscillates between privileges and pressure-points, Elliott suggests that many pastors are apt to feel that they have "treasure in jars of clay" (2 Cor 4:7). Against this backdrop, he then invokes the five ministerial metaphors of the Anglican Ordinal, but in reverse, in order to assess, not how clergy can manifest what they mean to others but rather how they themselves can be recipients of "shepherding," "service," "watching," "teaching," and "stewardship." The discussion centers on three main principles—pastors adhering more rigorously to self-care; pastors being more effectively cared for by those in episcopal oversight church authorities; and, most of all, pastors finding a rhythm of life whereby they can be ministered to by Christ himself, the one who is the ultimate shepherd, the perfect servant, the vigilant sentinel, the faithful messenger, and the wise steward.

As a final contribution to the Anglican perspectives, Pat Storey documents some of her at times poignant reflections on what it means to be a bishop. Storey was the first woman to be elected as an Anglican bishop in Ireland or Britain, and she speaks with the wisdom of significant lived experience. Whereas the call to be a bishop implies acting as *pastor pastorum*—the pastor who is charged with caring for the other pastors—much of Storey's treatment of the topic bears upon issues that inhibit this, challenges such as the burden of administration; the weight of educational, ecclesial, or statutory processes; and, perhaps most demanding of all, the duty to enact discipline when complaints are made against members of the clergy. Storey writes honestly of personal loneliness, and she suggests that the task of oversight requires more substantial support, greater scope for delegation, the provision of induction training, and ongoing professional development.

In the final section, "Pastoral Skills," seven authors offer important contributions on specific areas of pastoral competence. In a delightful narrative piece, Robin Stockitt considers the matter of pastoral visiting. Stockitt invokes a number of cameos from his own experience of local church ministry, and he brings out of these a list of helpful pastoral principles: the need for "safety" and "authenticity"; the importance of "listening"; "presence"; "cultural" awareness; the recognition of "limits"; and, perhaps most notably, the skill of "improvisation," which can acknowledge the uniqueness of every individual pastoral encounter. The chapter ends with Stockitt's critique of what he sees as misplaced metaphors for pastoral ministry such as "doctor, psychotherapist, handyman, coach, and lawyer," and his assertion of that which is preferable, namely, that pastors see themselves as "fellow pilgrims" alongside their flock.

In his chapter on "Pastoral Care in Marriage," Drew Gibson walks the reader through a *tour de force* of practical pastoral awareness in relation to marriage preparation and the daily cut and thrust of married life itself. Gibson broaches the understanding of marriage as "covenant," suggesting that it can act as a witness to the surrounding culture, and he notes the imperative of viewing marriage as part of an extensive network of other relationships. While Gibson's firm belief is that marriage ought to enable both spouses to flourish, he equally recognizes with a wise pastoral heart that difficulties do emerge, and in such circumstances he cautions pastors against overreaching their own ability when there may be an urgent need to refer a couple to other professional agencies.

The issue of "Ministry in a Healthcare Setting" is addressed by Columba Toman, OP. Guided for the most part by his own Catholic theological perspective, Toman explores three key principles of effective hospital ministry: "dignity," "community," and "vocation." The "hearts that see," of which his title speaks, are described very simply as those who minister to the sick by looking on them with the eyes of Christ, and Toman applies his thinking in particular to the challenging matter of end-of-life care. Whereas the role of hospital chaplaincy carries a clear sense of specialism, readers with a general interest in more regular pastoral ministry will undoubtedly derive much benefit from Toman's many useful insights.

Closely related to Toman's topic is Daniel Nuzum's chapter on "Bereavement Care." Nuzum writes out of his own professional expertise in dealing with trauma, grief and loss, and he concentrates much of what he says on the need for pastoral "accompaniment." Underlying any experience of loss is a natural sense of "attachment" to loved-ones, and hence, with the rupture that is caused by death, there is a need for the pastor both to help the bereaved to face into their new present-day reality, and to proclaim to them hope as found in the doctrine of the communion of saints. Nuzum speaks candidly of how impactful grief can be, and he prudently identifies a range of appropriate pastoral "supports": the funeral service itself, communal gatherings, memorial events, and other symbols, all of which also offer their attendant and "multisensory" rituals. Bereavement care, he posits, is about "acknowledgment" of pain, "making of meaning," and the establishment of "continuing bonds," and, given this, Nuzum emphasizes the importance of ongoing care long after such rituals have been enacted in order that memories can be sustained.

In chapter 12, John Alderdice discusses "collaborative ministry" as informed by the thinking of John Wesley and early Methodism. Alderdice observes that, at its best, pastoral ministry will seek to prioritize enabling others and releasing their gifts, so that this in turn can become a means of bringing more lay persons into Christian service. In the eighteenth-century Methodist revival movement, Wesley was guided by important pastoral principles such as the need for house-to-house visitation, the importance of the minster's spiritual and theological development, and the prioritizing of good relationships with other denominations. Since what mattered most for Wesley was a sense of call, a display of virtuous love, and an emphasis on people ahead of programs, Alderdice infers an application of all these principles to the contemporary church and not least given the reality of declining numbers in many Western contexts.

A second Methodist voice is that of Laurence Graham who opens up a subject that is of increasing importance in the twenty-first century: "Ministering Cross-Culturally to Those on the Margins." Against the backdrop of rising levels of migration as a global phenomenon, Graham adduces a number of theological perspectives for pastors who may find themselves dealing with different nationalities within their congregations.

Uppermost here are a strong belief in the fundamental unity of the body of Christ and the need for forthrightness with regard to latent attitudes of racism. Graham has dealt extensively with migrants in his own ministry, and he notes how those arriving from elsewhere are simultaneously strong and weak—strong in that they have chosen to leave home; yet vulnerable insofar as they know little of their new surroundings. As pastors may seek to engage with this sensitive issue, he advises that they should be mindful of dealing with vastly differing spiritual values, and, for this reason, Graham insists on the need to avoid making generalized assumptions.

Finally, Christina Baxter offers the reader a thoughtful piece that explores how the practice of mentoring might assist in pastoral ministry. Baxter relates some of her own formation as she revisits the years of her early Christian discipleship, and in particular she notes the influence of "significant" others in her spiritual development. Along with this, Baxter faces into what can be some of the perilous pitfalls of unwise and insufficiently regulated mentoring arrangements. Most of all, however, she calls for this aspect of pastoral work to be understood as a grace of the Holy Spirit—the one who is love, who brings conviction, who ministers truth, and who instills power, insight, knowledge and freedom—suggesting that he often accomplishes these very things through the relationships that are established between a mentor and a mentee.

Concluding Comments

The contents of this book address many aspects of pastoral ministry across a broad canvas of biblical witness, historical tradition, the theological framework of Anglican heritage, and the multiple areas of necessary skill. Given the breadth of what pastors do daily, it would be impossible to cover every base. Nevertheless, our hope as editors is that those who serve in pastoral ministry may find in what follows renewed strength and enhanced vision for everything that their calling represents within the church and to the world. To be a pastor is a lofty privilege and an onerous responsibility, and, moreover, the way in which the cultural context, especially in the West, now militates against religious faith and belonging has rendered that task even more challenging. Such is the scale of the pastoral calling that it is sometimes said, if an individual can countenance doing anything else over the course of their life, that other thing is what they ought to do. And yet, as already mentioned, the promise and sufficiency of grace does not change. Ultimately, pastors do not serve in their own strength; rather they live according to the truth of what Jesus himself declares: "Apart from me you can do nothing" (John 15:5). As a final word, therefore, perhaps the most crucial thing is to insist that, come what may, and even though it may feel like having "treasure in a jar of clay," pastoral ministry at its best will want to point people consistently to that same Christ. In his exposition of the "Collects for Eastertide" according to *The Book of Common Prayer*, Ashley Null makes the following telling observation:

> [Pastors] are sheepdogs, not the Shepherd. Their task is to learn to know their Master's signals. At his direction, they are to identify who needs the Shepherd's help and to bring them to him at just the right time so that the Master can directly intervene in the lives of his flock.[11]

---

11. Null, *Eastertide*, 29.

Biblical and Theological Principles

1

Pastoral Care in the Christian Tradition

Cynthia Bennett Brown

Introduction

THE PURPOSE OF THIS chapter is to outline pastoral care in the Christian tradition. It is impossible to summarize two thousand years of practice in one chapter, and, indeed, entire books have done this well elsewhere.[1] The approach instead will draw on three criteria that inform Christian pastoral care across the ages. Each criterion will be introduced and then illustrated from different eras of church history with examples to invigorate thinking and practice in the twenty-first century. Reference to primary literature is dictated by the methodological decision to take specific documents as portals into the period's practice. While each source is extensive in its analysis, it can obviously only be drawn on to a limited extent.[2]

We state it simply at the outset: pastoral care in the Christian tradition must always be an expression of the good news of God's divine mercy for the world. If it is not this in the first instance, it is not *Christian*

---

1. Any reflection on the history of Christian pastoral care must include at least these four surveys: McNeill's *A History of the Cure of Souls*; Clebsch's and Jaekle's *Pastoral Care in Historical Perspective*; Oden's *Care of Souls in the Classic Tradition*; and Purves's *Pastoral Theology in the Classical Tradition*. They inform our comments here but merit direct engagement as well.

2. McNeill is right when he notes that sources on the subject are "almost limitless"! *History*, x.

pastoral care. It may be pastoral care in a generic sense, but it does not sit within the Christian tradition. What makes pastoral care specifically Christian is faith in the message of the good news of the Gospel of Jesus Christ, which holds out more than just a disembodied salvation but also the promise of healing, blessing, and the reality of reconciliation with God and neighbor. Of course, not everything the church has done through the centuries has been reflective of its Lord. Our aim in this brief survey of pastoral care, however, is to attend to those approaches that have been consonant with the Gospel and that we can imitate in our own time and place.

This brings us to this chapter's logic and structure. We identify three criteria that characterize pastoral care as Christian, and these determine the sections below. *First, pastoral care is soul care.* While it addresses felt needs, it also looks beyond them to the ills and well-being of the soul; it remains incomplete without attention to the spiritual reality that underpins human existence. *Secondly, pastoral care expresses Christ's compassionate response to suffering.* This includes existential troubles of all kinds: temptations, grief, loss, hopelessness, anxiety, to name but a few examples, and it does so reflecting the love of God in Christ. Even with the suffering that sin brings to the Christian disciple, which must be taken with the utmost seriousness, soul shepherding is always reflective of the humble, empathetic, and un-condemning ministry modelled by Jesus himself. *Thirdly, pastoral care is both an expression of and invitation into the church.* In a broad sense it can be defined as "the practical outworking of the church's concern for the everyday and ultimate needs of its members and the wider community."[3] The perennial debate as to whether or not it is or should be used as a tool for evangelism is not my primary concern here;[4] rather, the emphasis is this ministry within the faith community of the body of Christ.

Definitions

Etymologically "pastor" originates in the Latin term for shepherd, *pāstōrum*, and reflects the pastor-shepherd metaphor in Scripture. Examples include YHWH as the psalmist's shepherd (Ps 23), some of Israel's

---

3. See Hurding, "Pastoral Care, Counselling."

4. Senkbeil sees the two as inseparable: "Winning souls and tending souls go together." *Care of Souls*, 9.

kings as wicked shepherds (Ezek 34:2), Jesus as the Good Shepherd (John 10), early church leaders as shepherds of God's flock (1 Pet 5:2), and the Lamb on the throne as shepherd (Rev 7:17). Beyond this familiar image of the shepherd, pastoral care has been called more specifically *cura animarum*—"cure of souls." This care of the soul refers to both the healing and the means by which the healing is effected, and is, according to one theologian, "the foundational description of pastoral ministry."[5] Such care includes the whole of the human person, body, soul, and spirit, with particular attention to the person's interior life with God. Thus, Benner defines soul care as "the support and restoration of the well-being of persons in their depth and totality, with particular concern for their inner life."[6] Clebsch and Jaekle offer further precision: "The ministry of the cure of souls, or pastoral care, consists of helping acts, done by *representative Christian persons*, directed toward the *healing, sustaining, guiding, and reconciling* of *troubled persons* whose troubles arise in the *context of ultimate meanings and concerns*."[7] These categories—healing, sustaining, guiding, reconciling—have been used often in subsequent publications to define the precise activities of the Christian pastoral carer.[8]

As we trace common characteristics of pastoral care across the Christian tradition, we recognize that it remains a diverse ministry with a range of expressions dictated by context, resources, needs, and skill. It is informed by doctrinal categories such as anthropology, hamartiology, Christology, soteriology, and ecclesiology, and in our own day is located within the discipline of practical theology. Oden comments on the complex work of good pastoral care as "the constant interweaving of scriptural wisdom, historical awareness, constructive theological reasoning, situational discernment, and personal empathy."[9] In other words, it has been simultaneously a simple and a sophisticated calling across the church's story. The following pages are an introductory sketch of that endeavor.

---

5. Senkbeil, *Care of Souls*, 63.
6. Benner, *Care of Souls*, 23.
7. Clebsch and Jaekle, *Historical Perspective*, 4; emphasis original.
8. See, for example, Benner, *Care of Souls*, 31; also Egan, "Pastoral Care Today."
9. Oden, *Care of Souls*, 12.

Pastoral Care is Soul Care

The shepherd needs great wisdom and a thousand eyes to examine the soul's condition from every angle.

—John Chrysostom

Chrysostom's (d. 407) vivid image of the pastor's thousand eyes suggests the urgency of soul care in the patristic period. We see from the earliest years of the church that pastoral care was part and parcel of Christian faith and incorporated physical provision for the hungry, sick, marginalized, and destitute as well as spiritual nurture for believers. One excellent text on the apostolic church's pastoral care is Rodney Stark's *The Rise of Christianity*. He comments in chapter 4, "Epidemics, Networks, and Conversion," on the role this ministry played in the growth of the church in the early centuries, and in particular how Christians were caring for the poor, marginalized, and ill amid crises from which others were fleeing for their lives. One result of this was the church's growth in response to its witness of kindness, mercy, generosity, and grace that gave expression to the message of Jesus Christ in a most convincing manner.

In the pre-Constantinian church, the demands of Christian discipleship were high and reminders of its costliness in the lives of the saints were frequent. Failures of faithfulness were threats to both the person and community, and provision for confession of sin, repentance, and a return to a life of holiness was a priority for clergy. This was informed by an anticipation of Christ's imminent return, the reality of persecution and martyrdom, and the need for a way of life that would promote and enable earnestness in the inner person. Given what was at stake, soul shepherding was serious business. It was deeply concerned with supporting believers' faith for life and death, trusting that perseverance would win the crown of eternal salvation.

As early as the second century we see the evolution of extra-canonical literature to inform and support such faithfulness. The *Didache*, for example, is concerned with directing believers to be grounded in a life devoted to love of God and neighbor.

> "Watch" over your life: do not let "your lamps" go out, and do not keep "your loins ungirded"; but "be ready," for "you do not know the hour when our Lord is coming." Meet together frequently in your search for what is good for your souls, since "a

lifetime of faith will be of no advantage" to you unless you prove perfect at the very last.[10]

Also extant are letters exhorting believers to endure periods of acute persecution.[11] Sources from the Eastern Church also evidence this priority on the individual's salvation as their counselling practices "consistently move from external concerns to inner 'psychological' issues to innermost spiritual conflicts."[12] The endurance of the whole person was always in view across varied early efforts of pastoral accompaniment, and the Holy Spirit was regarded as the agent of personal, spiritual, emotional, and psychological healing.[13]

The fourth century legalization of Christianity brought with it an increased potential for compromised discipleship. Christian monasticism, organized from the third century, grew as means to evade easy concession to the world. The specific practice of spiritual direction became an early tool of clergy and religious to attend to those under their ministry.[14] Asceticism of the body for soul health characterized all forms of monasticism, both solitary and communal; exact practices differed only in the type and extent that was required. From the third century, "cognitive disciplines of Scripture, fear of God, and prayer,"[15] alongside physical disciplines of fasting, silence, and celibacy, were prerequisites for ecclesial office, and by the sixth century many of these came to be expected in the soul care of the laity as well.[16]

We cannot survey pastoral care in any period, least of all the patristic, without particular attention to Gregory the Great (c. 540–604). The raft of literature about Pope Gregory I testifies that he lived his vocation as a pastor with integrity, devotion, and humanity, attributes made evident in his books and correspondence. He was strongly empathetic and saw this characteristic as essential for clerical office as well as for effective pastoral care.[17] Gregory's ongoing impact is best discerned via his book *Liber*

10. *Teaching of the Twelve* 16.1–2:155.
11. Hurding draws attention to examples like the second-century text the *Shepherd of Hermas* that addressed this question and to Cyprian's letters of the third century; see Hurding, "Pastoral Care, Counselling," 87.
12. Marcu, "Orthodox Christian Church Fathers," 85.
13. Marcu, "Orthodox Christian Church Fathers," 84.
14. Demacopoulos, *Five Models*, 1.
15. Dilley, *Monasteries*, 295.
16. Demacopoulos, *Five Models*, 2.
17. Moorhead, *Gregory the Great*, 1–48.

regulae pastoralis, written to Archbishop John of Ravenna c. 590, which quickly became a primary and authoritative source on the subject.[18] His contribution is not entirely novel among church fathers in that, like Chrysostom, Ambrose, Augustine, and Benedict with his *Rule*, Gregory is attentive to the integrity, spiritual health, and practical challenges of his spiritual leaders. He recognizes different personalities among clergy and laity alike and their unique needs for spiritual guidance.[19] For example, in book 3 of *Pastoral Rule* we find advice on how men and women, young and old, rich and poor, are not to be guided identically because they all have different conditions that need to be taken into account when offering pastoral consolation.[20] Similar consideration is needed with the happy and the sad, who require different "admonishments" and "those lacking in shame are to be admonished in one way and the sensitive in another."[21] His list extends to instructions for the quiet and those who talk too much as well as the "indolent" and "the impulsive."[22] We might think awareness of personality and emotional shape is a fruit of modern psychology, but Gregory was modelling this facet of pastoral care from the sixth century.

How can our pastoral care bring people to soul healing? This is a critical question and a perennial one. It is not simply a matter of eloquent style to use a Latin phrase for our pastoral care; it must truly be *cura animarum* or else it is not Christian. This first element of Christian pastoral care through the ages reminds us that it retains the whole person as its object—body, soul, mind, and emotions. Such a prompt is profitable,

---

18. *The Book of Pastoral Rule*, though the title is also translated as *Pastoral Care*.

19. Demacopoulos, *Gregory the Great*, 53–56. There is one citation from Augustine that is also referenced to this effect in McNeill, *History*, 100, but I have not been able to locate it in an original source and thus cannot quote Augustine here. Benedict, however, is certain. He writes, "For in his teaching the Abbot should always observe that principle of the Apostle in which he saith: 'Reprove, entreat, rebuke' (2 Tim 4:2), that is, mingling gentleness with severity, as the occasion may call for, let him show the severity of the master and the loving affection of a father. He must sternly rebuke the undisciplined and restless; but he must exhort the obedient, meek, and patient to advance in virtue. But we charge him to rebuke and punish the negligent and haughty. Let him not shut his eyes to the sins of evil-doers; but on their first appearance let him do his utmost to cut them out from the root at once. . . . The well-disposed and those of good understanding, let him correct at the first and second admonition only with words; but let him chastise the wicked and the hard of heart, and the proud and disobedient at the very first offense with stripes and other bodily punishments." Saint Benedict, *Rule*, 2.

20. Gregory, *Pastoral Rule*, 3.2.

21. Gregory, *Pastoral Rule*, 3.3, 7.

22. Gregory, *Pastoral Rule*, 3.14, 15.

even essential, in our late modern, materialist context, and the pastoral wisdom of the earliest centuries of our faith is a treasure trove towards this end.

Pastoral Care Expresses Christ's Compassionate Response to Suffering

Let the priest be discreet and cautious that he may pour wine and oil into the wounds of the one injured after the manner of a skilful physician, carefully inquiring into the circumstances of the sinner and the sin, from the nature of which he may understand what kind of advice to give and what remedy to apply, making use of different experiments to heal the sick one.

—FOURTH LATERAN COUNCIL[23]

Suffering is universal and Scripture testifies that addressing and healing human pain and anguish is a priority of the triune God. This concern in turn becomes a defining feature of God's people, whether of Israel and her care for the widow, orphan, and alien in her midst, or of the early Christian community in its countercultural expression of Christ's self-giving love. The church's ministry in the world, then, must at the very least attend to those in hardship, for the purpose of preservation in body and soul. This most important task of the cure of souls is illustrated across the long Middle Ages as people sought salvation from incessant threats of war, famine, and plague, as well as the perpetual anxiety these realities created for the majority of the population. Though vital, it was not just the sacraments that ministered solace, but also a plethora of consolation literature from across the social spectrum.[24] Common themes include the assurance of divine sovereignty over calamity, the importance of perseverance in faith, the communion of saints, and the possibility of physical healing in this life.[25]

The omnipresent reality of daily hardship, and the desire to make sense of it, elicited a range of expressions of pastoral care. Assuaging

---

23. Cited in Stansbury, *Companion to Pastoral Care*, 263.
24. Consolation literature can be found across each era of the Christian tradition, and it is not unique to the Middle Ages.
25. Rittgers, *Reformation of Suffering*, 24.

spiritual misery was crucial to medieval *cura animarum*. The association between sin and suffering, while not the only explanation for the latter,[26] was a part of the Western worldview. Both elements needed to be addressed in pastoral care. In the sacraments of confession and extreme unction, for example, the soul's guilt and shame were acknowledged and forgiven, and the believer's contrition expressed in appropriate penance. Preaching was likewise a means of pastoral care, not just for the purposes of instruction but also for assurance of God's presence and care across life's trajectory, whether long or short. Progress in the spiritual life hinged around belief that certain vices would send someone to hell or purgatory, and conversely that certain virtues would contribute to salvation.[27] Relief from physical suffering was sought through touching holy relics, to the point of upper classes procuring their own set of artefacts to cure specific diseases.[28] Shrines grew up around those relics considered to be potent, and prayers to certain saints likewise were regarded as healing, usually for the illness from which the saint died.

This sacramental emphasis was complemented by "the practical spirituality of Bernard of Clairvaux (1090–1153) and Hildegard of Bingen (1098–1179), and the commitment to the poor and outcast which characterized the mendicant orders of Dominic Guzman (c. 1170–1221) and Francis of Assisi" (1181–1226).[29] Jeffries notes, for example, the importance of medicants' "vigorous pastoral activities" across Ireland in the late Middle Ages alongside the ministry of parish priests,[30] emphasizing pastoral responsibility as not simply the care of the soul but also charitable action in response to physical need. The spiritual duty of clerics appears, at least on paper, straightforward: instructing parishioners on the basics of Christian faith and life. This catechesis included education on the seven deadly sins, the ten commandments, the seven articles of faith, and the seven corporal works of mercy. While such knowledge was considered essential for salvation, in practice the celebration of the sacraments was the real lifeblood of medieval Christian practice, with

---

26. Rittgers is clear that "the fact of suffering was held to be the result of sin, especially original sin, but this did not mean that each instance of suffering could be causally linked to a specific sin and its divine punishment." *Reformation of Suffering*, 8.

27. Campbell, *Rediscovering Pastoral Care*, chapters five and six.

28. Clebsch and Jaekle, *Historical Perspective*, 35.

29. See Hurding, "Pastoral Care, Counselling," 87.

30. See Jeffries, "Parish and Pastoral Care," 224.

particular attention given to confession and penance.[31] The Fourth Lateran Council (1215) testifies to this preoccupation with the care of souls. Rittgers goes so far as to say that "the emphasis on *cura animarum* at Lateran IV was unprecedented in the history of Western Church councils" because it offered to parochial priests and the *cura animarum* a recognized place in the church and highlighted the need for priests to be properly trained in this "art."[32]

Such personal pastoral ministry could prove problematic when it came to caring for certain groups. Beth Alison Barr's insightful study of vernacular literature from thirteenth-century England yields two conclusions. First, pastoral care of men and women attended to sins that all shared, in response to which spiritual attention was offered regardless of gender. Secondly, textual evidence recounts how women were at times charged with specific sins in a manner different to their male counterparts. Unsurprisingly, perhaps, one of those was sexuality. On the one hand, women were a potential danger to the celibates' vow, whether temptation was intentional or incidental. In this way, pastoral care of women, in the confessional for example, required vigilance on behalf of priests to avoid sexual transgression. Sometimes such vigilance prevailed; at other times it failed and the woman was deemed doubly sinful. Nevertheless, Barr observes, this reality did not prohibit relevant and effective pastoral care of women. "The picture that emerges is relatively bright. . . . Middle English pastoral literature reveals priests concerned about women . . . painting a more realistic picture of women than was often found in general Church ideology."[33]

The fifteenth century introduces a genre of text related to the pastoral care of the dying, such as Jean Gerson's essay "On the Art of Dying," Caxton's book *The Arte and Crafte to Knowe Well to Dye*, and Woorde's *The Crafte to Live Well and to Dye Well*. Across these and other *ars moriendi* sources, death is viewed as a spiritual event in which "malign and gracious spirits contend for the soul. Death is, indeed, commended in the manner of the old consolation literature; but the dying man has his 'great and grievous temptations, greater than those he has met hitherto.'"[34]

---

31. For a helpful summary of the evolution of these sacraments from the patristic period into the Middle Ages, see McNeill, *History*, 88–111.

32. Rittgers, *Reformation of Suffering*, 13.

33. Barr, *Pastoral Care of Women*, 3.

34. McNeill, *History*, 158–59.

Perseverance through life's vicissitudes included care for the soul in the certain yet unpredictable hour of death.

How can our pastoral care bring people to Christ as the supreme pastor of their souls in life and death? Suffering's omnipresence across time and space requires sustained attention from those who represent Christ. It is not Christian if it does not do this. We in the West do not endure the same trials of our medieval forebears, so certain emphases will differ; however, themes such as divine sovereignty, perseverance in faith, the role of fellow believers in adversity, and the possibility of physical healing in this life are consistent with the Gospel of Jesus Christ and so remain in our practice of pastoral care.

Pastoral Care is both an Expression of and Invitation into the Church

The goal and end of this seeking and leading to Christ of lost sheep . . . is to bring them into the fold of Christ, so that they give themselves wholly to Christ . . . hear his voice in all things, and use all those things which the Lord has appointed for furthering the salvation of his sheep.

—Martin Bucer

According to McNeill, it was "in matters concerning the cure of souls [that] the German Reformation had its inception."[35] Both early and late Protestant initiatives consciously prioritized pastoral care in their theology and practice. One Protestant objective towards this end was integration of the believer into a healing community and subsequent service through that community for the purpose of the kingdom of God in the world. Indeed, McClure argues that while certain practices such as spiritual direction or assuaging suffering are shared with other religions across the centuries, Christian pastoral care is defined by its context of the faith community.[36]

Key sources are the "piety-theology" texts—*Frömmigkeitstheologie*—which, in Protestant hands, were edited away from the medieval

---

35. McNeill, *History*, 163.
36. See McClure, "Pastoral Care."

justification of suffering as the judgment of God and a source of sanctification towards compassionate consolation of the sufferer.[37] These were accompanied by the *Kirchenordnungen*—church orders that were produced to guide new forms of worship, faith, and polity according to evangelical priorities. They encompassed the breadth of church and social life, including redefining what pastoral care involved and how it should be exercised. According to Rittgers, these ordinances replaced the medieval *summa* in their breadth and aim, which was to guide the faithful in the ways of salvation and, furthermore, to invite the unsaved into the Protestant faith. They are valuable to us in that they detail the prescribed spiritual care of the early Reformation period, but even in the sixteenth century itself they were influential because there was no systematic education for clergy on *cura animarum* in university training.[38]

A closer look at Strasbourg reformer Martin Bucer's booklet *Von der waren Seelsorge*[39] is instructive here. He identifies five tasks of soul care taken from Ezek 34:16: "Searching for the lost, bringing back the strays, binding up the wounded sheep (that is, those who have fallen into sin), strengthening the weak, and guarding and feeding the healthy sheep."[40] The first goal of this ministry is evangelism, reconciling lost sheep to the true shepherd. Its second goal follows: the pastoral discipline of those already in the sheepfold so that they grow in faith and life. This care includes the binding up of the weak and hurting as well as directing the healthy. Bucer's concern was that Christians would experience Christ as Lord of the church corporate and as shepherd of his disciples.[41] This emphasis on Christ is what makes pastoral care true and what renders the work of the church so imperative as it is Christ himself who ministers through it.

The Reformers recognized that the need for spiritual and personal reassurance of salvation continued even though confession and penance were no longer deemed requisite for salvation. Of course, sermons and catechisms alike were influential towards this end but attending to

---

37. Rittgers, *Reformation of Suffering*, 5–7.

38. Rittgers, *Reformation of Suffering*, 163–65.

39. The full title with English translation is: *Von der waren Seelsorge, vnnd dem rechten hirten dienst, wie der selbige inn der Kirchen Christi bestellet, vnnd verrichtet werden sollen* [On the true pastoral care and the correct shepherd-service, how this is to be established and carried out in the church of Christ].

40. Bucer, *Concerning*, 212. On pages 70–73 Bucer briefly explains this fivefold ministry of pastoral care and then elaborates on this framework in the rest of the book.

41. Van der Waat, "Wholehearted Commitment," 252.

personal pastoral needs was also key. Ministries of consolation such as letter-writing and visitation are evidenced across the period in a variety of expressions, including through women. Katarina Schutz Zell is one such example. Her public ministry in Strasbourg alongside her husband-pastor Matthew was extensive, including hospitality for refugees, relief of physical suffering, succor in spiritual trials, teaching the Reformed faith, and exhortation through print, all of which "became the hallmarks of Schutz Zell's life."[42] She is one example of the newly discovered vocation of being a "pastor's wife," in which service to God was not confined to the taking of religious vows. Katherine Luther, Argula von Grumbach, and Marie Dentière are three other examples of this vital force of the Reformation.[43]

These texts and women illustrate two things: 1) pastoral care is central to the church's purpose as the body of Christ; and 2) it was a ministry for which one did not have to be ordained.[44] The priesthood of all believers was expressed in the inclusion of laypeople as agents of spiritual support. Since all Christians were baptized into Christ, all shared his ministry of mutual care, whether physical or spiritual. This corporate responsibility for each other was reflected not just in the Magisterial Reformation but in Quaker, Pietist, Methodist and Baptist communities as well.[45]

Alongside the pastor's core ministry of preaching was the essential work of home visitation where clergy engaged personally with parishioners to enable them to apply Scripture to their own situations. Calvin comments, "The office of a true and faithful minister is not only to teach the people in public, which he is appointed to do as pastor, but also, as much as he is able, to admonish, exhort, warn, and console each person individually."[46] This included care for physical needs, but it was ultimately about care of souls. "For Calvin, Christian ministers were expected to provide intensive, personal, spiritual support that would nurture the parishioners' Christian understanding and spirituality over the course of a lifetime, from cradle to grave."[47] In busier parishes these home visits might happen just once a year, but they were considered central to

---

42. See McKee's introductory remarks in Zell, *Church Mother*, 17.

43. Much more could be said here! See Stjerna, *Women and the Reformation*.

44. DeVries offers a concise and constructive article on this emphasis: "Models of Mutual Pastoral Care."

45. McNeill, *History*, ix.

46. Calvin quoted in Manetsch, *Calvin's Company*, 256.

47. Manetsch, *Calvin's Company*, 256.

pastoral care, and form the foundation of a Reformed approach to pastoral ministry in which elders play a key role. This model is still present today in many denominations.

Beyond this, evolution of the clerical office can be seen, for example, in Calvin's "company of pastors." In his *Ecclesiastical Ordinances* (1541) we read of the establishment of three named offices in the Genevan church beyond pastor—those of doctor, elder, and deacon, all intended to imitate the offices of the early church. While the pastor preached and administered the sacraments, the doctor taught local congregations as well as future pastors with an eye to sound doctrine. Elders were appointed for the work of pastoral care—"to take care of the life of everyone, to admonish in a friendly manner those whom they [saw] weakening or leading a disorderly life, and, where it [was] needful, to make a report to the company which [would] be deputed to apply brotherly correction."[48] Alongside them, deacons were connected to the pre-existing roles associated with the local hospital, which served as a kind of social welfare center, specifically in ministries of physical care required by the city's destitute.[49]

Moving into the early modern period, one of the most cited books on pastoral ministry was Richard Baxter's *The Reformed Pastor*. The "reformed pastor" is less a designation of churchmanship and more a category of minister who is spiritually alert so as to do his shepherding work diligently. Thus, Baxter exhorts his readers,

> Take heed unto yourselves lest you be void of that saving grace of God that you offer to others and be strangers to the effectual workings of the gospel you preach . . . so that you will be that which you persuade your hearers to be, believe that which you persuade them daily to believe, and have heartily accepted that Christ and Spirit whom you offer unto others.[50]

No fewer than thirty-two times in chapter 1 alone, Baxter exhorts his readers to attend to their own sanctification lest their ministry or even their salvation be compromised.

Baxter takes Acts 20:28, with its injunction of watching over self as well as the congregation, as the impetus behind pastoring every person

---

48. Calvin quoted in Manestch, *Calvin's Company*, 29.
49. Manestch, *Calvin's Company*, 30.
50. Baxter, *Reformed Pastor*, ch. 1.

in his congregation,[51] and, indeed, his responsiveness to individual persons is what Purves suggests as "Baxter's greatest genius as a pastor."[52] He recognized the significant demand of such soul care and advised employment of a pastoral assistant when required. Baxter himself lived out this devotion assiduously along the same lines as Calvin. He made a commitment to visit every family personally at least once a year—no small task with a parish of eight hundred families—by setting aside two days a week to do this. He viewed this individual, spiritual instruction to be at the heart of ministry—"personally catechizing and instructing everyone in [the] parishes who [would] submit to it."[53] The result of Baxter's pastoral care was the growth and spiritual renewal of the congregation to which he was so committed.

We see across the ages that pastoral care was exercised by a range of people—ordained, lay, religious, married, men, women—and in a variety of individual and communal contexts, but, insofar as it is Christian, it is the expression of the body of Christ. Reconciling, directing, providing, teaching, visiting, feeding, preaching, evangelizing, reforming are all forms of shepherding, each in its own way alleviating suffering, caring for the soul, and integrating people into healing church communities. This differentiates it from counselling, for example, where the individual is cared for by another individual for a limited period of time. It is also different to ministries such as support groups or food banks because, while these can unequivocally express the love of Christ, they also are services that function within a client–provider arrangement that can militate against deep, personal knowing. "The Church of Christ is the assembly and fellowship of those who are gathered from the world and united in Christ our Lord through His Spirit and word, to be a body and members of one another, each having his office and work for the general good of the whole body and all its members."[54] In Christian pastoral care, the church itself as the body of Christ is central to soul care and to the healing of the soul that is its ultimate aim. The question that needs to be asked is

---

51. See Baxter, *Reformed Pastor*, ch. 2.

52. Purves, *Pastoral Theology*, 111.

53. Baxter, *Reformed Pastor*, ch. 7. Chapter 8 expounds the objections to this personal catechesis he anticipates from his ministerial colleague, and chapter 10 offers "the best directions I can give" to succeed in this task.

54. Bucer, *Concerning*, 72–73, cited in Van der Watt, "Wholehearted Commitment," 241.

whether church communities continue to express such pastoral care. This is not an easy question, but our care is not Christian if it does not do this.

Conclusion

Pastoral care is not the unique purview of the Christian faith; religions and philosophies older than Christianity engaged in the practice long before the advent of the church.[55] This can also be seen in our own day where the term is applied to what goes on in the workplace[56] and education.[57] This is important to acknowledge as we work to care faithfully for others in the name of Christ. As Barnes observes, Christian pastoral care is "to witness the work of the Holy Spirit in bringing people back to life through their union in Christ."[58] It is part of a bigger picture of the kingdom of God and the flourishing of individuals, communities, and the entire created order. Only the Spirit can effect the fullness of this shalom.

We mentioned in our first section that the earliest Christian communities were intentional in their ministries of care, and the Spirit was at work through them to grow the church. This witness continued in each era, through different means and expressions, all imperfect yet still used by God. Much has changed through the ages, however, and this is evident in our own time. The multiplication of subjects in the late modern university means that pastoral care has been divided into specialisms.[59]

---

55. One helpful summary of pre-Christian pastoral care can be found in McNeill, 1–66. See also Cajthaml's (*Care of the Soul*) extensive treatment of Jan Patočka's analysis of very early, even pre-Christian, soul care as well as modern inheritance of this. Also, see Benner's reference to soul care in ancient Greece and Judaism in *Care of Souls*, 21–34.

56. For example, the employment social media platform LinkedIn describes it using terms familiar to the Christian tradition: "Pastoral care performs many essential functions: healing, sustaining, guiding, reconciling and nurturing. Each function is directed towards providing care to the worker in need and helping them to achieve their prime potential by resolving any issues they have and by overcoming any impedance to their learning." See Noorani, "Pastoral Care."

57. For example, Taylor & Francis have their own academic journal to address the subject called *Pastoral Care in Education*, which states as its goal that it is "directed at teachers/educators, professionals, researchers and academics who are concerned with the pastoral care, emotional health and wellbeing of children and young people across all formal and informal education settings." See Taylor & Francis, "Pastoral Care in Education."

58. M. Craig Barnes quoted in Van der Watt, "Wholehearted Commitment," 133.

59. A succinct survey of this dissolution of pastoral care by the mid-twentieth century is Scharfenberg, "Babylonic Captivity."

This has had two consequences: 1) it has become in some cases a vocation apart from the Christian faith, the name of Christ, and intentional cooperation with the Spirit of God; and 2) healing practices differentiate between body, mind, emotions, relationships, etc., with little attention to the integration of the whole person, including the soul. Specifically in the twentieth century, Christian pastoral care was profoundly influenced by the burgeoning discipline of psychology, with contributions from sociology as well. This is no bad thing, as much excellent cross-fertilization between the disciplines means that this practice has been enriched in numerous ways.[60] We must ask ourselves, however, how such engagement can *enhance* our practice of Christian pastoral care and where it might dilute or detract from the goal of caring for the vulnerable who need healing, sustaining, guiding, and reconciling. In the end, we could go so far as to say that it is the presence and work of the Holy Spirit that is the single most defining feature of pastoral care in the Christian tradition. Without the work of the Spirit, we cannot be reconciled to God in Christ, and without such reconciliation, the soul is not cured. It is the Holy Spirit alone who deeply heals.

Biblical testimony and the story of the church, as we have seen, witness to the important role that individuals and communities play as agents of the Spirit's work. This brings us to the Christian pastoral carer as a channel through which the Spirit ministers. A host of sources address the character, abilities, and intention of the pastor as soul physician. Marcu's commentary on the counselling practices of the Orthodox Church Fathers draws specific attention to Spirit-filled examples such as Basil the Great, John Climacus, Simeon the New Theologian, Moses the Ascetic—the list goes on.[61] Indeed, in a sober assessment of his own pastoral call, Gregory of Nazianzus writes, "A man must himself be cleansed, before cleansing others: himself become wise, that he may make others wise; become light, and then give light: draw near to God, and so bring others near; be hallowed, then hallow them; be possessed of hands to lead others by the hand, of wisdom to give advice."[62] He recognized that a fundamental requirement of an effectual pastor is the slow process of

---

60. A glance at chapter titles in summary texts such as the *Wiley-Blackwell Companion* as well as the flotilla of specialist sources that are published every year eloquently evidences this.

61. Marcu, "Orthodox Christian Church Fathers" is one such source.

62. Gregory of Nazianzus, "In Defence," 2.71.

deification,[63] fostered by a patient attentiveness to one's inner life as a reflection of the nature of God himself. The pastor must know God and be made into the likeness of Christ through the work of the Spirit to "minister the things of God," and this cannot be hurried.[64]

We have surveyed three defining features of pastoral care in the Christian tradition: it is the cure of souls, it expresses Christ's compassionate response to suffering, and it is an expression of and invitation into the life of the church. God by his Spirit, and through his people, has been active across the centuries and remains so today. The story of our forebears reminds us that our cooperation with God requires obedience and humility, courage and wisdom, skill and love. And so we return to the image of shepherd, the Good Shepherd, with which we started. As we seek to be faithful in playing our role in this vital ministry of *cura animarum*, may Christ be our model, may the Spirit be our strength, and may our care of souls be always for the glory of God and the coming of his kingdom.

---

63. This is Gregory's term within the context of the Eastern understanding of salvation, what in Protestant terms is more familiar as sanctification.

64. Purves, *Pastoral Theology*, 12.

2

Love and Pastoral Ministry: A Case Study of Paul the Pastor

Patrick Mitchel

This chapter explores the relationship between love and pastoral ministry through the lens of the apostle Paul. This approach raises some questions. Why a case study on Paul in particular? If Paul is a good example of pastoral ministry in action within the New Testament (and the case will be made below that he is), a second question emerges: How does Paul's theology and experience of the risen Christ shape his pastoral practice? A third question concerns love in Paul's pastoral ministry: What is so important about this virtue rather than other important Christian themes such as, for example, forgiveness or grace? Answering these three questions will open up a fourth: What have Paul's pastoral priorities and theological convictions to teach us about pastoring in local churches today?

Why Paul as a Case Study of New Testament Pastoral Ministry?

Two books published closely together a few years ago, *Paul as Pastor*[1] and *Pastor Paul*,[2] highlighted a lack of attention on his pastoral ministry within New Testament scholarship. Those that did exist tended to discuss

1. Rosner et al., *Paul as Pastor*.
2. McKnight, *Pastor Paul*.

his pastoral practice within selected letters.[3] This is not the place to explore the reasons why, but my hunch is that it is the result of treating Paul's letters primarily as a source of theological beliefs—whether Christology, pneumatology, election, justification, eschatology, sexual ethics, the future of Israel, atonement, leadership, or whatever. While valuable, the predominance of this orientation unintentionally marginalizes the social contexts of his letters, which are written to teach, encourage, warn, and exhort believers in Jesus Christ to live their lives together in a way "worthy of the calling to which you have been called" (Eph 4:1).[4]

What it means to live worthily is spelt out in numerous places, most beautifully in Eph 5:1–2—"Therefore be imitators of God, as beloved children, and walk in love, as Christ loved us and gave himself up for us, a fragrant offering and sacrifice to God." The word for "walk" here is *peripateō*, a typical Jewish term for a way of life. Rather than walk as they used to, "dead through trespasses and sins" (Eph 2:1), now, as beloved children of God, they are to imitate him by walking in the self-giving and loving way of Jesus.

We shall return to love and pastoral ministry in Paul, save to say here that *the ultimate goal of Paul's mission is relational and pastoral*—to see believers conformed to the way of Christ.[5] Elsewhere Paul talks of believers being transformed into the image of Jesus (Rom 8:29; 1 Cor 15:49; 2 Cor 3:18; Col 3:10). This is what McKnight has termed "Christoformity"[6] and is what Paul has in mind when he describes the goal of his apostolic mission as that which will "bring about the obedience of faith among all the gentiles for the sake of his name" (Rom 1:5).

So, while Paul has a God-given task of proclaiming the gospel of Jesus Christ,[7] he understands the ultimate purpose of his apostolic mission in pastoral terms—that of transformed lives. Brian Rosner notes that "without exception, Paul's letters were motivated by pastoral concerns. All thirteen letters traditionally attributed to Paul bear this out."[8] James

---

3. One notable exception is a slim but significant treatment: James Thompson's, *Pastoral Ministry According to Paul*.

4. See also Phil 1:27; Col 1:10; 1 Thess 2:12; 2 Thess 1:5, 11. All Bible quotations are from the NRSV unless otherwise stated.

5. For broader discussion of Christian maturity as the overall purpose of Paul's pastoral ministry see Patrick McGlinchey's chapter 3 of this book.

6. McKnight, *Pastor Paul*.

7. Proclaiming the gospel is a major theme in Paul's letters. See for example 1 Cor 9:16—"Woe to me if I do not preach the gospel."

8. Rosner, "Household Setting," 17.

Dunn contends that "as a pastor as well as theologian, Paul was inevitably concerned with the outworking of his gospel . . . Paul never spoke other than as a pastor."[9] For N. T. Wright, Paul "was a pastor, and a pastor's pastor"[10] and "all Paul's theology is . . . pastoral theology."[11] Mark Roberts concludes that "there is little doubt Paul was what one would call a pastor. The work of shepherding churches, helping them grow in Christ and to have Christ formed in them, was an essential aspect of his apostolic mission."[12] James Thompson argues that "Paul's pastoral ambition, as he states consistently in all his letters, is community formation."[13] Thompson defines Pauline pastoral ministry as *"participation in God's work of transforming the community until it is 'blameless' at the coming of Christ."*[14]

Despite this consensus, two objections raise their heads. First, Paul may have been a pastor, but what sort of pastor? If someone asked you what makes a good or bad pastor you might say the former is a servant leader; someone who seeks to imitate the Lord in concern for the spiritual well-being of those under her care, even at cost to herself. The latter as someone power hungry, manipulative, or narcissistic, who uses their position to promote their own selfish agendas at cost to others supposedly under their care. Some scholars have made such charges against Paul. He is oppressive (Castelli), controlling (Moore) and manipulative (Shaw). Marion Carson, taking a case study of 1 Thessalonians, deals with each criticism.[15] While it is naïve to hold Paul up as a model of a perfect pastor, she concludes that

> Paul should be seen as a benevolent leader, driven by theological rather than selfish motives. Against Castelli and Moore, we have contended that he is not concerned with his own self-advancement or the control of others, but by a genuine desire to serve God and nurture his converts. Against Graham Shaw we have argued that Paul is not maliciously manipulative.[16]

---

9. Dunn, *Theology of Paul*, 626.
10. Wright, *Faithfulness of God*, 452.
11. Wright, *Faithfulness of God*, 556–69.
12. Roberts, "Pastor, Paul As," 755.
13. Thompson, *Pastoral Ministry*, 20.
14. Thompson, *Pastoral Ministry*, 20; emphasis original.
15. Carson, "For Now We Live," 23–41.
16. Carson, "For Now We Live," 41.

Thus, Carson argues, Paul can be seen as "an appropriate role model for today's pastoral leaders."[17]

Second, we should note that Paul never refers to himself as pastor,[18] and so we need to acknowledge that in calling Paul a pastor "one is applying a term from experience that Paul did not use for himself."[19] As we shall see below, there are ample grounds to support this move.

How does Paul's Theology and Experience of the Risen Christ Shape his Pastoral Practice?

Our second question is how is the apostle's pastoral practice embedded within his theological vision of new-creation life in Christ? As hinted earlier, too often these two strands, pastoral and theological, have become artificially separated in Pauline studies. The result has been the formation of "two Pauls"; one of church life and the other of academia, existing in virtually separate worlds, a reality captured amusingly by Pauline scholar Douglas Campbell:

> I sometimes wonder what Paul would make of the conferences at which scores of highly learned people sit around and debate for hours tiny semantic nuances in his preserved writings. I expect he might be patient with this exercise for a while, but then at some point I'm pretty sure he would jump up—possibly wielding a whip—and shout: "For goodness sake! Haven't you read what my writings actually say? You're not meant to be sitting around debating them. You are meant to be out there doing what they tell you to do—meeting people and fostering Christian communities in service to your Lord. Get off your backsides and get moving!" Doubtless this challenge would be accompanied by the sounds of tables being overturned and piles of pristine books crashing to the floor.[20]

What follows is a sketch attempting to integrate both "Pauls": the pastor and the theologian. The crucial point to grasp is this: *Paul is both a pastor and eschatological theologian.* By eschatological I mean a set of theological convictions that can only be properly understood with

---

17. Carson, "For Now We Live," 41.

18. The Greek word for shepherd is *poimēn*, which Paul uses rarely and never in referring to himself.

19. Roberts, "Pastor, Paul As," 749.

20. Campbell, *Pauline Dogmatics*, 4.

reference to God's future that has burst into the present in the teaching, life, death, resurrection, and ascension of Jesus Christ. This "messianic eschatology" is key to interpreting the pastoral teaching he gives his congregations.[21] This means that we need to look *behind* any specific moral commands to Paul's underlying eschatology. A useful framework for doing this is to start with the dramatic impact of the *past* (a crucified and risen Messiah), how it revolutionized Paul's vision of the *future* (judgment and resurrection), and (our main focus) how *past and future together shape his pastoral ministry in the present*.[22]

Past Messianic Eschatology

Paul is persuaded that the past events of Jesus' death, resurrection, and ascension are evidence that God's future now exists in the present. Those "in Christ" have already been raised from spiritual death to new life (Rom 6:2–11; 2 Cor 5:17; Gal 6:14–15). This is pictured in multiple ways, one being through the image of being buried with Christ in baptism and subsequently raised with him (Rom 6:3–4; Col 2:12). The old self has been crucified with Christ (Rom 6:5–6), setting believers free from sin and its enslaving power (Rom 6:6–7, 17–18; 7:6) to live righteously for God (Rom 6:13). In this vein, Paul can talk of his own experience that "the world has been crucified to me, and I to the world" (Gal 6:14).

The role of the Spirit in Paul's experience and thinking is crucial (Rom 5:5). The gift of the Spirit has united believers within the body of Christ (1 Cor 12:13), empowering them to live the Christian life in the present. It is the Spirit who bestows new life to both Jews and gentiles through faith in Christ, thus fulfilling God's promise to Abraham (Gal 3:14). Repeatedly this is depicted as a decisive past event (Rom 8:1–2, 10; 2 Cor 3:6). Similarly, the Spirit is talked of in eschatological terms as "first-fruits" (Rom 8:23), "guarantee" (2 Cor 1:22; 5:5; Eph 1:14), and "seal" (2 Cor 1:22); all images designed to encourage believers that they already belong to God and their future is therefore assured.

---

21. For fuller discussion see Mitchel, "Eschatology," 265–79.
22. Mitchel, "Eschatology," 266.

Future Messianic Eschatology

Paul's thinking about the future revolves around the implications that Jesus is the risen and reigning Lord. His future coming (*parousia*, 1 Cor 15:23; 1 Thess 2:19; 3:13; 4:14; 5:23; 2 Thess 2:1, 8–9) will involve God's final victory over all malevolent and destructive powers, including sin, Satan, the flesh, death, the world, and a rogue's gallery of other evil forces.[23] God will "crush Satan" (Rom 16:20) and the Lord will destroy the "lawless one" at his *parousia* (2 Thess 2:8). At "the end" every ruler and authority and power, including death, will be destroyed (1 Cor 15:24–26, 56) "so that God may be all in all" (1 Cor 15:28).

At the *parousia* all in Christ will, whether awake (living) or asleep (already dead), by God's power, experience resurrection (1 Cor 15:51–52; Phil 3:21; 1 Thess 4:13–18). However exactly understood, Paul's emphasis is that the resurrection body is fitted for the age to come where believers will be able to see God "face to face" (1 Cor 13:12). On a cosmic scale, creation itself will be liberated (Rom 8:19–23). Thus, Paul can pray with the Corinthians in confident hope, "Our Lord, come!" (1 Cor 16:22).

Present Messianic Eschatology: Snapshots of Paul's Pastoral Practice

We can now turn our attention to Paul's pastoral ministry among the young churches under his care. As a pastor he wants believers to develop an "eschatological double vision"—looking back at Christ's first coming while simultaneously looking forward to his *parousia*.[24] Richard Hays describes this as a process of converting their imaginations to think eschatologically in order to live faithfully in the present.[25] Since Paul was an itinerant missionary writing letters to scattered churches over fifteen years or so, what emerges is an unsystematic educative program addressing all sorts of ethical and practical issues. What follows are a series of snapshots of Paul's pastoral ministry in action. They are deliberately not in any particular order. As you read them, keep an eye out for how his

---

23. These include rulers and authorities (*archai* and *exousiai*), powers (*dynameis*), cosmic powers (*kosmokratores*), dominions (*kyriotētes*), spiritual forces (*pneumatika*), "elemental spirits" (*stoicheia*) of the world (Gal 4:3, 9; Col 2:8, 20) and the enigmatic "lawless one" of 2 Thess 2:1–12.

24. Mitchel, "Eschatology," 272–73.

25. Hays, *Conversion of the Imagination*.

messianic eschatology guides believers to make good moral choices in the overlap of the ages.

a) However real evil powers are, since they have already been decisively beaten, believers are empowered to resist them in the present. One example of many is Rom 6:12 where, since believers have been made alive in Christ, they are not to "let sin exercise dominion in [their] mortal bodies." Another is in Colossians where rulers and authorities opposed to God have been disarmed, shamed, and vanquished by the cross (2:14–15). The pastoral implications of God's victory are spelt out memorably in Rom 8 where nothing in the present or future—neither affliction, distress, persecution, famine, nakedness, peril or sword nor death, angels, demons, rulers, powers—has the capacity to separate believers from the love of God in Christ the Lord (Rom 8:35–39). These verses have encouraged countless generations of Christians over millennia.

b) Paul often worries pastorally over the spiritual progress of believers under his care. He fears that the Corinthians will be led astray "from a sincere and pure devotion to Christ" (2 Cor 11:3) and later in the same chapter acknowledges that he is "under daily pressure because of [his] anxiety for all the churches" (2 Cor 11:28).

c) In Galatians he is like a mother worrying over a self-destructive teenager, calling them his "little children" for whom he is in "pain of childbirth until Christ is formed" in them. He wishes he could be with them since he is "perplexed" about them (Gal 4:19–20). He feeds the Corinthians with milk since they are "infants in Christ" (1 Cor 3:1–2) and he reminds the Thessalonians that "we were gentle among you, like a nurse tenderly caring for her own children" (1 Thess 2:7).

d) To this motherly image can be added that of a father. Most often his fatherly role is that of a spiritual parent, uniquely responsible for believers' birth in Christ and subsequent development (e.g., 1 Thess 2:11–12). Like a father in the Greco-Roman world, his role is to instruct and guide his children but with a crucial difference: rather than honor, status, or material progress, the *telos* of Paul's fatherhood is towards Christoformity. At times he has no hesitation in holding himself up as a model to imitate (1 Cor 4:16; 1 Cor 11:1; Phil 3:17; 1 Thess 1:6; 2 Thess 3:7, 9), but this is qualified in that all believers are called to imitate God

LOVE AND PASTORAL MINISTRY: A CASE STUDY OF PAUL THE PASTOR   39

(Eph 5:1), and Paul himself is a co-imitator of Christ: "Be imitators of me, as I am of Christ" (1 Cor 11:1).

e) One of the most significant Pauline pastoral images is that of brothers (*adelphoi*), occurring 127 times in Paul and 271 times in the New Testament making it the most common term for Christians.[26] It is best translated "brothers and sisters" since it is an inclusive term for all believers. The dominance of this household metaphor points towards the conclusion that Paul wanted the first Christians to think of themselves *primarily* as a family of siblings, even more than "believers," "disciples," "the Way," "church," "saints," or "Christians."[27]

It is difficult for us to appreciate how radical were the implications of this "flat" community status in the hierarchical and status-driven structures of the ancient world. Paul's pastoral goal is that the new communities of believers—whether male, female, slave, free, Jew, gentile, rich, poor, young, old, educated, or not—would be marked by the love, affection, and mutual care characteristic of close siblings who share the same Father and who follow the same Lord. For Paul, such unity is far from a pleasant optional "add-on" to "belief" in the gospel, it is the very goal of that gospel and "hard evidence" of the presence of Christ and his Spirit within the church in a hostile world.

f) It is within this sibling framework that Paul's frequent "one another" language is best understood. Positively, they are to love one another (1 Thess 3:12; 4:9; 2 Thess 1:3; Rom 12:10; 13:8); to pursue one another's good (1 Thess 5:15); and to bear with one another in love (Eph 4:2). We could multiply examples, but the point is made.[28] Negatively, they are not to divide by creating leadership factions within the community (1 Cor 1:10–13); or to take each other to court (1 Cor 6:1–11); nor are the wealthy to show contempt for the poor—the issue behind Corinthian division at the Lord's Supper (1 Cor 11: 17–22). Such "one another behavior" describes what it is to be a follower of the self-giving Christ (Phil 2:6–11).

g) Another pastoral metaphor Paul employs is that of a "skilled master builder" who lays a foundation on which others can build (1 Cor 3:10). This involves teaching and encouraging believers to build up one

26. McKnight, *Pastor Paul*, 61.
27. Rosner, "Household Setting," 14.
28. For fuller description see Mitchel, "Solus Spiritus," 71–102, especially 99.

another (1 Thess 5:11; Rom 14:19; Eph 4:11–12) and so build up the body of Christ. Again, the objective remains consistent—Christoformity via "knowledge of the Son of God" so that believers would grow "to the measure of the full stature of Christ" (Eph 4:13).

h) Paul does not pastor alone. His letters are peppered with references to his coworkers and other colleagues in pastoral ministry.[29] These are clearly deep relationships forged in the heat of ministry. In a chapter on friendship in Paul, McKnight concludes that the apostle's "love for his friends is in his face, on his tongue, in his letters, and everywhere revealed."[30] Marion Carson observes that Paul "does not seem to set himself up as a remote figure, unapproachable and aloof. Despite his conviction that his authority stems from God, he is conscious of his vulnerability and need of those to help him in the task. Leadership, Paul is well aware, requires mutuality."[31]

i) Repeatedly evident is a caring pastor's joy in the people with whom he ministers. He longs to see the Roman believers (Rom 1:11–12) and closes the Epistle, hoping that "by God's will I may come to you with joy and be refreshed in your company" (Rom 15:32). He tells the Corinthians that "I have great pride in you; I am filled with consolation; I am overjoyed in all our affliction" (2 Cor 7:4). No letter is as overflowing with pastoral delight as Philippians. He prays with joy for them (1:4); tells them that "I long for all of you with the tender affection of Christ Jesus" (1:8); and calls them his "brothers and sisters, whom I love and long for, my joy and crown" (4:1). Similarly, the Thessalonians are his hope, joy, crown, and glory before the Lord (1 Thess 2:19–20) with whom he is "determined to share . . . not only the gospel of God but also our own selves" (1 Thess 2:8). And he has tender words for Philemon telling him that "I have indeed received much joy and encouragement from your love" (Phlm 7).

---

29. Those named coworkers include people like Priscilla and Aquila, Urbanus, Timothy, Titus, Epaphroditus, Clement, Jesus called Justus, Philemon, Mark, Aristarchus, Demas, and Luke. Numerous other dear friends and fellow workers for the Lord are named in Rom 16, including Junia, a female apostle and several other women.

30. McKnight, *Pastor Paul*, 46. It is worth noting that, perhaps because of Greek ideas of friendship, Paul carefully avoids calling fellow believers his friends, preferring brotherly love (*philadelphia*). McKnight is aware of this arguing that Paul reframed friendship in light of God's love for us in Christ (41–46).

31. Carson, "For Now We Live," 41.

j) Prayer plays a central role within Paul's pastoral ministry. Often this takes the form of heartfelt and constant prayers for the churches (e.g., 2 Cor 13:7-9; Eph 1:16; Phil 1:9; Col 1:3, 9; 1 Thess 1:2; 3:10; 2 Thess 1:11; 2 Tim 1:3; Phlm 4, 6). But this is not a one-way relationship; he also frequently asks the believers to pray for him (Rom 15:30; 2 Cor 1:11; Phil 1:19; Col 4:3; 1 Thess 5:25; 2 Thess 3:1; Phlm 22). The picture is one of mutuality as pastor and church serve God together.

k) It would be easy to overlook how Paul's letters themselves represent a form of pastoral care. As an itinerant missionary he frequently found himself distant from churches he had either founded or over whom he had apostolic influence. His extraordinary use of personal representatives (like Phoebe to Rome) helped to maintain pastoral relationship and deliver Epistles carefully tailored to the everyday pastoral and theological issues facing each church community. Letter writing, notes Dunn, meant that "Paul's theology was always wrapped around with the greetings, thanksgivings, and prayers of letter openings, with the travel arrangements, personal explanations, and farewells of letter closings."[32] While often physically distant, he was not a distant pastor.

l) Paul has much to say on what constitutes appropriate sexual behavior for believers in the context of the Greco-Roman world. Larry Hurtado makes the point that Paul expressed "a stance diametrically opposed to the prevailing attitudes of the time, and he intended to distinguish sharply what should be the sexual behavior of believers, particularly males."[33] Again, his pastoral teaching is framed through his messianic eschatology. The Corinthians *have been* washed, sanctified, and justified (1 Cor 6:11). *Now* their bodies are not their own but belong to the Lord—they are joined with him through the Spirit, are temples of the Spirit, and *will be* resurrected. Therefore, in the *present* they are to glorify God in their bodies. This means fleeing from sexual immorality (*porneia*) such as visiting prostitutes (1 Cor 6:12-20).[34] Similarly, in Gal 5:19 *porneia* is one of the "works of the flesh" and in Col 3:5 it is "earthly" and is to be "put to death."

---

32. Dunn, *Theology of Paul*, 736.
33. Hurtado, *Destroyer of the Gods*, 163.
34. Hurtado notes that Paul's use of *porneia* goes beyond the specific issue of prostitution and embraces a diverse range of illicit sexual activities. *Destroyer of the Gods*, 160-65. See also 1 Cor 5:1-12; Eph 5:3, 5; 1 Thess 4:3.

m) Talk to any pastor and he or she will almost certainly say that the job seems inevitably to involve personal criticism and relational tension. Paul was no exception. This reality is captured most viscerally within 2 Corinthians, but is present in 1 Corinthians and elsewhere.[35] There are two sides to any conflict and, despite 2 Corinthians being a complex letter to untangle,[36] it is clear that Paul and the Corinthians had long term relational difficulties that had become acute, probably because of the arrival of "super-apostles" (2 Cor 11:5) from outside Corinth.[37] The point I want to make here is that a real test of pastoral integrity is someone's response to criticism—even if unfair. Paul is obviously deeply stung by their rejection, so his reaction as a pastor-theologian is revealing.

Relationally, he does not wash his hands of a troublesome church but remains committed to them even at personal cost. Despite their pain and his, he takes the risk of reaffirming his love for them, most poignantly in 2 Cor 12:15—"I will most gladly spend and be spent for you. If I love you more, am I to be loved less?" (see also 2 Cor 2:4; 6:6; 8:7; 11:11).

Theologically, he develops a future-oriented theology of weakness and strength to point the Corinthians away from himself and towards the paradoxical nature of the gospel. The Corinthians had been infected by the power structures of the Roman world.[38] Status and honor were drivers in their love of impressive appearance and speech, leaving little room for Paul's sufferings and at least some finding "his bodily presence . . . weak and his speech contemptible" (2 Cor 10:10). In response, he writes that "we have this treasure in clay jars, so that it may be made clear that this extraordinary power belongs to God and does not come from us" (2 Cor 4:7). He is not to be rejected for his outward weakness, rather God has placed his power within "cracked pots" (Paul's description of his people and himself in 2 Cor 4:6) who are "afflicted," "perplexed," "persecuted," "struck down," "being handed over to death" (4:8–11), and whose "outer nature is wasting away" (4:16). Instead of measuring by temporary fleshly standards, the Corinthians need to look beyond Paul to God himself: "For we do not proclaim ourselves; we proclaim Jesus

---

35. Most notably with the "foolish Galatians" (Gal 3:1–3) who now viewed Paul as an "enemy" (4:16) after being "bewitched" by Judaizers whom Paul wishes would "castrate themselves" (5:12).

36. White, "Second Letter," 181–94; Barnett, "Paul as Pastor," 55–69.

37. For a likely reconstruction of the chronology of these difficulties see White, "Second Letter."

38. McKnight, *Pastor Paul*, 153.

Christ as Lord and ourselves as your slaves for Jesus' sake" (2 Cor 4:5). Because of the resurrection to come, present experience of weaknesses and trials are dramatically reinterpreted as "our slight, momentary affliction . . . producing for us an eternal weight of glory beyond all measure" (2 Cor 4:17–18; cf. Rom 8:18). This is the paradoxical way of the cross that the pastor in Paul hopes will subvert the Corinthians' imaginations and lives in the present.

n) Often overlooked in more systematic studies of Paul's beliefs is how personally important to him was the collection for the saints in Jerusalem from congregations in Achaia, Macedonia, and Galatia. The collection occupied his attention for several years and it can be argued that it was this pastoral priority that eventually cost Paul his life.[39] Dunn proposes that "the collection sums up to a unique degree the way in which Paul's theology, missionary work, and pastoral concern held together as a single whole."[40]

Various theories have been proffered as to what motivated Paul,[41] but our focus here is on a fascinating example of a pastor-theologian in action. A potentially mundane practical issue (a financial collection) is treated with considerable theological depth and pastoral sensitivity. Themes of grace, future hope, gospel, imitation of Christ, invitation, persuasion, worship, love, joy, and generosity abound. Four points can be made.

First, Paul is concerned to ensure equality between givers and recipients (2 Cor 8:13–15). While not stated explicitly in this text, the pastoral implication is clear. All believers belong to one another within the body of Christ. Equality extends beyond a local congregation to where there is known need. Second, the collection is described as a gift or grace (1 Cor 16:3; 2 Cor 8:4, 6–7, 19). The gentile churches of Macedonia had shown the way in modelling the transforming power of God's grace in their lavish giving to their fellow believers in Jerusalem (2 Cor 8:1–6). For Paul, such costly generosity is an admirable sign of living now in light of the future and he invites the Corinthians "to excel also in this generous undertaking" (2 Cor 8:7). Paul's pastoral concern is that God's grace should

---

39. The collection led him to a final visit to Jerusalem in the face of well-founded doubts about possible arrest (Rom 15:31). The consequence was transportation to Rome and eventual execution.

40. Dunn, *Theology of Paul*, 707. The collection forms an important close to Romans (15:14–32) and forms major sections of 2 Cor 8–9 and 1 Cor 16:1–4.

41. See Downs, "Collection," 136–39.

create gracious people. Third, the gift is a form of sharing or fellowship (2 Cor 8:4; Rom 15:26) in the service (Rom 15:25, 31; 2 Cor 8:4, 19–20) of the saints in Jerusalem. There is a form of "spiritual debt" to honor the church there (Rom 15:7). The sense is of an exchange: a material blessing given in return for a spiritual blessing received. For Paul, such giving not only fosters unity between Jewish and gentile believers but embodies the heart of his apostolic mission. Fourth, it is significant that the collection is framed by Paul in 2 Cor 9:12 as ministry or liturgy suggesting an act of worship.[42] God "loves a cheerful giver" who gives in response to God's provision of "every blessing in abundance" so that they "may share abundantly in every good work" (2 Cor 9:7-8). The pastoral implications of this cycle of grace for Paul are significant. Financial giving is a good work of grace and orientated to God (2 Cor 9:12).

Notice how, in most of the examples discussed above, there is a potentially thin dividing line between exhorting believers to changed behavior and lapsing into exhausting moralism. When I was a student at theological college, I remember being assigned reading from F. F. Bruce's intimidating tome on Paul. I do not think I took much in, but I was attracted to the title (and still am)—*Paul: Apostle of the Free Spirit*. For whatever reasons, as a youngish Christian I had not heard a lot about freedom or the Spirit! Bruce's title was carefully chosen because he understood Paul intimately after a lifetime of study. This is what he wrote in the introduction.

> Where love is the compelling power, there is no sense of strain or conflict or bondage in doing what is right: the man or woman who is compelled by Jesus' love and empowered by his Spirit does the will of God from the heart. For (as Paul could say from experience) 'where the Spirit of the Lord is, there the heart is free' (2 Corinthians 3:17).[43]

Bruce's words remind us that for Paul the Christian life begins by personal encounter with God's love (Gal 2:20), is empowered by the Spirit, and is lived in light of future hope. He is not a pastor wielding a big stick, forcing people into behavioral change by sheer force of will. In this vein, let us now turn to our third question and the central role of love within his pastoral ministry.

---

42. McKnight, *Pastor Paul*, 91–94. Downs, "Collection," 139.
43. Bruce, *Free Spirit*, 21.

What is So Important about Love within Paul's Pastoral Ministry?

As Paul moves continually from theology to pastoral instruction, at least five points can be made to support the case that this process is always framed by love.

First, a general observation: an examination of the place of love in Paul's letters shows it is perfectly justifiable to call him, alongside John, an "apostle of love."[44] He and John are the two major New Testament authors on love, far outstripping all others,[45] with each contributing distinct perspectives on Christian love and pastoral ministry. Thompson notes that it is the central place of love in Paul's ethic that set him apart from ancient moralists.[46]

Second, if there are three strands of love in the Bible (God's love for humanity; human love for God; love for one another within the covenant people of God),[47] Paul's focus is overwhelmingly on the third, "horizontal" strand.[48] This should not be surprising. As we have seen, his pastoral priority is to build up diverse communities of believers imitating the way of Jesus in the "present evil age" (Gal 1:4). Love fulfils the law (Rom 13:10; Gal 5:14) and is the primary objective of his apostolic mission. Nowhere is this made clearer than in 1 Cor 13 where the Corinthians (and Christian readers today) are warned bluntly that their obsessions with knowledge, prophecy, faith, status, and inspired speech together mean that they are in danger of missing the entire purpose of the Christian life. If love is not present, they gain *nothing*.[49] Love is described in a series of fifteen verbs (eight depicting "unlove" and seven depicting love). Love is, in other words, an active choice to imitate the love of God in Christ—a costly commitment to act for the good of others.[50]

---

44. Mitchel, "Solus Spiritus," 99–101. Campbell devotes five chapters to love in Paul's life and teaching in his *Pauline Dogmatics*.

45. Paul uses the noun *agapē* (love) seventy-five times, the verb *agapaō* (to love) thirty-four times, and the adjective *agapētos* (beloved) twenty-seven times together making up over 42 percent of the usage of these words in the New Testament. Morris, *Testaments of Love*, 138. John's Gospel and 1 John alone have ninety occurrences. Overall, Paul and John's writings contain about 75 percent of the New Testament's *agap*-related words.

46. Thompson, *Moral Formation*, 180.

47. Mitchel, *Message of Love*, 269–84.

48. For excellent discussion, see Thompson, *Moral Formation*, ch. 7 on "Putting Love into Practice."

49. For more discussion on love in 1 Cor 13, see Mitchel, *Message*, 205–20.

50. Oord, a prolific, if controversial, theologian of love, defines love this way: "To

Third, the shape of love in Paul is Christological. Unlike in our modern world, love in Paul is not a vague idea but is patterned on the Messiah's self-giving example: "God proves his love for us in that while we were still sinners Christ died for us" (Rom 5:8). Cruciform love gives shape to the entirety of the Christian life.[51] So, as Paul moves from theology to practice, it is Christological love that guides his thinking, emotions, and teaching.[52] Followers of Jesus are to imitate his example of costly self-giving love (e.g., Eph 5:2; 1 Thess 1:6; 2:14–15; and especially Phil 2:5–11). As Gary Burnett puts it, "Again and again in his letters, Paul urged these little communities of Christians to live in ways that exhibited kindness, generosity and compassion, bearing one another's burdens and imitating the self-denying, serving love of Christ."[53]

Fourth, not only is love central to Paul's ethics in the here and now (Rom 13:8–10; 1 Cor 13; Col 3:14), it is integral to future hope. This becomes explicit in 1 Cor 13:8–13. When "the complete" (*to teleion*, 1 Cor 13:10) arrives it is love (*agapē*), rather than the temporary virtues of faith and hope, which is the greatest (1 Cor 13:13). Love in the present is a foretaste of the future. It is no wonder, then, that Paul commands them to "pursue love" (1 Cor 14:1) and in his closing exhortations says, "Let all that you do be done in love" (1 Cor 16:14).

Fifth, a fascinating aspect of Paul's pervasive theology of spiritual conflict is that love is God's chosen "weapon" in a cosmic battle with destructive forces of evil. Nowhere is this clearer than in Galatians and the war between the flesh and the Spirit. The flesh produces destructive "desires" that are contrary to the Spirit (5:16–17) and result in destructive "works of the flesh" characteristic of those who will not inherit the kingdom of God (5:19-21). In utter contrast, "those who belong to Christ Jesus have crucified the flesh with its passions (*pathēma*, passion) and desires" (Gal 5:24). Liberated from the power of the flesh, they are to use their freedom to serve one another in love rather than indulge the flesh (5:13). Walking by the Spirit will enable believers not to gratify the desires of the flesh (5:16). It is no accident that the first descriptor of the

---

act intentionally, in relational response to God and others, to promote overall well-being." *Pluriform Love*, 28.

51. Mitchel, "Love," 663.

52. A scholar who blazed the trail here is Furnish in his *Theology and Ethics in Paul*, followed up with his seminal work *The Love Command of the New Testament*.

53. Burnett, *Paul's Gospel of Love*, 17.

fruit of the Spirit is love (5:22). Paul can even say that the "only thing that counts is faith working through love" (5:6).

Pastoring Today

Our final question is what have Paul's pastoral priorities and theological convictions got to teach us about pastoring in local churches today? An initial answer is "a lot," but in saying that I want to offer a qualification. While involved in local church leadership, I am a college lecturer not a pastor. Researching and writing this chapter has been a joy, sparking off all sorts of connections and implications for pastoral ministry today that are sketched below. But I am well aware that pastoring is a complicated and challenging task. I do not presume to tell pastors how to do their job, nor could I. It is not easy to draw straight lines from Paul's context to that of the twenty-first-century Western world. The ten observations below are based on how Paul understood and practiced his own pastoral calling (and perhaps you can add others). They are offered as a resource to those engaged in the good work of pastoral ministry.

1. Ultimate "success" in pastoral ministry for Paul seems clearly defined: transformation of his communities into the likeness of Christ. If the overriding goal for pastors is therefore not external markers (numerical growth, buildings, programs, impressive budgets, events, and so on), but rather the calling to nurture Christoformity within a church community,[54] this will have significant implications for how pastoral ministry is conceived and practiced. Pastoral ministry will involve pastoral care for individuals, but a pastor will be primarily concerned with how the whole church is fulfilling its calling to reflect the character of Jesus in the world.

2. We have seen that in pastoral ministry, for Paul, everything is theological. The challenge for modern pastors is to do similar creative work of seeing all of life through the lens of messianic eschatology. In other words, to help people understand their lives as located within an eschatological drama shaped by what God has done in Christ in the past and will do in the future and then live accordingly. Such a vision is deeply subversive within the materialist and capitalist culture of the twenty-first century. It is also liberating—it centers

---

54. McKnight, *Pastor Paul*, 4.

the Christian life on God rather than on the illusion that we humans are in control of history.

3. Paul's objective was to create missional communities of people across ethnic, religious, gender, and social divisions who loved one another while worshiping a God of self-giving love. Such a vision was an outlandish, but ultimately deeply attractive, proposition in the stratified ancient world.[55] Similarly today, in an increasingly ethnically diverse and individualized culture, one of most powerful testimonies to the inclusive love of God is a racially, culturally, and socially mixed community of believers. This will also speak to a culture that is, with good reason, deeply cynical about the integrity and motives of Christian churches. While love's primary purpose is to participate in the love of God,[56] and neither has conversion as its primary goal nor is any guarantee of evangelistic success, it is missionally essential.

4. Linked to the above point, there is no contradiction between experiencing God's undeserved love and the expectation of an obedient response. This was true for Paul personally and it characterized his entire apostolic mission. While it is popular to talk of God's "unconditional love," this language needs care. It can give the impression that the call to Christoformity is an optional bonus to saving faith. It is more accurate to say for Paul, while God's love is unconditioned (not dependent on any condition of the recipient), it is not unconditional.[57] While God's love is offered as an immeasurable gift of grace, transformation is the *purpose* of the gift. For pastors today this means imitating Paul in having high expectations of spiritual growth and maturity and continually setting that liberating vision before their congregations.

5. Pauline pastoral practice is shaped by an acute awareness of an apocalyptic conflict between divine and evil forces behind the scenes of everyday life. A key pastoral priority is therefore learning from how Paul "took fully into account the reality both of living in a hostile

---

55. Hurtado, *Destroyer of the Gods*, 64–65. He writes that "the emphasis on God's love and the appeal of an answering 'love ethic' characterizing Christian conduct comprise something distinctive" in the ancient world.

56. Gorman, *Becoming the Gospel*, 96.

57. The language of "unconditional" / "unconditioned" is taken from John Barclay who used it in *Paul and the Gift* with reference to grace in Paul.

world and of living between two worlds."⁵⁸ Believers can choose to "keep in step" with the Spirit or follow the "desires of the flesh." Such a perspective may seem bizarre to the modern secular mind, but it is at the heart of New Testament faith. Eugene Peterson, the pastor's pastor, argued that modern pastors "must be apocalyptic" because it is their job to talk about reality as it really is: "Apocalypse is arson— it secretly sets a fire in the imagination that boils the fat out of an obese culture-religion and renders a clear gospel love, a pure gospel hope, a purged gospel faith."⁵⁹

6. Christoformity does not happen easily. Pastoral ministry at times requires a combination of courage and wisdom to challenge damaging behavior and attitudes. Paul demonstrated both in response to a bewildering array of complex theological and ethical issues. When behavior needed correction, he tackled the problem head-on. No one said pastoring is easy! Pastoral ministry today may face very different questions, but the same challenge remains. For example, just as Paul stood uncompromisingly against the sexual ethics of the Greco-Roman world, pastors today face the task of articulating a faithful Christian sexual ethic distinct from that of Western liberalism. A pastor will offer pastoral care, *but his or her ultimate task is not primarily therapeutic*. It will often involve calling for confession, repentance, and changed behavior so that believers will live lives worthy of the gospel. Such change takes time; effective pastoring is a marathon more than a sprint.

7. Our seventh point is the flip side of the sixth and links back to the conclusions of Marion Carson. Paul was a benevolent leader who loved his churches passionately: he crafted extraordinary letters, prayed, shed tears, was in anguish, rejoiced, and grieved over his communities. As a theologian of love, liberty, and personal responsibility, he used his apostolic authority to teach, inspire, persuade, and encourage Christoformity. When criticized, he responded by developing a theology of humility and suffering consistent with the cross. Being a pastor is not a job of professional detachment; it is a calling that involves a person's whole being in relationship with others who are simultaneously brothers and sisters in the Lord. It

---

58. Dunn, *Theology of the Apostle*, 736.
59. Peterson, *Contemplative Pastor*, 41.

matters just as much, if not more, *how* someone pastors as to what they say in preaching and teaching.

8. Paul forged deep relationships with a network of men and women coworkers during his years of itinerant mission. Pastoring is best done with others, in relationships of honesty and transparency. It is ironic that modern church structures can leave pastors isolated and lonely, with little pastoral support in a culture that sees little or no value in their calling. A wise pastor will seek out other pastors to meet with, share, pray, talk, and be open with. Eugene Peterson writes about "The Company of Pastors," a group he hosted for twenty-six years, as a "place to form and nurture a pastoral identity that had theological and biblical integrity. . . . We needed one another. There was too much in American culture that was hostile to who we were."[60]

9. Paul encouraged his mission churches towards generous giving to the poor saints in Jerusalem. Developing generosity exemplified themes of grace, love, worship, joy, and thanksgiving and formed an integral element in Paul's overall goal of developing Christoformity. Such a perspective poses a radical challenge of our contemporary privatization of money with its relentlessly "this-worldly" perspective. For contemporary pastors, this means the topics of generosity, money, and caring for others are not off the table.

10. Finally, returning to Paul's building metaphor, he constructs in mutual partnership with people in his churches. Everyone has a specific role within the body. All are gifted by the Spirit to serve. No task is reserved exclusively for leaders. "Communal transformation includes the recognition that . . . the entire community works to build a lasting structure."[61] In other words, pastoral ministry then and now does not revolve around one person. While this is well known, it is a truth with continuing implications. It confronts any notion of the indispensable "celebrity pastor" or of pastoral ministry being the sole domain of the ordained minister. A healthy pastoral culture is not self-protective but encourages and releases men and women to be involved in pastoral ministry together for the glory of God.

---

60. Peterson, *Pastor*, 159.
61. Thompson, *Pastoral Ministry*, 162.

3

Christian Maturity as the Goal of Pastoral Ministry

Patrick McGlinchey

Introduction

ALFRED, LORD TENNYSON LONG ago penned this famous line which I found immediately compelling the first time I read it: "And ah for a man to arise in me, That the man I am may cease to be!"[1] Although the phrase was old-fashioned, and I had little clue as to what the poet precisely had in mind, it spoke to me of a deep dissatisfaction I felt with my own life. I was a committed Christ follower and yet was so frustrated at my inability to live up to this calling that at times it felt like I needed to become an altogether different person. While this mindset may appear pessimistic, it has some resonance with the church's perspective on human nature. As an Anglican minister who has occasionally led the 1662 service of Evening Prayer, I was aware that the ancient language of the church encouraged me to take seriously the profound flaws in my own make-up. The General Confession opens with these words:

> Almighty and most merciful Father; We have erred and strayed from thy ways like lost sheep. We followed too much the devices and desires of our own hearts. We have offended against thy holy laws. We have left undone those things which we ought to

1. Tennyson, *Maud and Other Poems*, 1.10.6.

have done; And we have done those things which we ought not to have done; and there is no health in us.²

While this sentiment is doubtless true, the general tenor of both the New Testament and this particular prayer is not to focus on the gloomy news about our shortcomings, but to invite us to embrace the possibility of new beginnings. This is the case because the goal of Christ's ministry in our fractured lives is to radically remake us. C. S. Lewis, in *Mere Christianity*, makes this claim about what the New Testament teaches regarding Christ's plan for us:

> Now we begin to see what it is that the New Testament is always talking about. It talks about Christians "being born again"; it talks about them "putting on Christ"; about Christ "being formed in us"; about our coming to "have the mind of Christ."
>
> Put right out of your head the idea that these are only fancy ways of saying that Christians are to read what Christ said and try to carry it out—as a man may read what Plato or Marx said and tried to carry it out. They mean something much more than that. They mean that a real Person, Christ, here and now, in that very room where you were saying your prayers, is doing things to you. It is not a question of a good man who died two thousand years ago. It is a living Man, still as much a man as you, and still as much God as He was when He created the world, really coming and interfering with your very self; killing the old natural self in you and replacing it with the kind of self He has. At first, only for moments. Then for longer periods. Finally, if all goes well, turning you permanently into a different sort of thing; into a new little Christ, a being which, in its own small way, has the same kind of life as God; which shares in His power, joy, knowledge and eternity.³

My aim over the next few pages will be to fill out what Lewis so impressively synthesized in just a few sentences. For although written as a script for a radio broadcast during wartime, his words could sum up what the church's ministry ought ultimately to be about, that is, the forming of little Christs. Indeed, the initial goal of the chapter will be to show that Lewis's thumbnail sketch of God's purposes for us really does correspond with New Testament teaching. However, my aim will not be to stop there. Ultimately, I will be exploring two further questions. What are the best

2. *BCP* 2004, 86.
3. Lewis, *Mere Christianity*, 161.

conditions in which we can become little Christs? In other words, what hints does the New Testament give about what best facilitates the kind of growth and transformation described by Lewis? And finally, in the main section of the chapter, I will attempt to outline what it means to be a little Christ, that is, a mature Christian stamped by the character of Christ. We will explore what this will look like and ask how it might inform the Church's ministry.

Being Formed in the Image of Christ as the Goal of New Testament Ministry

The process of being "made mature in Christ" is probably best understood through the lens of the New Testament's teaching on salvation.[4] This is because the two are so profoundly intertwined. It is impossible to talk about salvation without at the same time referencing God's transformative work within us. We can see this through the key New Testament words used to characterize salvation—"save," "sanctify," and "glorify." The present tense of these three words highlights the fact that salvation is an ongoing interior process (i.e., "I am *being* saved, I am *being* sanctified and I am *being* glorified").[5] This idea is also evident in the New Testament's employment of other words that are related to sanctification. A prime example is *summorphoó* ("make conformable to") which speaks of being transformed into the image of Christ.[6] Its use by Paul in Rom 8:29 shows that conformity to this image is not only God's present intention for those in the church, but also his underlying eternal purpose ("For those God foreknew he also predestined to be *conformed* to the likeness of his Son" NIV). It is no surprise, then, that at some key points in Paul's letters we find a reiteration of this pastoral goal that the apostle wanted to keep at the forefront of his readers' minds. We find it in this moral exhortation to the Colossians: "Do not lie to each other, since you have taken off your old selves with its practices and have put on the new self, which is being renewed in knowledge in the image of its Creator" (Col 3:9–10 cf. Eph 4:22–24 NIV).

The other significant Greek term employed is the word for maturity itself (*teleos*). This is the word that is translated as "perfect" in the King

---

4. See the discussion in Carter, "Personality and Christian Maturity."
5. Carter, "Personality and Christian Maturity," 195.
6. Carter, "Personality and Christian Maturity," 196.

James Version's rendering of Matt 5:48, although in most other passages modern translations opt for the designation "mature." The Christian psychologist John Carter, commenting on the use of "perfect," notes that it is "noncomparative in character" and refers simply to "the development of the potential of the object."[7] Drawing on the Authorized Version's translation of Matt 5:48—"Be perfect as your Father in heaven is perfect"—he makes the observation that Jesus' exhortation is not to be as divine or as holy as the heavenly Father, but to be as "complete" or "fully developed" as he is. This sense of the term *teleos* is confirmed by the fact that it was used in secular Greek to describe fruit that had reached the stage of ripeness. We might summarize Carter's position by saying that the New Testament's focus on maturity centers on individual Christians having their potential as image bearers developed so that they will ultimately be conformed to the image of God. We see this idea expressed below in terms of "actualization," a favorite phrase of psychologists of Carter's generation:

> Therefore, most clearly salvation is the process which allows the believer to begin to actualize his full potential: to be what he was created to be, to become what he is—a son of God, being in the image of Him who created him.[8]

Becoming Mature

As Lewis has already indicated, we are not called simply to mimic the behavior and example of Jesus as others have sought to emulate certain key figures in their search for intellectual or moral maturity. The relationship with Jesus is richer and more complex than this. It starts with an acknowledgment of our own incapacity. In words that echo the citation from Tennyson, Paul himself expresses intense frustration at the seeming intractability of his own nature: "What a wretched man I am! Who will rescue me from this body of death?" (Rom 7:24 NIV). Paul's answer is that deliverance comes through the work of the Spirit of God. We see how Paul conceptualizes this in his discussion of conversion and its aftermath in 2 Corinthians:

> But whenever anyone turns to the Lord, the veil is taken away. Now the Lord is the Spirit, and where the Spirit of the Lord is,

---

7. Carter, "Personality and Christian Maturity," 197.
8. Carter, 'Personality and Christian Maturity," 196.

there is freedom. And we all, who with unveiled faces contemplate the Lord's glory, are being transformed into his image with ever increasing glory, which comes from the Lord, who is the Spirit. (3:16–18 NIV)

It is clear from Paul's general teaching that while the Spirit is the agent of change in the lives of Christians, the foundation for his work is the believer's union with Christ. This is arguably the defining idea of New Testament spirituality and the one that makes most sense of how transformation occurs.[9] But what might that union consist of and how does it facilitate change in the person? I want to suggest that it happens in two closely related ways that involve both the interior life and our relationships within the body of Christ. At this point, the account becomes slightly more autobiographical. One of the most transformative events of my own life was a silent eight-day spiritual retreat undertaken at a center in Wales (St. Beuno's). The combination of solitude and attentiveness to God's voice enabled me to encounter Christ in a way that was more real than at many other points in my Christian experience. During this time of "unusual" availability to the Lord, I learned truths about myself that my hectic lifestyle and distracted mindset had successfully hidden from me. Moreover, this encounter enabled me to lay a deep foundation of prayer and active listening that kept the transformation ongoing long after the retreat had ended.

I want to suggest the kind of encounter I have described was never meant to be an exotic experience available only to aficionados of a particular brand of spirituality. On the contrary, I had stumbled into a pattern of solitude and spiritual discipline that Jesus and Paul had modelled out and that was intended for everyone.[10] Our transformation is rooted in times spent in solitude with God and facilitated through profound self-honesty during the time of prayer. Without this kind of attentiveness our own unruly natures will keep us happily distracted and deaf to the things we may most need to hear. Moreover, that in-depth and ongoing relationship with God which is premised on earnest engagement with the spiritual disciplines and self-honesty, may be forever lost to us if we do not set

---

9. For example, James S. Stewart, in one of the classic studies in Pauline spirituality, wrote that "union with Christ, rather than justification or election or eschatology, or indeed any of the other great apostolic themes, is the real clue to an understanding of Paul's thought and experience." Stewart, *Man in Christ*, vii.

10. For a more detailed discussion of this theme, see Elliott and McGlinchey, *Perspectives on Prayer*, 15–21.

in place the habitual practices that empowers authentic discipleship. This interiority is the indispensable foundation of spiritual transformation and without it real growth is impossible. Hence, the church's task, both in its teaching ministry and its small group work, is to inculcate these spiritual insights and facilitate direct engagement with the practices that bring about such spiritual renewal.[11]

However, this is not meant to function alone. The *relationality* that defines our interior union with Christ also characterizes another aspect of our lives used by God to bring about transformation. We find this second emphasis also prevalent in Paul's letters. Here the quest for spiritual maturity is also attained communally through shared spiritual gifts and ministries that are exercised for the benefit and growth of the whole church (e.g., Eph 3:11–13 cf. 1 Cor 12:7–11).[12] Gordon Fee argues that Paul conceived of God's redemptive work in corporate terms because this idea was embedded in his biblically informed consciousness. The God of the Hebrew Bible was a God whose overriding purpose was the fashioning of "a people for himself," and, for Paul, this dynamic goal also characterized God's purposes for the church. According to Fee,

> "To be saved" in the Pauline view means to become part of the *people* of God, who by the Spirit are born into God's *family* and therefore joined to one another as one *body*, whose gatherings in the Spirit form them into God's *temple*. God is not simply saving diverse individuals and preparing them for heaven; rather he is creating a *people* for his name, among whom God can dwell and who in their life *together* will reproduce God's life and character in all its unity and diversity.[13]

While Fee's bracketing out of the individual or solitary aspects of faith may seem odd at first sight (actually, I do not believe he is questioning the centrality of the interior life as outlined above), there are reasonable grounds for acknowledging how essential the witness, encouragement, inspiration, and enabling of others can be to any individual's

---

11. Excellent resources to facilitate this area of the church's ministry can be located on the Renovaré website. See renovare.org.uk.

12. See also Jenkins, *Christian Maturity*, 4 where, commenting on Pauline teaching, he states, "[Christian] maturity is known only in relationship. Our humanity is co-humanity. As 1 Corinthians 12 and Ephesians 4 emphasize, the gifts of the Spirit are given to each only for the sake of all, because it is together and not separately that those who follow Christ achieve mature manhood."

13. Fee, *Spirit*, 71–72. For a popular discussion of the same theme, see Bolsinger, *It Takes a Church*.

growth in faith. The old tale from the Hebridean Revival of "the single ember" highlights just how much the liveliness and reality of anyone's faith depends on their connectedness to others who irradiate that same faith. The ember burns brightly when placed alongside other embers but turns lifeless and cold when separated from them and left on its own. The old pastor's physical action in removing the coal from the fire was enough to convince the erring parishioner of his need for involvement with his fellow believers. Maturity in faith comes invariably as part of an interactive and interdependent relationship with other members of the body of Christ. There is no special transformative track for those who willfully disengage from the life of the church. As James Davison Hunter astutely observed, "Character outside of lived community, the entanglements of complex social relationships and their shared story, is impossible."[14] Redemption as "the people of God" and not as solitary saints is God's enduring purpose for any community of faith that draws its inspiration from the witness of the Old or New Testament.[15]

Maturity, Relationality, and the Trinity

This brief discussion of the nature and means of Christian maturity ends where the chapter began. At the outset we made the claim that God's great pastoral goal was to restore human beings to the divine image. But what is that image and why does relationship with God and others seem to play such a key role in its restoration? I believe that the most satisfying answer to those questions was supplied by Karl Barth in the *Church Dogmatics*. Adopting a *sensus plenior*[16] approach to the Genesis narrative, Barth suggests that humanity possesses the image of God by virtue of the fact that the male/female relationship (or interhuman relationships, more broadly) reflect the life of the Trinity. Although qualities such as rationality and creativity belong to each individual human being and may to some degree mirror the nature of God, human beings' resemblance to

---

14. Hunter, *Death of Character*, 227 cited in Smith, *Called to Be Saints*, 183.

15. For a helpful "fleshing out" of how this vision of corporate life might be realized within a congregation, see appendix A ("Congregations and Transformation") of Smith's, *Called to Be Saints*.

16. "That additional, deeper meaning, intended by God but not clearly intended by the human author, which is seen to exist in the words of a biblical text (or group of texts, or even a whole book) when they are studied in the light of further revelation or development in the understanding of revelation." Brown, *Sensus Plenior*, 92.

God is most fully shown in their capacity for interpersonal relationship and mutual self-giving. Barth writes, "In God's own being . . . there is a counterpart . . . an open concentration and reciprocity [of persons]. Man is the repetition of this divine form of life; its copy and reflection."[17] Barth's insight about males and females created together as the image of God to live lives of reciprocity reflects perfectly what has been said above about the centrality of relationship. Moreover, such a view of the image of God is necessarily instructive for our understanding of maturity. Restoration of this image must involve human beings relating to each other in ways that mirror the triune life of the Godhead. Hence, most of our final section will be devoted to these divine relational qualities (e.g., love, self-giving, and the desire and movement towards unity and mutual harmony). We shall also touch on other related themes such as personal and social holiness and, ultimately, joy—that luminous quality that marked Jesus' own ministry at unique points and is one of the hallmarks of a transformed personality.

The Make-up of Christian Maturity

The following section outlines the key traits of Christian maturity and their biblical and theological foundation. They emerge in Scripture as ideals that are impossible to attain by unaided human effort, but which are realizable by the ministry of the Spirit in synergy with our practice of the disciplines and our common life together.

A Capacity to Love

The core characteristic of Christian maturity and the one to which we will devote most attention is the ability to *love*. The Bible witnesses at numerous points to the primacy of this unique and awe-inspiring capacity. To love God wholeheartedly and our neighbor as ourselves is also the most fundamental thing asked of us (Mark 12:28–32). However, love is not a quality generated independently by individuals but has its roots in the *imago Dei*. Moreover, on account of love's pre-eminent role within the divine relationships, it serves as the blueprint for our own life together. As Gordon T. Smith observes,

---

17. Barth, *Doctrine of Creation*, 3.1:185.

> God is not a solitary being; rather, the divine being is a union of three persons bound together by the mutuality of love. In like fashion we affirm and celebrate that the human person is not a spiritual monad but a being designed to live in interdependence and communion with others.[18]

This call to live in communion raises basic questions about what constitutes the expression of love. The temptation is to focus exclusively on 1 Cor 13 with its richly textured description of love. However, there may be merit in considering first the earthly ministry of Jesus. This is where we find the genesis of the New Testament teaching on love and arguably some of its most unsettling implications for the life of faith. Jesus ministered within a deeply polarized society riven by political and religious division. Much of the popular religion of the time baptized this division and gave sanction for what was essentially hatred of enemies. We can therefore envisage the consternation with which these original words of Jesus may have been greeted:

> You have heard that it was said, "Love your neighbor and hate your enemy." But I tell you, love your enemies and pray for those who persecute you, that you may be children of your Father in heaven. (Matt 5:43–45a)

The imagined indignation of that first-century Palestinian audience might well be replicated today in our own increasingly polarized world. However, it may be precisely amid such a political maelstrom that the real nature of love becomes most apparent. These words from one of the most inspiring texts of the 1960s (Martin Luther King Jr.'s *Strength to Love*) demonstrate not only the practical realism of Jesus' command to love enemies but also the necessity of it for real Christian maturity:

> I am certain that Jesus understood the difficulty inherent in the act of loving one's enemy. He never joined the ranks of those who talk glibly about the easiness of the moral life. He realized that every genuine expression of love grows out of a consistent and total surrender to God. So, when Jesus said, "Love your enemy," he was not unmindful of its stringent qualities. Yet he meant every word of it. Our responsibility as Christians is to discover the meaning of this command and seek passionately to live it out in our daily lives.[19]

---

18. Smith, *Called to Be Saints*, 128–29.
19. King, *Strength to Love*, 50.

In outlining King's vision, I should reiterate the fact that only *in union* with Christ does the believer move beyond the ideal set out in *Strength to Love* and start to live the reality of Christ's words.[20] King enjoins his readers to develop and maintain the capacity to forgive, noting that those who are "devoid of the power to forgive are devoid of the power of love."[21] This practice of forgiveness is a lifestyle and involves the believer consistently taking the initiative even when they are the injured party.[22] The outcome of such forgiveness is a reconciled relationship in which the past no longer functions as an obstacle to the good working of the present relationship.[23] Built into the movement towards reconciliation is the acknowledgment that the enemy is not entirely defined by their evil actions.[24] Moreover, the ultimate goal of loving one's enemies must always be the transformation of hatred into harmony. As King puts it,

> Love is the only force capable of transforming an enemy into a friend. We never get rid of an enemy by meeting hate with hate; we get rid of an enemy by getting rid of enmity. By its very nature, hate destroys and tears down; by its very nature, love creates and builds up. Love transforms with redemptive power.[25]

While this language appears to set a very high bar for the Christian, I think we would be unwise to see it as marking an idealized standard of spiritual maturity not found elsewhere in the New Testament. Paul's words in 1 Cor 13 also embody this radical concept of love and are every bit as challenging to normal standards of goodness as the message of the Sermon on the Mount (Matt 5–7).[26] What Paul does superbly well is give a full-orbed description of the love that appears in its most dramatic form in love of enemies. His style of language (hidden in most translations) reminds his readers that love is expressed in concrete actions rather than functioning as an abstract quality.[27] This same point is made with homiletical flair by Ray Stedman:

20. This idea is gestured to by King in his stress on the need for "total surrender." See King, *Strength to Love*, 50.
21. King, *Strength to Love*, 50.
22. King, *Strength to Love*, 50.
23. King, *Strength to Love*, 51.
24. King, *Strength to Love*, 51.
25. King, *Strength to Love*, 54.
26. See Bornkamm, *Paul*, 218, where the workings of love "are set in complete contrast to the natural man's acts and go far beyond what he can ever achieve."
27. See Bender, *1 Corinthians*, 224. "Paul defines love by listing a number of its

> Love is not an ethereal thing; it is not just an ideal that you talk about. It is something that takes on shoe leather and moves right down into the normal, ordinary pursuits and aspects of life. That is where love is manifest.[28]

Paul sees this manifestation not only in the display of patience and kindness but in the absence of those vices that persistently undermine and damage human relationships. Love, in other words, is comprehended in what we do and do not do.[29] The *patience* Paul has in mind here is a behavior largely exercised towards people and not circumstances. This is borne out by the older translation "long-suffering" in the Authorized Version. It is a quality of forbearance that allows the person not to act in anger or retaliation towards the one who has injured them. If this might be called the passive face of love (refraining from doing the harmful thing), then its active outworking is *kindness*—the expression of care and goodness even towards those who do harm.[30] Articulated in these terms, we can see the continuity between Jesus' costly call to love (expounded by Martin Luther King Jr.) and the implications of Paul's own vision for the mature life of love.

Before moving on to briefly consider those other Trinitarian-inspired traits of Christian maturity and their related themes, it will be instructive to list the behaviors that evidence love's absence. These are as accurate in their depiction of love as the previous positive demonstrations. They include these seven defining attributes of unloving actions: *envy* (being jealous of what others have); *bragging* (having "an inordinate desire to draw attention to oneself"[31]), *pridefulness* (being conceited and overly sure of oneself), *rudeness* (acting in an unseemly and disrespectful way), *self-seeking* (pushing for one's own way), *easily triggered anger* ("touchiness"[32]), *resentfulness* (unable to forget or let go of hurts), and *rejoicing in wrongdoing* (celebrating evil and enjoying the injustice

---

essential forms of action. While most translations list these as adjectives (patient, kind, etc.), he actually defines love in terms of verbs of action—for example, 'love shows patience,' 'love displays kindness,' and so on. Love is not characterized by a random list of qualities but set forth as the embodiment of concrete actions that define its character. Noting here that love is not merely goodwill but manifested in actions."

28. Stedman, "Supreme Priority."
29. Barrett, *First Corinthians*, 303.
30. Barrett, *First Corinthians*, 303.
31. Fee, *First Corinthians*, 637.
32. Barrett, *First Corinthians*, 303.

perpetrated on others).[33] The ability to do, and then not do, some of what Paul describes here is only possible as the fruit of a deep relationship with God and presupposes profound personal engagement with our own interior lives. The ensuing qualities will often emerge subliminally, and the loving person may not carry around any such self-perception.

A Self-Giving Pattern of Life

Against the logic of our own human categories, the triune God of Scripture may be rightfully described as a *servant*. This becomes apparent when we consider some of the defining ways in which God's ministry and activity are recounted in Scripture. The most quoted verse in the Bible asserts that "God so *loved* the world that he *gave* his one and only Son" (John 3:16; emphasis added). Hence, while Greek philosophy might make great play of God being impassible and emotionally untouched by any other reality, the desire of the writer of John's Gospel is to communicate the huge cost involved in God the Father initiating the incarnation. This was an act of supreme sacrifice on the part of the Father. Likewise, the ministry of the Son is characterized as one of utter self-giving. For example, Paul urges the recipients of 2 Corinthians to remember that Jesus Christ, although he was rich, became poor for our sake (2 Cor 8:9). However, this act of self-abnegation was not merely a voluntary exchange of habitats (the choice to swap a heavenly existence for an earthly one), but a steady, unwavering commitment to give of himself absolutely on behalf of others, culminating in the sacrifice of the cross. This was the import of the great Christological hymn in Phil 2:5–11 where the depths of Christ's self-sacrifice are spelt out against the backdrop of the human situation and the inner life of God. Servanthood was so innate to the incarnate life of the Son, and so much an encapsulation of what should define the redeemed human state, that Jesus' final dramatic gesture towards his disciples was the act of foot washing. This was not the ceremonial act of servanthood that it has become in contemporary Christianity (which ironically marks out the *most important* person in the room), but an uncomfortable and self-denying act that defied every notion of human worth and value. This closing gesture was the ministry of Christ beautifully summed up and set forth as the pattern for his future disciples. Similarly, the third person of the Trinity, the Holy Spirit, also emerges within the pages of Scripture as

---

33. Bender, *1 Corinthians*, 227.

servant-like. This is particularly clear from his self-effacing ministry ("he will not speak of himself") and work as Paraclete within the Gospel of John. The standard translation of Paraclete as "Helper" underscores the degree to which the ministry of the Triune God subverts human notions of power and position.

How does the kind of self-giving we have been discussing above express itself in a human being who is genuinely following Christ? J. I. Packer captures perfectly the mindset that Christ seeks to instill in his followers:

> What work does Christ set his servants to do? The way that they serve him, he tells them, is by becoming the slaves of their fellow servants and being willing to do literally anything, however costly, irksome, or undignified, in order to help them. This is what love means, as he himself showed at the Last Supper when he played the slave's part and washed the disciples' feet.[34]

Truly servant-like behavior is always the product of the Holy Spirit's ministry and most assuredly not a collection of performative actions undertaken for the approval of others. As Packer further explains, "Only the Holy Spirit can create in us the kind of love toward our Savior that will overflow in imaginative sympathy and practical helpfulness towards his people."[35] Without that divine stimulus, any number of human motives can lie behind our "good actions." We can be influenced by social expectation, a craving for recognition, or simply the impact of our whims or moods (i.e., we may choose to do the helpful thing when we feel like it). However, real self-giving will not be dependent on our frame of mind but will be a consistent pattern of behavior born out of the practice of the spiritual disciplines and the energizing power of the Spirit working in synergy with this.

A Passion for Unity

This may seem an unlikely trait to highlight so prominently in a list of spiritual characteristics that definitively mark out Christian maturity. Suspicion of the ecumenical movement and/or robust confidence in one's own style of theology, whether this be Roman Catholic, "Reformed," Pentecostal, dispensationalist, or even liberal and progressive, will often

---

34. Packer, *Your Father Loves You*, 62.
35. Packer, *Your Father Loves You*, 62.

mean that the call to unity has little appeal. Indeed, the default reaction is often the assumption that others must gravitate towards *our* position before any worthwhile dialogue is even possible. A passion for unity, then, can seem unrealistic or wrongheaded or theologically compromised or far removed from matters of more immediate concern for the church, depending on our vantage point. Moreover, given the prevalence of this outlook, one might even be tempted to question whether there is any value at all in promoting this trait as an indispensable aspect of spiritual maturity.

Such misgivings have to be measured against two vital considerations that are often missed by the churches. First, if our being made in the image of God is meant to reflect the inner life of the Trinity and the divine priorities within that life, there can hardly be any greater ecclesial or individual goal than the quest for unity enjoined by Jesus in his high priestly prayer in John 17:

> I ask not only on behalf of these, but also on behalf of those who believe in me through their word, that they may all be one. As you, Father, are in me and I am in you, may they also be in us, so that the world may believe that you sent me. (John 17:20–21 NRSV)

Reflection on this prayer underscores for me the dissonance between Jesus' own vision for the church and the almost unthinking toleration of disunity and division that characterizes the mindset of so many ecclesial communities. Thankfully, some prominent theologians have acknowledged the contradiction and invited the church to take stock of its manifest failure in this area. Geoffrey Wainwright highlights what he calls "the absurd disunity among Christians"[36] and urges his readers to grasp what the church is meant to be. "If Christ is the revelation of self-giving love, the body of his followers must be expected to exhibit a unity in which the members are bound to one another by the ties of mutual self-giving love."[37] Lutheran theologian Peter Leithart, in a similar vein, calls us to recognize that Jesus' plea for unity has not diminished or become less binding over time. The churches have simply institutionalized their disobedience in the face of Jesus' radical call.

> This is what Jesus *wants* for his church [i.e., for it to be genuinely united]. It is *not* what his church is. The church is divided. It is

36. Wainwright, *Doxology*, 123.
37. Wainwright, *Doxology*, 122.

not that the church has remained united while groups falsely calling themselves churches have split off. It is *not* that we are spiritually united while empirically divided.

The church is a unique society, the body of Christ and the temple of the Spirit. But it is a visible society that exists among other societies. That visible society is divided, and that means the *church* is divided. This is not as it should be. This is not the church that Jesus desires. So long as we remain divided, we grieve the Spirit of Jesus, who is the living Passion of the Father and Son.[38]

The second important consideration to bear in mind also has its roots in the high priestly prayer of Jesus. At the close of the passage cited above, Jesus draws a striking correlation between the visible unity of the church and the effective proclamation of the gospel to the world. It must rank as one of the most stunning charges ever given by an authoritative founder to have subsequently been so roundly ignored. Only in the last sixty years has Jesus' plea for unity been taken seriously by major segments of the church. It is a happy coincidence that the evangelical who most embodied a passion for Christian unity and made it a prerequisite for participation in his evangelistic campaigns (Billy Graham), and the Catholic Pontiff most dedicated to spiritual ecumenism and the healing of the breach with Protestantism (John Paul II), stood side by side in a historic service at Kraców Cathedral in 1978 where Graham proclaimed the gospel at Cardinal Karol Wojtyła's (the city's archbishop) invitation. The unity exhibited there (so rare that it earned a mention in the British national news) was a momentary glimpse of how rapprochement, rooted in an orthodox understanding of Christ and the gospel, can speak powerfully to the world. A passion for the visible unity of those who believe in the historic faith should be a trait of those properly formed in Christ.

A Personal and Social Holiness

The archetypal characteristic of the mature Christian is a quality of holiness that sets them apart from those around them. Of course, being different to others is no guarantee that one is genuinely holy. Church people can exhibit the worst features found in the Gospels—Pharisees, looking down on those they consider "moral outcasts"—with the same coldhearted disdain. It was this disposition among the watching Pharisees

---

38. Leithart, *End of Protestantism*, 1.

that inspired the parables of Luke 15 (i.e., the lost sheep, the lost coin, and the lost son). Indeed, taking our lead from Jesus' gospel ministry, I would suggest that the qualities that drew "sinners" to Christ are the ones which tell us most about the nature of true holiness. Looking at Jesus' manner of life in the Gospels, we discover characteristics that both challenge and inspire—love for the Father, compassion for the outsider, an attractive goodness that enticed individuals to live differently, and a fundamental integrity that expressed itself in the refusal to embrace falsehood, self-aggrandize, use or manipulate others, or be drawn into any other form of moral dysfunction. While these qualities may appear off-putting as a standard for the ordinary Christian to aspire to, we must remember that they were lived out by one whose humanity was the model for our own restored human nature.

The caption heading "A Personal and Social Holiness" may be misleading as personal holiness also has a social dimension, and some may not understand the distinction. What were the terms intended to convey? The first point to note is that holiness is understood largely in personal or individual terms. It is something that is felt to show itself in the narrow ambit of our personal interactions. It is thought to be entirely about the struggle to overcome our own *individual* sin. However, this category of sin is quite distinct from another expression of sin that the Hebrew Bible places great emphasis upon. When the Old Testament writers talk about God's justice and righteousness, their focus is on society and the way it is ordered. They saw that things were not as God intended, and that individuals were badly damaged by an unjust social reality that impeded their ability to live life as God had purposed. Hence, the passionate preaching of Amos against societal blindness to the oppression of the poor (e.g., Amos 2:6–8; 5:10–12; 8:4–6) and the development of the concept of Jubilee in Lev 17–26 to put right embedded injustices in Israel were two ways in which the negative impact of "structural sin" was addressed.

This challenging expansion of the call to holiness rooted within the Torah and the prophets has influenced the fourth Anglican mark of mission, which calls the church "to transform unjust structures of society, to challenge violence of every kind and pursue peace and reconciliation."[39] It has also inspired one of the most telling quips ever made about people's blindness to structural sin. Archbishop Hélder Câmara, the former bishop of the diocese of Recife in Brazil, commented, "When I give food to

---

39. Anglican Communion, "Marks of Mission."

the poor they call me a saint. When I ask why so many people are poor, they call me a communist."[40] The reaction of Câmara's critics illustrates how individuals can ignore the systemic nature of injustice and view any attempt to eradicate it as an insidious ideology. True holiness, while never negating the significance of individual sin, will always be concerned that those whose lives have been blighted by injustice will know freedom. The holding together of these two priorities is essential when our polarized culture will valorize only the importance of personal morality *or* social justice but not grasp the need to integrate both.

Joy

The final trait of Christian maturity we will examine is joy. Its nature is vastly different from its synonym happiness since the latter is determined by realities external to the person. Happiness is contingent on things being well while joy can be known amid the most trying of circumstances. Perhaps the miracle of Paul's Letter to the Philippians is the joy experienced by the apostle while under house arrest in Rome. Joy is a theological virtue, one of the fruits of the Spirit and an end-product of living the pattern of life explored earlier in this chapter. As we take our union with Christ seriously, practicing the disciplines and having our capacity for love and works of service honed by the Spirit, this unique quality of joy will become increasingly evident in our personality.

Smith characterizes joy as the ultimate mark of the mature Christian. It is not simply an additional virtue to be added to the others, but the ultimate virtue which testifies to the deep work of God in our characters. Smith cites the words of an Eastern Orthodox theologian, Alexander Schmemman, to illustrate the overarching significance of joy in the believer's life:

> I think God will forgive everything except the lack of joy; when we forget that God created the world and saved it. Joy is not one of the components of Christianity, it is the tonality of Christianity that penetrates everything.[41]

Joy has many expressions. It is present in our anticipation of final redemption and the beatific vision. It accompanies us as we reflect on God's work in our own lives and his gracious purposes for the future. It

---

40. Goodreads, "Hélder Câmara."
41. Schmemman, *Journals*, 25–26.

functions as the sign of his presence when an inner peace overrides our feelings of fear or disarray. It is evidence of divine liberation when we are able to truly enjoy nature, beauty, humor, and all the goods of this world with unfettered gratitude. It expresses itself in a warmhearted humanity that enlivens human relationships. This is the gift and the fruit of the Christian life which we are called to make our strength (Neh 8:10).

Conclusion

What has our study taught us about the goal of pastoral ministry and its attainment? Three key lessons have emerged over the course of the chapter. First, while pastoral ministry is often "in the moment" (i.e., a response to an immediate pastoral need), we have been reminded that there is a clearly articulated pastoral goal which all are called to serve within their ministry contexts. This is each individual church member's *maturity in Christ* (i.e., their restoration to the divine image). This idea of *maturity* as the focus of pastoral ministry is communicated with great clarity by Paul in his discussion of the ascended Christ's gifts to the church in Ephesians.

> The gifts he gave where that some would be apostles, some prophets, some evangelists, some pastors and teachers, to equip the saints for the work of ministry, for building up the body of Christ, until all of us come to the unity of the faith and of the knowledge of the Son of God, to maturity, to the measure of the full stature of Christ. (Eph 4:11–13 NRSV)

Secondly, fulfilment of this calling must involve the church creating the means by which the process of transformation can take place in individuals. This involves inviting and equipping them to undertake a serious interior journey with Christ. Here a combination of self-honesty and life-giving spiritual practices can enable them to grow out of their spiritual immaturity and increasingly take on the character of Christ. They will begin to become little Christs. However, as that above citation from Paul reminds us, this is not simply a private journey of transformation. The process by which Christians are changed necessarily involves the ministry of others. However, this will only be effective as Christians exercise their gifts for the benefit of their fellow believers. Their bare presence in the church building or meeting place will not by itself minister life to those around them. Vibrant worship (both sacramental and informal), life-giving teaching, practical and emotional support in times of trouble and the experience of a common life will be the real means by which Christ's image is further restored and God is experienced as present among his people.

Thirdly, the centrality of "relationship" (divine/human and in the life of the church) to the process of transformation may tell us quite a lot about the divine image to which we are being restored. Following Karl Barth, I suggest that our image bearing rests not primarily in our individual capacities like creativity and intelligence, but in our relationality. Human beings are made in the image of a triune, relational, self-giving God and we are most like him when our human relationships reflect the pattern of the Trinitarian life. This is hugely important for our understanding of what it means to be re-made in the image of God. This image reveals itself most tellingly in how we relate to other human beings. Hence, qualities like love, servanthood, the vision for and commitment to unity within the body of Christ and holiness (demonstrated at both a personal level in our normal interactions and in our concern for righteousness and justice within society) are the truest indicators of moral transformation and the life of Christ being present.

As a way of bringing the chapter to a close, I wish to describe briefly the character of a little Christ. Their capacity to love will be most evident at that point where other people's willingness to love has run aground. They will be characterized by an astonishing capacity to exercise moral restraint in the face of provocation or disrespect. Forgiveness will be their most practiced art. There will be an air of humility in interpersonal dealings and a palpable absence of ego. Their acts of service will be genuinely costly and invisible to everyone else. While never compromising any vital belief, they will long to be faithful to Christ's final plea for visible Christian unity. This will involve approaching every "mere Christian" (in Lewis' terminology) with respect and openness, seeking to draw them into closer fellowship in the Lord. Their kindness and trustworthiness at a personal level will be matched by a passion for righteousness and a longing for God's shalom in the world. Underlying all these wonderful traits will be a profound and lasting inward joy. We long for Christ's work in us to bring this new person fully into being.

"And ah for a man to arise in me, That the man I am may cease to be!"[42]

---

42. Tennyson, *Maud and Other Poems*, 1.10.6.

Anglican Perspectives

4

The Bible and Pastoral Ministry: "Two Facets of One Reality"

William Olhausen

Introduction

Eugene Peterson said, "Pastoral work properly originates, as does all Christian ministry, in the biblical sources."[1] While such an observation may make pastoral ministry appear straightforward, it also begs important questions about the relationship between the two. How should one address such an expansive theme as the Bible and pastoral ministry? I was greatly helped by a small book of disparate essays and addresses written by the late archbishop of Canterbury, Michael Ramsey.[2] In the final section of the book, entitled "Concerning the Ministry," three of the addresses have a direct bearing on our theme: "The Call of Christ," "Pastors and Teachers: An Ordination Charge," and "A Devout, Learned, and Useful Clergy." Taken together, they go a long way in identifying the essentials of Anglican ordained ministry. What is striking is the way Ramsey's understanding of the ordained ministry insists on the essential unity of Bible and pastoral care and truth and love, what he calls "two facets of one reality."[3] Without prejudice to the many and varied ministries of all

---

1. Peterson, *Five Smooth Stones*, 1–2.
2. Ramsey, *Durham Essays*.
3. Ramsey, *Durham Essays*, 121.

believers, I have attempted to put together something of a framework to understand the ways in which the Bible and pastoral ministry interact within, primarily, the Anglican tradition, though the lessons can be much more widely applied.

An Anglican Understanding of the Pastoral Task

When *The Oxford Dictionary of the Christian Church* was first published in the 1950s, there was only one small entry for those things that we might consider falling within the semantic range of "pastoral care." The word used then was the Latin *pastoralia*. Here is the entry:

> The branch of theology concerned with the principles regulating the life and conduct of the parish priest. Among the subjects which it normally includes are:
>
> i. the methods of public worship and administration of the sacraments;
> ii. preaching and sermon construction;
> iii. the care of the sick and dying;
> iv. the study of moral theology.
>
> All exponents of the subject are agreed that the personal training of the pastor himself [sic] in prayer and devotion to his calling are the precondition of all success.[4]

This definition is arresting and feels countercultural at a time when it is so easy to be mesmerized by, and caught between, the Scylla of relevance and innovation on the one hand, and the Charybdis of compliance and administration on the other.[5] It is also worth noticing the fourth element in the above definition. The study of moral theology is increasingly becoming a lost art. Under the heading of "moral theology" we would certainly want to include ongoing theological reflection, but it also entails the increasingly important task of apologetics within the fields of public or political theology, the critical task of re-presenting the gospel in the public square. What the definition of *pastoralia* misses is

---

4. Cross, ed., *Oxford Dictionary*, 1023. Further light is shed on pastoral ministry in the dictionary's entry for "The Visitation of the Sick" on p. 1426.

5. This is not to suggest that contextualization or excellence in administration are really monsters. They become monsters for the pastor who has been distracted or unnecessarily burdened by those things that do not primarily belong to the vocation of the pastor-teacher.

the ongoing ministerial task of enabling discipleship.[6] This certainly takes place in corporate worship, but it also needs to happen in midweek fellowship or home groups, as well as the incidental encounters between pastor and members of the parish church. We see this emphasis in the Ordinal. Deacons are "to strengthen the faithful, search out the careless and the indifferent. . . . When called upon to do so, they may . . . give instruction in the faith."[7] Priests are to "teach and to admonish, to feed and to provide for the Lord's family."[8] Bishops are to "guard the faith" and to teach and govern those committed to their charge "after the example of the apostles."[9]

Every Christian tradition authorizes ministers according to some interpretation of the biblical witness, especially the New Testament. This is informed, and sometimes distorted, by time, place, and local ecclesiology. Consequently, there might be things we would want to say about why the Anglican understanding of the ordering of ministers draws strongly on the Pastoral Epistles (1 and 2 Timothy and Titus).[10] Along with being "learned in the Latin tongue"(!), *The Book of Common Prayer* outlines further criteria attaching to the authorization of ministers; namely, they be "called, tried, examined and admitted."[11] The admission to the ministry must be accompanied by "publick prayer with the imposition of hands." These additional criteria attach both to the "lawful" status of the minister (bishop, priest, or deacon) and, importantly, to the empowering for "the said functions." The qualification for ministry and the actual act of ordination, like the ordering of ministers, rest equally on an interpretation of the Bible.[12]

6. See, for instance, Anglican Communion, "Intentional Discipleship."
7. *BCP* 2004, 555.
8. *BCP* 2004, 532.
9. *BCP* 2004, 576.
10. The formalization or institutionalizing of these three orders was not fully settled until at least the third century, but there is Scriptural warrant for them. See Walcott, *Annotated Book*, 665. However, it is also worth noting that the Pastoral Epistles are indicative of a more settled and institutionalized church polity. Other church traditions might appeal to the Gospels, to the Book of Acts or other Pauline letters. Many of the new churches are drawn to the five-fold ministry model of apostles, prophets, evangelists, pastors, and teachers. In Christendom, there is less perceived need for "apostles," prophets, and evangelists. There is an argument for saying that alongside the pastor-teacher vocation, these are also ministries that need retrieving for the Western church today.
11. From the Preface to the Ordinal in the *BCP* 1662, 518.
12. On the qualifications for "ordained" ministry and the laying on of hands, the

According to Ralph McMichael, the "vocation of Anglican theology is to bring people into the presence of God, and then see what happens,"[13] and David Hansen suggests that pastors need to be "parables of Jesus Christ to the people we meet."[14] In different ways, Hansen and McMichael remind us that ministry is deeply relational because it originates in a very personal encounter with God. This is reflected in the service of ordination. In his charge, "The Call of Christ," Ramsey reminds the ordinands of the question asked by the bishop of every candidate at the beginning of an ordination service: "Do you believe in your heart that God has called you to the office and work of a deacon in his Church?" The candidate replies: "I believe that God has called me." Ordination is therefore premised on a personal experience of God's summons and an acknowledgment that this call is to God's work in a church that belongs to God. Ramsey interprets this divine call in Christological terms. It is "a call to *him* (Christ), to be with *him*, to share *his* mission and ministry."[15] He continues, "All vocations are from God; all alike involve a call to be Christ-like; all are equally sacred; but the minister of word and sacrament shares in Christ's own as apostle and shepherd. In the last resort the call is not to a profession but to *him*."[16] Graham Tomlin helps us to understand this vocation within a much larger divine plan cast in terms of priesthood: humanity's priestly ministry to the creation; the church's priestly ministry to humanity; and the ministry of priests (authorized ministers) to the church. While all these priestly responsibilities find their vocation in Christ, the Great High Priest, Tomlin writes, "The focus of ordained ministry is first and foremost the Church: it is to enable the Church to be the Church."[17] Instead of speaking about priesthood, Ramsey reflects the Ordinal's emphasis on the vocation of the pastor-teacher, which he calls "one of the glories of our Anglican tradition."[18] Without prejudice to any other ways of understanding ordained ministry, the office of

---

Pastoral Epistles are particularly in view (especially 1 Tim 3:1–12; 2 Tim 1:6-7; and Titus 1:5–9). "Overseers" and "deacons" are mentioned in 1 Tim 3. "Elder" (presbyter/priest) is mentioned in Titus 1:5 and 6 and appears to be interchangeable for "overseer" (bishop). For "overseers," see also Acts 20:28; and Phil 1: 1.

13. McMichael, *The Vocation of Anglican Theology*, 24.
14. Hansen, *Art of Pastoring*, 11.
15. Ramsey, *Durham Essays*, 118; emphasis original.
16. Ramsey, *Durham Essays*, 119; emphasis original.
17. Tomlin, *Widening Circle*, 119.
18. Ramsey, *Durham Essays*, 123.

pastor-teacher invites us to investigate more closely the relationship of Bible to pastoral ministry.

The Loves of a Pastor-Teacher

The reason the office of pastor-teacher is so helpful is because it holds together that which should never be separated: "The tasks of the pastor and the teacher are like two facets of one reality: they interpret one another. . . . The lover of human lives who for their sake studies the mysteries of God: the student of truth whose books are marked with the love of human lives—that is the great tradition which our Ordinal sets before us."[19] Ramsey underlines the imperative to know and love one's congregation, "to care for them." At the same time, pastoral love "is rooted in the truth," which the pastor is called to teach.[20] It is this truth that gives depth and requires restraints. In other words, the love called forth from a pastor is a love that needs to be disciplined by truth. It is reasonable to ask what Ramsey means by truth. Anglican thought has often been drawn to the language and theology of John's Gospel. In that Gospel, truth is not the Bible as text but is the one whom the text reveals: the Word made flesh. This approach to truth has some considerable benefits, including an avoidance of any tendency towards Protestant scholasticism, fundamentalism, or literalism. Identifying truth with the person of Christ is not only faithful to the New Testament witness, but it also reminds us that this truth must show itself in the action and practice of everyday life and especially in pastoral ministry. However, this personal conception of truth does not rule out some version of (critical) realism. In other words, the Gospel witness to Christ was indeed a witness to events in the world. Archbishop William Temple could say, "If the whole story is a myth its quality as revelation is destroyed. The Gospel is that 'The Word was made flesh,' and being incarnate so spoke, so acted, so died and so rose from death."[21] Elsewhere, Temple can simply say, "The life of Christ is a momentary manifestation of eternal truth."[22]

How does this truth-shaped love express itself? First, it will be "reverent" love because people are made in the image of God. Ramsey exhorts

---

19. Ramsey, *Durham Essays*, 121.
20. Ramsey, *Durham Essays*, 122.
21. Temple, *Readings in John's Gospel*, xiii.
22. Temple, *About Christ*, 63.

us to "never forget that great doctrine."[23] Gregory Dix, too, understood the *imago Dei* as an expression of God's love: "Man is the creature of Love, made for Love's purpose. And that purpose is the *return* of love."[24] In loving people, we also love them enough to see their vulnerabilities and weaknesses. This is how Dix expresses it: "This is the deep mystery of my being, that I am at once both created and free. The whole tragic possibility of sin lies here. I am able of my own nature to go against the very Being of That upon Which I am utterly dependent—and yet I do not immediately destroy myself in so doing. This is the painful mystery of man's existence."[25] It is the pastor-teacher who must attend to this painful mystery, the deep surgery needed in every human soul. This is the critical task that demands a clear love for God's truth: "In serving them in the name of God's love, you must needs be serving them in the name of God's truth."[26]

Secondly, Christian love is costly. It is a love that involves a letting go of and dying to certain impulses and behaviors. The minister's vocation is a reminder that we have been bought at a price, our bodies no longer belong to us (1 Cor 6:19–20). We are to be living sacrifices (Rom 12:1). In very practical terms, Ramsey urges wisdom and discernment when it comes to friendships in the parish. He warns against our own need to be liked, approved of, or admired: "You are sent to be the teacher of the truth, and it is easy to be popular for superficial reasons and to forget to look again and again at our crucified Lord and ask that our boast may be only in him."[27] Ramsey notes again, "Where there is a zeal for the truth combined with a love for souls commended by holiness of life, *there* souls are won and edified."[28] Our churches desperately need to see and experience the reality of souls won and edified. This points us to a further way in which the pastor-teacher is to love: they will be devoted to the apostles' teaching (Acts 2:42).

Thirdly, the pastor-teacher must cultivate a love for the tradition. Ramsey's third address is inspired by a phrase from a prayer taken from the benediction in the liturgy used at the coronation of Queen Elizabeth II: that the monarch may enjoy "a devout, learned, and useful clergy." The

---

23. Ramsey, *Durham Essays*, 122.
24. Dix, *Image and Likeness*, 21; emphasis original.
25. Dix, *Image and Likeness*, 20.
26. Ramsey, *Durham Essays*, 122.
27. Ramsey, *Durham Essays*, 122. Cf. 1 Cor. 2:2.
28. Ramsey, *Durham Essays*, 124; emphasis original.

phrase is taken from the First Letter to Timothy (4:16). Ramsey explains: "Take heed to thyself: that is *devoutness*. Take heed to the teaching: that is the call to *learning*. Thou shalt save them that hear thee: that is to be *useful*—towards the greatest ends."[29] To be learned is not necessarily to be a scholar or an intellectual, but it is, argues Ramsey, to be someone who "constantly wins fresh knowledge and fresh understanding of the Faith which he teaches."[30] He cites Christ's own "utter consecration to the truth."[31] Ramsey charges the ordinands to "Make friends with the greatest writers, in Biblical exposition, in Christian doctrine, in the classics of Christian spirituality."[32] Importantly, he also commends pastors "to make a special study of one book of the Bible every year."[33] And once again he reminds us that taking heed of our teaching is precisely because we have a pastoral duty of care to our congregations. With the considerable assistance of Ramsey's wisdom, we have a clearer understanding of the ideals of Anglican ministry. We need now to acknowledge the very real challenges to realizing the vocation to be pastor-teachers, and the greatest challenge has been the contested status of the texts upon which that vocation rests: the Bible.

Challenges to the Ministry of the Pastor-Teacher

Two challenges, representing pastoral ministry and the Bible respectively, are clear: 1) confusion about the purpose and practice of pastoral ministry; and 2) a crisis of confidence in the status of the Bible. Ramsey has helped us to see more clearly the vocation of the pastoral task, but this beautiful ideal rests on the Bible as Christian Scripture. In his book, *The Word of Life*, William Challis wrote about the relationship between the Bible and pastoral ministry. In the preface, he describes three types of ministers: first, the minister who has lost confidence in the Bible and has no expectation of it having anything useful to say to their congregation; secondly, the minister who holds a high regard for the authority of the Bible but rarely attempts to make any meaningful connection for people between Sundays; and, thirdly, the minister who holds a high regard for

---

29. Ramsey, *Durham Essays*, 126; emphasis original.
30. Ramsey, *Durham Essays*, 127.
31. Ramsey, *Durham Essays*, 128.
32. Ramsey, *Durham Essays*, 127.
33. Ramsey, *Durham Essays*, 128.

the authority of the Bible and insists on opening it for every pastoral encounter. Challis concludes,

> All three styles of ministry are inadequate. The first is barely Christian, the last barely human. The one fails to offer people anything that truly speaks of God and contains no element of transformation in Christ. The other can seem irrelevant, or indeed crass and insensitive. The second style of ministry is more complex to assess, but it is clearly dualistic. There are probably many of us who have managed to maintain such a style of ministry over many years, but further reflection, and pastoral practice, make it appear increasingly unsatisfactory.[34]

Challis was writing almost thirty years ago, but his assessment, in general terms, remains true: integrating Bible and pastoral ministry in contextually sensitive and life-giving ways is not easy and is rarely practiced well. Challis argues that "Bible and pastoral care belong together. . . . The reality of pastoral experience must be allowed to meet our biblical understanding."[35] In Anglican terms, Challis was calling for a renewal of the office of the pastor-teacher.

The Bible and Reason

We need to say something more about Challis's first example, the minister who has lost confidence in the Bible. It is often said that Anglicanism has a distinctive approach to thinking about faith and the life of faith, which privileges Scripture, tradition, and reason. The seventeenth-century Anglican scholar, Richard Hooker, is probably the person most closely associated with the development of this approach. Much ink has been spilled to defend or critique Hooker's view, especially, of reason. According to Nigel Atkinson, Hooker owed his understanding of reason to Luther and Calvin and the Continental Reformers.[36] Drawing a distinction between the laws or spheres of grace and nature, reason properly belongs to the sphere of nature and is God-given, part of what it means to be made in the image of God. But, unaided, reason is not sufficient to understand spiritual things. In other words, reason is certainly competent to gain all sorts

---

34. Challis, *Word of Life*, xvi.
35. Challis, *Word of Life*, xvi–xvii.
36. For Atkinson's view on Hooker and reason see Atkinson, *Richard Hooker*, 1–33, (especially 27–33).

of empirical or natural knowledge. This is both a high view of reason and a recognition of the limits of reason when it comes to understanding the mysteries of the gospel, which by their very nature are revealed. For this reason, Hooker was not a proto-rationalist, but neither can he be accused of fideism because biblical revelation is not the only type of knowledge; there are things we can know, especially about the natural world, without the assistance of biblical revelation. It is also worth remembering that for Hooker, as for all the Reformers, the critical scholarship of the humanists was extremely important.[37] The intellectual blossoming of Renaissance humanism allowed them to draw on all that was helpful in the sphere of reason in their theological task. The nature of the relationship that holds between reason and faith (nature and grace) has generated much scholarly disagreement and ecclesial divisions. For Christians, the risk of falling into some sort of dualism can only be overcome by a robust doctrine of creation in which every creature, in its rightful creation order, is a good in and of itself.

In relation to faith and the interpretation of the Bible, we can therefore thank God for the tools of reason and critical thinking as we bring them into conversation with the revelation of the Gospel. For instance, critical thinking helps us to make arguments and to assess arguments for their strengths and weaknesses. This is a life skill, but it is especially important in academia and when it comes to studying the Bible or reading a textbook on theology. Getting to grips with the rigor of reasoning is not easy. It is like mastering a new language or a new skill—it takes "devotion" and "learning" to quote Ramsey.[38] Thankfully, the church has more resources and more learning than ever to assist the pastor-teacher to take up and read. Training for ministry can happen in a confessional context—one in which biblical studies is taught from a faith perspective. There is no reason why this cannot also be critical, but, clearly, it assumes a certain Christian worldview without asking the student to, as it were, build from the ground up. The more usual way for training ordinands in the Anglican tradition, in Ireland and in England, is a hybrid model where some teaching is looked after by the theological college and some

---

37. Atkinson, *Richard Hooker*, 11. For instance, it was a recovery of classical learning and a developing historical consciousness that led them to question the status and authority of certain beliefs and traditions alien to the original biblical witness, the true source of the Church's authority. This privileging of origins, *ad fontes*, meant a new-found interest in the biblical languages.

38. Ramsey, *Durham Essays*, 126–27.

subjects are taught by a university department where individual lecturers may or may not share a Christian faith. There are strengths and weaknesses in both models, but the hybrid model will take students on a journey that they may find difficult or with which they will not meaningfully engage. Regrettably the hybrid model has often produced hybrid clergy who have taken on board enough information to leave them either disorientated by an apparent disconnect between the Bible of the pew and the Bible of the academy, or giddy from the process of disenchantment. Alternatively, the ordinand who has been warned that they will "lose their faith" at theological college may fail to engage critically or even meaningfully with their studies. Leave to one side those for whom academic work is very demanding; this is the path to fundamentalism, or some other sort of arrested development, and it very often comes back to bite the minister, or worse, their congregation. Some parts of the church, even some senior clergy, attach little value to study. Theological college is something to be endured before being released to do the proper business. This is, I suggest, a betrayal of the call to be a pastor-teacher and presents serious challenges to the second leg of the Anglican three-legged stool: tradition[39].

The Bible and Tradition

We have seen how the pastor-teacher needs to cultivate a love for the tradition. We need now to say something more about what tradition is and why it is so important for the pastor-teacher. Dietrich Bonhoeffer said that we need to have some idea of who God is before we even read the Bible.[40] He is saying that the Bible needs a context within which to be read and understood. Think, for instance, of the occasion when the Ethiopian eunuch asks Philip the deacon to explain the meaning of Isa 53: "About whom, may I ask you, does the prophet say this is, about himself or about someone else?" (Acts 8:34).[41] Notwithstanding the high doctrine of Scripture that our Anglican tradition confers, we need to hold

---

39. Tradition can be a loaded word and there are differing ways of understanding exactly what it means and what its relationship to Scripture might be. In Anglicanism, tradition is understood to be in a continuing conversation with reason and the interpretation of Scripture. It certainly includes Christian wisdom accumulated and proved since the time of the primitive church.

40. Bonhoeffer, *Meditating on the Word*, 44.

41. All Scripture quotations in chapter 4 taken from the NRSV.

articles 6 and 7 of the Thirty-Nine Articles of Religion together with the sometimes-forgotten authority of human agents. In his commentary of the Thirty-Nine Articles, Bicknell includes this significant observation of Richard Hooker's:

> For whatsoever we believe concerning salvation by Christ, although the Scripture be therein the ground of our belief; yet the authority of man is, if we mark it, the key which openeth the door of entrance into the knowledge of Scripture. The Scripture could not teach us the things that are of God unless we did credit men who have taught us that the words of Scripture do signify those things.[42]

Hooker's observation reminds us of the interdependent relationship between Bible and human agency. We call this dynamic "tradition."

In the middle of a theological argument, and in exasperation, someone might say, "You simply don't know the tradition!" This is probably true for most pastor-teachers today.[43] There are several reasons why this is not ideal and why, I am sure, Ramsey encouraged a group of Durham ordinands to build into their ministries time to read the great works of theology alongside a deep study of at least one book of the Bible each year. The first and most important reason that the pastor-teacher should have some awareness of the tradition is because it is the ideal context for reading and interpreting the Bible. How the church has read the Bible previously illuminates our understanding today. This is closely connected with the second reason why this forgetting of the tradition is a threat: without an understanding of the tradition, it becomes very difficult to think theologically. The history of art might serve as an analogy. To interpret great pieces of art you need to know from where their inspiration came: Which pieces of art are they talking to, reacting, or alluding to? So much of art, literature, and music is text on text. Tradition in the general sense provides the framework of meaning. Only by familiarizing ourselves with a tradition can we teach and think across time and space.

One of the great strengths of Anglicanism has been the way the great scholar-bishops, whether they have been evangelical, catholic or liberal, have had a good understanding of the tradition. Not everything

---

42. Hooker quoted in Bicknell, *Thirty-Nine Articles*, 129.

43. This is one reason why there have been moves to retrieve the vocation of the pastor-theologian or scholar. See, for instance, Hiestand and Wilson, *Pastor Theologian*; and their edited volume *Becoming a Pastor Theologian*; or Vanhoozer and Strachan, *Pastor as Public Theologian*. See also Center for Pastor Theologians, "Vision & Mission."

they have said or written is right or true, but in the conversation, wisdom emerges, and new possibilities or insights begin to take shape. To put this another way, meaningful improvisation can only happen when someone knows that they are improvising! If the pastor-teachers forget the tradition we will continue to lose where we are in the conversation and we forget how to speak with theological wisdom and integrity to our dioceses or congregations. With the Bible, tradition is also under threat from intellectual and cultural fashions as we experience now the full blossoming of modernism: a forgetting of history, relativism, and individualism, including the insistence on personal "rights" and identity politics.[44] This eating away at community, and with it the idea of the communion of saints, destroys the context within which together the church can understand themselves as the people of God and sit under the authority of God's word. The great lifeline we have is our liturgy, our times of corporate worship, because it is there that congregations engage with and participate in the tradition.

In Anglicanism, our worship typically involves musical praise, confession and absolution, reading and expounding of Scripture, creedal affirmations, intercession, and celebration of the sacraments. Ministry to the church flows from these times together because biblically informed worship gives a sense of identity and purpose to a given church community and provides the vocabulary and grammar for the pastor-teacher.[45] To put it another way, the Bible, liturgically performed, iterates the divine–human drama within which the believer is invited to participate—with the loving direction of the pastor-teacher—when we leave the church building. Recall Graham Tomlin's comment, it is the task of the priest (pastor-teacher) to help the church be the church. Someone who knew this well and who was an exemplar of biblical pastoral ministry was Eugene Peterson. Peterson once noted, "That which begins in the prayer and praise and preaching of worship continues in pastoral work: the rescue operation that is announced in the gospel of salvation becomes a health operation in the way of pastorally guided discipleship."[46]

44. Ironically, these phenomena are often indicative of a loss of identity, a loss of security, and a loss of purpose or meaningful action.

45. It is very important to remember that the *BCP* itself represents the ideal resource for the pastor teacher: the application of scriptural truth for worship and pastoral care. We might therefore have explored our theme by expounding the logic and grammar of the liturgy for Holy Communion. A larger study might want to revisit a pastoral commentary on the prayer book in its entirety.

46. Peterson, *Five Smooth Stones*, 32.

He provides the example of the Song of Songs, reminding us that it is read in most traditions of Judaism at some point within the Passover celebration. In the Song of Songs the great story of salvation finds its existential purchase in the most intimate of human relationships: "the love lyrics of the Song are a guard against every tendency to turn living faith into a lifeless 'religion.'"[47] Similarly, the pastor-teacher must insist that the gospel, our exodus, is a word of life and meets people in their particularity. As Peterson puts it, "Pastoral work is a commitment to the everyday: it is an act of faith that the great truths of salvation are workable in the 'ordinary universe.'"[48] This, according to Challis, is the element of the pastor-teacher vocation most often missing in many of our parishes. We turn now to explore in more detail the sourcebook of these "great truths of salvation": the Bible.

The Bible as Scripture: The Disclosure of the Word[49]

In a seminal essay on the Bible, Karl Barth said, "The question, What is within the Bible? has a mortifying way of converting itself into the opposing question, Well, what are you looking for, and who are you, pray, who make bold to look?"[50] We, too, might pause to consider these questions: When we open the Bible, who or what are we expecting to find? We might also consider our own status as ministers and reflect on our spiritual poverty, the weakness of our humanity, and the partial and limited extent of our understanding. We are like the people of Israel in Ps 95 who must first worship, bow down, and kneel in acknowledgment of God and of our own status as sheep of his pasture.[51] Only then are we ready to apprehend the word. Memorably, Barth went on to describe the Bible as "a new world, the world of God."[52] This is the world in which

---

47. Peterson, *Five Smooth Stones*, 32.

48. Peterson, *Five Smooth Stones*, 33.

49. The phrase, "disclosure of the word" is taken from the title of a book by Francis Martin: *Sacred Scripture: The Disclosure of the Word*.

50. Barth, *Word of God*, 2.

51. The allusion to Ps 95 is apposite. We often say it together in Morning Prayer as the first canticle, the Venite. It represents a template for the journey of a worship event. It begins with praise as we declare together great truths about who God is. This reorientates the believer to the right order of the world. And in finding themselves in the presence of their Lord and creator, the only response is to "bow down in worship" (Ps 95: 6-7). In this posture of awe-inspired humility, the word can be heard.

52. Barth, *Word of God*, 34.

God is made known and God's Spirit can pour into our hearts the love of God, by whom we cry, "Abba! Father!" (Rom 8:15). This is the formative experience of faith upon which pastoral ministry can then appropriately follow because ministry is the sharing of this Spirit-ordained love. This is how Barth expresses it: "But God is also that spirit (that is to say, that love and good will) which will and must break forth from quiet hearts into the world outside, that it may be manifest, visible, comprehensible: behold the tabernacle of God is with men!"[53]

Capturing the pastoral telos of the Bible, Dix has said, "The Bible is nothing else but the story of the absolute and eternal significance of man, of each single man, to the everlasting God."[54] Similarly, Article 7 of the Thirty-Nine Articles of Religion states, "Both in the Old and New Testament everlasting life is offered to mankind by Christ."[55] Reflecting the consistent witness of the New Testament, the article also points to a unique relationship between the Bible and the second person of the Trinity. For instance, in St. Luke's account of the Emmaus Road, we read this: "Beginning with Moses and all the prophets, he interpreted to them the things about himself in all the scriptures" (Luke 24:27).[56] Hebrews opens with these words: "Long ago God spoke to our ancestors in many and various ways by the prophets, but in these last days he has spoken to us by a Son, whom he appointed heir of all things, through whom he also created the worlds" (Heb 1:1–2). The First Epistle of John opens similarly: "We declare to you what was from the beginning, what we have heard, what we have seen with our eyes, what we have looked at and touched with our hands, concerning the word of life" (1 John 1:1). The prologue of John's Gospel introduces the incarnation as a new creation. Temple wrote,

> The Word of God does not consist of printed propositions; it is living; it is personal; it is Jesus Christ. That living Word of God speaks to us through the printed words of Scripture; and all our study of those printed words helps us to receive it. But the point

---

53. Barth, *Word of God*, 49.

54. Dix, *Image and Likeness*, 18. This foundational doctrine is taken from Gen 1:26–27. Dix takes these verses as the basis for a series of retreat addresses.

55. *BCP* 2004, 779.

56. While all the Gospels clearly situate their accounts of Jesus within his Jewish context, the fulfilment motif is most prominent in Matthew's Gospel.

of vital importance is the utterance of the Divine Word to the soul, the self-communication of the Father to his children.[57]

When we think about the Bible and pastoral ministry, we are thinking about the ways in which the ministry of the church enables and facilitates the hearing by faith of this "Word to the soul." To oversee the cure of souls, our own soul must know something of that cure. How much more alive is the sermon that we have already preached to ourselves? How much more meaningful the pastoral encounter when we have experienced a similar joy, a similar struggle, or a similar sorrow? This is when a familiarity with Scripture can inform our understanding and use of our prayer books, as well as providing us with the wisdom to engage new pastoral situations. Sometimes we might supplement the richness of the prayer book liturgy, drawing on a particular verse or passage when we pray. Sometimes it might be appropriate to reference a particular verse or reading, especially if it connects back to the Sunday readings and themes. There is no pastoral blueprint for every situation. Each moment, each human encounter, will have its own unique features. Through being with the church community in prayer and meditating on Scripture, the minister continues to cultivate a godly "feel for the game." We might think of the analogy of being match fit or battle ready. But there is something more too. There is a spiritual *je ne sais quoi*, a "sixth sense" by which the Spirit moves us to a word or an action. Again, a thorough understanding of the Bible's world reconfigures our thinking and our affections in ways that might facilitate this "living by the Spirit" (Gal 5:16).

The Bible's Witness to the Cross

A little earlier we saw how Karl Barth described the Bible as "a new world," and, famously, it is also a "strange new world."[58] But what makes it "strange"? For Barth, the strangeness was another way of talking about dialectic theology, the contrast between who we are and who God is; how we think and act and how God thinks and acts. At the heart of this strangeness is the witness of both Old and New Testaments to the cross. Following Barth, Bonhoeffer characterizes God as the one who is "altogether strange to us" and "who hides himself from us under the sign of the cross." He continues, "God's Word begins by showing us the cross.

---

57. Temple, *Readings in John's Gospel*, ix.
58. Barth, *Word of God*, 33.

And it is to the cross, to death and judgment before God, that our ways and thoughts . . . all lead."[59] The Ordinal speaks of the ordained minister as a shepherd and a servant. These two metaphors alert us to the specific character demanded of the minister. In John's Gospel, the Good Shepherd lays his life down for the sheep, and in the Synoptic Gospels the Son of Man came not to be served but to serve. This is the love of which the cross, supremely, speaks. C. S. Lewis has captured this love graphically:

> God, who needs nothing, loves into existence wholly superfluous creatures in order that He may love and perfect them. He creates the universe, already foreseeing . . . the buzzing cloud of flies about the cross, the flayed back pressed against the uneven stake, the nails driven through the mesial nerves, the repeated incipient suffocation as the body droops, the repeated torture of back and arms as it is time and after time, for breath's sake, hitched up. . . . God is a "host" who deliberately creates His own parasites; causes us to be that we may exploit and "take advantage of" Him. Herein is love. This is the diagram of Love Himself, the inventor of all loves.[60]

Two phrases stand out from this Lewis citation: "inventor of all loves" and "diagram of love." Both phrases agree that cross-shaped love tells us both who God is and how God works. This is ground zero for all Christians, but especially for the pastor-teacher. Only here will they find those truths that will assist ultimately in the curing of souls. Consequently, the pastor-teacher, the one who ministers ever conscious of the Bible's witness, must continue to search the Scriptures for God "under the sign of the cross." Otherwise, we will be unable to take our sheep to the one place where they can find the reservoir of benefits that are ours in God's diagram of love. This is precisely the pattern we see in the pages of the New Testament. Two examples will suffice: Paul's First Letter to the Corinthians, and the Letter to the Hebrews.

The Cross in First Corinthians

What makes 1 Corinthians such an important part of Scripture for the pastor-teacher is the example of the apostle Paul's explicit pastoral appeal to the cross in the opening chapter, which extends to the end of

---

59. Bonhoeffer, *Meditations on the Word*, 45–46.
60. Lewis, *Four Loves*, 116.

chapter 4. The presenting symptoms include "quarrelling" (1:11), factionalism (1:12–14), fascination with celebrity "wisdom" (1:17—2:16), judgmentalism (4:1–5), being "puffed up" (4:6), and triumphalism (4:8). The principles he sets out so carefully in these first four chapters provide the framework, the "diagram of love" to use again Lewis's phrase, for the series of issues and questions he proceeds to address in the rest of the letter. By the time he reaches chapter 13, Paul breaks into his celebrated hymn to love, his attempt to put into words the character of cross-shaped love. The cross reminds us of the terrible hypocrisy we exhibit when we "other" certain people in the church. The cross reminds us that we were "other" to God before the cross. The cross reminds us that we were not in the "in-crowd" before the cross, and that, in fact, there can be no "in-crowd." The cross makes a mockery of celebrity and any triumphalism that goes with it. Before the cross we were separated from God. The cross is God's redemption of us; we have been bought back "at a price" from our bondage to the flesh (1 Cor 6:19–20). We have a new Lord. Our bodies are under new management.[61] This side of the cross, from the horizon of the resurrection, we have a new vocation to be relationship builders, to be world changers, to perform the values of the kingdom in all areas of society. But whatever our circumstances, the status of our health, our relationships, or our work, we need to constantly go back to the cross to get our bearings, to be reminded of what God has done for us, his costly love, and to be reminded of what it means to follow Christ. Alister McGrath has written, "A theology of the cross treats the cross as the center of all Christian thought in that from its center radiate Christian statements on ethics, anthropology, the Christian life and so on. The doctrines of revelation and salvation, so easily detached from one another, converge on the cross."[62] This is a perfect summary of Paul's pastor-teacher approach.

The Cross in Hebrews

According to scholars, the Letter to the Hebrews can best be understood as a sermon rather than a letter. This should immediately alert us to its importance for the pastor-teacher. The predominantly Jewish church is experiencing a time of persecution and some of them were beginning to

---

61. Paul, therefore, exhorts the Corinthians to "glorify God in your body" (1 Cor 6:20).

62. McGrath, *Dictionary of Paul*, 193.

lose confidence in the gospel, tempted to fall away. The preacher takes the time to re-present the person and work of Jesus and the superiority of the new covenant over the Sinai covenant. The sermon is a Christological reading of Torah with a special focus on the ways in which Jesus fulfils the office of high priest, not according to the Levitical system but according to the order of Melchizedek (Heb 5:6; cf. Gen 14:18; Ps 110:4). This is the only time in the New Testament that Jesus' work is described in priestly terms. At the heart of the argument is the self-offering of Christ on the cross. This event above all others is the word spoken by God to us in these last days (Heb 1:2). Unlike the high priest, Jesus does not offer the blood of goats and calves but his own, securing an eternal redemption (Heb 9:12), thereby inaugurating a new covenant as far superior to the first as his self-offering is to the sacrifices of the high priest. The sermon's "speech act" is therefore a solemn warning to the church not to reject this word and so lose their salvation and the benefits of the new covenant anticipated by the prophet Jeremiah (Heb 10:16–17).

What lessons are there here for the pastor-teacher? Here are three: First, Hebrews is another witness to the centrality of the cross for the life and witness of the church; secondly, it deepens our understanding of, and so appreciation for, the ways in which Jesus fulfils the Old Testament; and so, thirdly, it sets an example to the pastor-teacher not only in how to preach Christ from the Old Testament, but also demonstrates the pastoral urgency of the message for the church, the necessary balm for the soul. Given the cultural and intellectual challenges, especially in relation to the Old Testament, ministers often avoid preaching the whole Bible, thereby losing a sense of the whole drama of God and depriving their congregations of an encounter with the full glory of Christ. Without the Old Covenant context, so much of the Gospels and the New Testament remains a closed book. We can only grasp partially the language and ideas in our liturgy and our hymnal, and, crucially, we lose sight of the logic of the cross.

Concluding Remarks

We have seen how the Bible and pastoral ministry are inextricably connected in the Anglican understanding of ordained ministry. In the vocation of the pastor-teacher, they are "two facets of the one reality": the lover of truth and the lover of people as God's image bearers. We took time to indicate the significant intellectual and cultural challenges to the Bible as Christian Scripture and for the tradition. The scandal of Christianity is the claim that God "hides himself from us under the sign of the cross," to recall Bonhoeffer's words.[63] This is a revelation that grounds and illuminates pastoral ministry in at least these three ways: first, it shows us the depth of God's care for us; secondly, it becomes the ideal for those who would answer the call to be servants and shepherds; and, thirdly, the cross sets out the criteria for assessing the integrity and quality of any given expression of pastoral ministry. Consequently, this ministry is dependent on the strange new world of the Bible in which the word is disclosed as "the diagram of love," "the inventor of all loves." This is the showing and proving of the Bible as Scripture.

> Lord God,
> the source of truth and love:
> Keep us faithful to the apostles' teaching and fellowship,
> united in prayer and the breaking of bread,
> and one in joy and simplicity of heart,
> in Jesus Christ our Lord.[64]

---

63. Bonhoeffer, *Meditating on the Word*, 45.
64. Post-communion prayer for the fourteenth Sunday after Trinity in the *BCP* 292.

5

Pastoral Care in the Anglican Ordinal

Harold Miller

An "ordinal" is essentially a set of liturgies to be used at ordinations. Within Anglicanism, there are three such liturgies: the Making of Deacons, the Ordering of Priests, and the Consecration of Bishops. One of the particular aspects of the Church of England at the time of the Reformation was that it retained the ancient practice of a threefold pattern of ministry, believing it to have clear biblical roots and to have been formulated and clarified in the first few centuries of the Christian church.[1] But the acceptance of that pattern did not mean that the reformed church was continuing a medieval theology of ministry. It was emphatically not doing so, and Thomas Cranmer was expressing what he considered to be a primitive understanding of the ministry of bishops, priests, and deacons, each with their different nuances. Cranmer's first Ordinal was completed in 1550, a year after his first *Book of Common Prayer*, and in what follows I have deliberately decided to respect Cranmer's original linguistic idiom in both the liturgical and biblical citations.

It would not be an exaggeration to say that Cranmer's revision of the Ordinal was done with the intention of making it a thoroughly pastoral document, with its understanding that the authority exercised by ordained ministers is essentially derived from the pastoral model in the

---

1. "It is evident unto all persons diligently reading holy Scripture and ancient Authors, that from the Apostles' time there have been these orders of Ministers in Christ's Church: Bishops, Priests and Deacons." *BCP* 1662, pref. to the Ordinal.

Scriptures. It was a move away from any sacerdotal concept of ordained ministry, which had been much to the fore in pre-Reformation ordinals.[2] Although Cranmer continued to use the word "priest" for the second of the three orders of ministers, he did not see the word as having any sacerdotal overtones, but rather as being etymologically derived from the Greek *presbyteros* (essentially "elder"). In the service for the Ordering of Priests in 1550, there were some ritualistic hangovers from medieval ordinals: for example, the bishop delivered not only the Bible but the chalice and paten *(porrectio instrumentorum)* to the newly ordained priest; but two years later, in 1552, all of that was simplified to the delivery of the Bible alone[3] (and in the case of deacons, the New Testament), emphasizing that the entire authority of ordained ministry derives from the authority of the Scriptures and is, as we shall see, an essentially pastoral authority.

As we explore the particular emphases in the Ordinal, with regard to pastoral ministry, we might well be surprised by what we find, not least as those who live at a time when the whole concept of pastoral ministry has become somewhat vague and often sentimentalized. We will look at pastoral ministry from a series of "angles" that come together to give us a fully orbed view of what it essentially is. We will examine all three orders of ministry, but mostly the presbyteral and episcopal liturgies, not least because bishops and presbyters derive from one essential order[4] and have as their focus the provision of care and oversight of souls. We will use the set Bible texts of the 1662 *Book of Common Prayer* to ground,

---

2. Sacerdotal means "priestly" in the medieval sense of the word "priest," that is, a person who offers the sacrifice of the Mass. This understanding is intentionally repudiated by Thomas Cranmer, both in his theology of the Lord's Supper and the ordination services.

3. The obvious is pointed out in the Church of England Liturgical Commission's commentary in *Common Worship Ordination Services*: "The rubric in the 1550 Ordinal, where the Giving of the Bible was first introduced . . . suggests that each ordinand was symbolically given the single Bible in use at the service, rather than an individual and personal copy." Of course, the cost of printing in 1550 would have made the latter prohibitive.

4. This reality was cemented by Bishop J. B. Lightfoot (1828–1889) in his pivotal *Essay on the Christian Ministry*, appended to his *Commentary on Philippians*, in which he argues coherently and persuasively that *episcopos* and *presbyteros* mean essentially the same thing in the New Testament, one being derived from the Greek civil world and the other from the Jewish world. This does not, of course, mean that the development of the threefold order of ministry in the first three centuries is inappropriate, but it is important to note that the distinction between deacons and presbyters is much greater than the distinction between presbyters and bishops, who were initially one order.

establish, and confirm the particular understandings of pastoral care that are pivotal in ordination liturgies. Important questions to ask are: What do these particular understandings of pastoral care mean for the church of the twenty-first century? How much is the understanding of pastoral ministry in contemporary ordination liturgies continuous with that in 1662? To do all this, we will look at a set of ten statements that sum up the focal aspects of pastoral ministry as understood in Anglican ordinals.

1. The Pastoral Image is a Major Theme in Anglican Ordination Liturgies. Ordained Ministry is a Ministry of Shepherding.

It goes without saying that the essential meaning of the word "pastor" is "shepherd." There are four key readings in the 1662 Ordinal that give a biblical grounding for the particular pastoral focus of the image of the shepherd. The first two of these are in the service for the Ordering of Priests and are framed in the context of the set epistle from Eph 4, which includes these words: "And he gave some apostles, and some prophets, and some evangelists, and *some pastors and teachers*, for the perfecting of the saints for the work of ministry" (4:11 KJV; emphasis added). These are, of course, the gifts poured out on the church by the ascended Christ, and central here is the joint gift of pastor-teacher, the two aspects of which are like two sides of a coin and utterly inseparable theologically.

Then, there are two alternative Gospel readings, both of which also focus on the role of shepherd. The first is Matt 9:36–38, where Jesus has compassion on the multitudes "because they fainted, and were scattered abroad, as sheep having no shepherd." So, Jesus asks his disciples to pray to the Lord of the harvest, that he would send laborers into the harvest. The second Gospel reading is even more strongly pastoral. It is from John 10:1–16, focused on two of the "I am" sayings of Jesus: "I am the door of the sheep" and "I am the good shepherd, the good shepherd giveth his life for the sheep."[5] Many of the themes in this Gospel reading will emerge

---

5. This passage has very strong resonances with Ezek 34, especially for those who first heard Jesus teach on this subject. In that Old Testament passage, the shepherds of Israel have become infamous for their lack of care for God's flock. In comparison to the bad shepherds of Ezek 34, Don Carson notes that Jesus lays down his life for the sheep. In his reflection on John 10, Carson notes, "This pushes the metaphor to the wall. In real life, a good shepherd risks his life for the sheep and may lose it. But he doesn't voluntarily sacrifice his life for the sheep." Carson, *For the Love*, Mar. 20.

more fully as we explore the different aspects of pastoral care drawn out in the Ordinal.

The third and fourth readings that illustrate the centrality of the pastoral motif are placed in the Consecration of Bishops. The first one, which is "For the Epistle"[6] is Paul's famous farewell charge to the Ephesian elders in Acts 20. Interestingly, in the original 1550 Ordinal, this reading was appointed for the Ordering of Priests. It is clearly applicable to both priests and bishops, as it is one in which the word *presbyteros* and the word *episcopos* are used interchangeably, speaking of the same people. The latter word is used specifically in relation to pastoral care: "Take heed therefore unto yourselves, and to all the flock, over which the Holy Ghost hath made you overseers, to feed the Church of God."[7] The final reading with the shepherd image is the first Gospel appointed for the Consecration of Bishops. This passage from John 21:15–17 describes Jesus' post-resurrection meeting with Peter and his thrice questioning of Peter's love for him. There, the instructions to Peter are, "Feed my lambs. . . . Feed my sheep. . . . Feed my sheep."

These Scriptures lay the foundation for other aspects of the liturgy that pick up the same metaphor, for example, in the exhortation read to those about to be ordained as priests:

> Have always therefore printed in your remembrance, how great a treasure is committed to your charge. For they are the sheep of Christ, which he bought with his death, and for whom he shed his blood.[8]

Another example is in the prayer immediately before the laying-on of hands:

> Who (referring to Jesus), after he had made perfect our redemption by his death, and was ascended into heaven, sent abroad into the world his Apostles, Prophets, Evangelists, Doctors, and

---

6. This is the phrase used when another reading (e.g. from Acts or Revelation) is used at the point where there is normally the Epistle. In more recent liturgies, it is simply described as the second reading or a similar phrase.

7. Acts 20:28 KJV, cited in the 1550 ordinal. The word *episkopos* in the Greek world of Jesus' day meant essentially a supervisor who was sent out on visitations to support churches and to check that everything is well. The ministry of an *episkopos* is more than immediately local. The gradual development of two different strands to the presbyter/bishop model probably begins with the special ministries of people like Paul, Timothy, and Titus and becomes formulated more clearly during the first three centuries of the Christian church.

8. *BCP* 2004, 532.

Pastors, by whose labor and ministry he gathered together a great flock in all parts of the world.⁹

Again, in the Consecration of Bishops, the theme is emphasized even more strongly, beginning with the opening Collect—"Give grace, we beseech thee, to all Bishops, the Pastors of thy Church"—and in the Exhortation while delivering the Bible:

> Be to the flock of Christ a shepherd, not a wolf; feed them, devour them not. Hold up the weak, heal the sick, bind up the broken, bring again the outcasts, seek the lost . . . that when the chief Shepherd shall appear ye may receive the never-fading crown of glory.¹⁰

The pastoral staff, delivered in the 1550 Ordinal and traditional to the role of bishop, clearly was also a symbol, not of power or jurisdiction but of the key pastoral charge that lies at the heart of being an overseer of the flock of Christ. In contemporary ordination services the bishop is given the pastoral staff at the end of the service with these words: "Keep watch over the flock of which the Holy Spirit has appointed you shepherd,"¹¹ and presbyters are sent out with the words, "Remember always with thanksgiving that the treasure now entrusted to you is Christ's own flock."¹²

2. Pastoral Care is a Responsibility Given by and Supervised by the Church. It is a Ministry of Careful Selection and Confirmation.

Of course, it is true that a whole variety of people in any church context will have and exercise pastoral gifts. There will be people gifted in leading house groups, teaching children, discipling young people, mentoring and spiritual direction, visitation, reaching out to people in need in a variety of ways, and the list continues. A critical part of ordained ministry is to discern, train, release and enable the people of God in the exercise of their spiritual gifts. The ordained minister in the church has a responsibility to ensure, in an overall way, that pastoral care is effective. All the

---

9. *BCP* 2004, 548.
10. *BCP* 2004, 549.
11. *BCP* 2004, 584.
12. *BCP* 2004, 573.

sheep must be fed, led, protected, and, if they have strayed, brought back into the fold.

All of that means that the exercise of the "cure of souls"[13] requires careful selection and supervision. In the ordination services the carefulness of that process is made public and even tested publicly. This is made clear, first, in the Presentation of the Candidates at the beginning of the ordination service. For example, in the 1662 service for the Making of Deacons, when the archdeacon presents the candidates to the bishop, the bishop says,

> Take heed that the persons, whom ye present unto us, be apt and meet, for their learning and godly conversation, to exercise their ministry duly, to the honour of God, and the edifying of his Church.[14]

The archdeacon replies, "I have enquired of them, and also examined them, and think them so to be."[15] That focus continues in more contemporary ordinals, for example, where the question is asked, "Archdeacon, are those responsible for their selection and training satisfied that they are called and ready to be ordained deacon in the Church of God?"[16] In more contemporary ordinals, the presentation is made by sponsors rather than the archdeacon, but the reality remains that ordinands are not people who are taking ministry onto themselves, but rather those who have been through a period of discernment by the wider church, and to whom pastoral ministry is now being entrusted.

This process of discerning, testing, and training is common to all the key Christian denominations where there is an ordained ministry. In the work on interchangeability of ministries between Methodists and Anglicans, it was noted by the Anglican Methodist Commission for Unity in Mission (AMICUM) in its agreements in the area of ordained ministry that "the orderly transmission of ordained ministry embodies

---

13. An old but very important term used in many Anglican legal documents. "Cure" simply means "care." It is the word from which "curate" comes, in the truest sense of that word, as in the Prayer for the Church Militant in the 1662 Communion service, when we pray for "all bishops and curates." Later use of the term "curate" applied it to "curates-assistant," but it really means those to whom has been committed the cure (care) of souls in a particular context.

14. *BCP* 2004, 519.

15. *BCP* 2004, 519.

16. *BCP* 2004, 554.

the truth that we do not take ministry upon ourselves but receive it from Christ through the Church."[17]

The fact that all of this may seem self-evident can hide the reality that there are many newer churches planted and led by self-appointed ministers, and this particular area of ecclesiology is in need of examination by those who are in interchurch conversations with them. The Anglican way of doing things in this area can sometimes seem to be overly institutionalized or controlled, but it bears important witness to the fact that pastoral ministry is a trust given by the church in continuity with the pastoral ministry of the Good Shepherd.

This particular aspect of testing, choosing, and examining is evident in the "laying on of hands" scenarios in the New Testament. Here are four examples:

> "Brothers and sisters, choose seven men from among you who are known to be full of the Spirit and wisdom. We will turn this responsibility over to them and will give our attention to prayer and the ministry of the word." This proposal pleased the whole group. They chose Stephen, a man full of faith and of the Holy Spirit; also Philip, Procorus, Nicanor, Timon, Parmenas, and Nicolas from Antioch, a convert to Judaism. They presented these men to the apostles, who prayed and laid their hands on them. (Acts 6:3–6 NIV)

> While they were worshiping the Lord and fasting, the Holy Spirit said, "Set apart for me Barnabas and Saul for the work to which I have called them." So after they had fasted and prayed, they placed their hands on them and sent them off. (Acts 13:2–3 NIV)

> [Paul to Timothy] Do not neglect your gift, which was given you through prophecy when the body of elders laid their hands on you. (1 Tim 4:14 NIV)

> [Paul to Titus] The reason I left you in Crete was that you might put in order what was left unfinished and appoint elders in every town, as I directed you. (Titus 1:5 NIV)

Of course, it would be very simplistic to say that these passages are speaking of ordination as it is understood in Anglican churches today,

---

17. AMICUM, *Into All the World*, 51. I had the personal privilege of cochairing that commission.

but what they do make clear is that pastoral authority is not taken upon oneself but is given by the church through the leaders of the church and after careful selection with the laying-on of hands and prayer. This lays a foundation for what is expressed in the ordination services.

In the 1662 Ordinal, the people are asked, as in a marriage service, if there is any impediment to the ordination of any of the candidates. The Ordinal in contemporary forms also now requires the assent of the people, not as a new idea but as one which is very ancient. The Church of England expresses it as follows: "The president then asks the congregation to consent to the candidates being ordained and their commitment to continuing support for them in their ministry." The practice of receiving the consent of the laity has been traditional at ordinations since the earliest times and is one of the ways in which expression is given to the concept of ordination as the action of the whole church and not just of the bishop or archbishop who presides. It is the congregation's assent that marks the "hinge moment" of the whole rite.[18] So, the foundation is laid for the reality that pastoral ministry is given by the church after careful selection and testing and not taken up in an individualistic way. This is a very important principle.

3. Pastoral Care is a Ministry of Gifting and Vocation to which the Ordained Person Offers their Life. It is a Ministry of Calling.

The choosing by the church and its representatives in no way undermines the fact that pastoral ministry is a vocation and a deeply personal vocation. The call to care for the sheep of Christ's fold must come from the heart of the individual and pervade the whole being of the person being ordained. It is no less than a call of God and certainly not just a job! It is also a recognition of a certain gifting in the ordinand. All of this is expressed in different ways in the liturgies, not least, for example, in questions asked of the candidate. In the Making of Deacons (1662), we have the following questions and answers:

> Do you trust that you are inwardly moved by the Holy Ghost to take upon you this Office and Ministration, to serve God for the promoting of his glory, and for the edifying of his people? I trust so. Do you think that you are truly called to this Office and

---

18. *Common Worship Ordination Services*, 131.

> Ministration, according to the will of our Lord Jesus Christ, and the due order of this Church? I think so.[19]

In the Ordering of Priests we have the following:

> Do you think in your heart that you be truly called, according to the will of our Lord Jesus Christ, and the order of this Church ... to the order and ministry of Priesthood. I think it.[20]

In the contemporary services:

> Do you believe in your heart that God has called you to the office and work of a deacon/priest/bishop in his Church? I believe that God has called me.[21]

The gifting aspect of calling is well expressed by the introduction to contemporary services, which sets the ordained ministry correctly within the calling and giftedness of the whole body of Christ. It says,

> St. Paul wrote: "Just as in a single human body there are many limbs and organs, all with different functions, so we who are united with Christ, though many, form one body, and belong to one another as its limbs and organs. We have gifts allotted to each other by God's grace."[22] Today, giving thanks for the variety of gifts and ministries that God has bestowed on the Church, we have come together to admit to the order of ... one whom we believe God has chosen for this particular ministry within the body.[23]

Ordained ministry is also a calling to lifelong service. It is both functional and ontological.[24] It is relational and sacrificial, and it would not be possible to fulfil the role of a shepherd without the assurance of God's call and the blessing of God's pastoral gifting. Aspects of this gifting will be recognized in the candidates before ordination, but ordination is also dynamically the work of the Holy Spirit, and we will pray for an increase in that gifting to be given *in* ordination. One of the ways in which this

---

19. BCP 2004, 523–24.

20. BCP 2004, 524.

21. Strangely, the wording is slightly different with regard to bishops. It is "Do you believe, as far as you know in your heart." BCP 2004, 575.

22. Rom 2:5–6.

23. BCP 2004, 553.

24. A long-term debate about ordained ministry is whether it is functional (i.e., people are ordained to *do* certain things) or ontological (i.e., there is a change in the very *being* of the ordained person).

balance is recognized in some of the new ordination services is in the candidate being vested in the vesture of the order into which they will be ordained before the service begins as a sign that the church is essentially recognizing a call and gifting from God. That was an idea firmly grounded in ancient tradition that was developed by the Berkeley Statement of the International Anglican Liturgical Consultation, which suggests:

> Candidates are vested before the service, entering already dressed for the ministry to which they have been called by the church, a practice adopted in the ancient Roman tradition.[25]

4. Pastoral Care and Teaching Always Go Together. It is a Pastor-Teacher Ministry.

One of the difficulties in writing a chapter on "Pastoral Care in the Anglican Ordinal" is that we have no clear definition of "pastoral care." Our natural inclination in this particular age is to assume that pastoral care is essentially to do with the softer and warmer aspects of ministry: for example, listening, counselling, peacemaking, visiting the sick, caring for the dying, caring for the poor, needy, and oppressed. All of that is true and vital. But it has to be recognized that the model of pastoral care in Anglican Ordinals, while containing all those aspects, has a much greater depth. In reality, all of those things could be done, perhaps not as well, perhaps sometimes better, by entirely secular people or agencies. The model of pastoral care in the Ordinal is deeply rooted in that exercised by Jesus Christ, the Chief Shepherd. It is a shepherding of souls which holds together in unity both elements of the pastor-teacher model of Eph 4:11. John Stott, commenting on this text, says that St. Paul numbers "pastors and teachers" among Christ's gifts to his church, since "the work of ordained presbyters is precisely to shepherd and teach Christ's flock."[26] "Pastors and teachers" are linked together by the one article in the Greek. This is one office with two dimensions, two sides of one coin. Darrell Brock, in his commentary on Ephesians, says,

> Pastors, as shepherds, were to lead, teach and protect the flock (Acts 20:28; 1 Pet 2:25; 5:1-4). In fact, pastors were expected to be teachers (1 Tim 3:2; Titus 1:9). These roles are catalysts that

---

25. Dowling and Holeton, ed., *Equipping the Saints*, 236, with further commentary 109-113.
26. Stott, *Message of Ephesians*, 165.

equip the rest of the body to do the work of the church. They are grouped together to make that point.[27]

This is vitally important for those who are ordained. Pastoring is teaching, and teaching is pastoring. What the word of God has put together, we should not tear asunder. Sometimes clergy say, "I'm a pastor but not a teacher" or "I'm a teacher but not a pastor," and of course some people have a gifting that make them better at one side of the coin or the other. But we cannot and must not see the two things as separate entities. During the time of the Commonwealth (1649–1660), people like Jeremy Taylor[28] emphasized teaching the Anglican faith from door to door, catechizing the people, and enabling them to continue to value *The Book of Common Prayer*, the use of which was banned during the period. Another way of putting this is that for clergy the homes of the people should be places of teaching and the pulpit should be a place of pastoring. Both hold together. Teaching without a pastoral heart can become dull and dry—even cold—and pastoring without the element of teaching can become indulgent and sentimental.

So, what has the Ordinal to say about these things? In one of the most famous parts of the 1662 Ordinal it is all held together with real beauty and balance. The bishop speaks these words to those about to be ordained priests:

> We exhort you, in the Name of our Lord Jesus Christ, that you have in remembrance, into how high a dignity, and to how weighty an office and charge you are called: that is to say, to be messengers, watchmen and stewards of the Lord: to teach and premonish, to feed and provide for the Lord's family; to seek for Christ's sheep that are dispersed abroad, and for his children who are in the midst of this naughty world, that they may be saved through Christ forever.[29]

Andrew Atherstone expounds those three images: messengers, watchmen, and stewards in his book on the Anglican Ordinal and adds to it the other term that was in the list in 1550: "pastors." He notes, as we have already seen, that this word "was omitted in 1662 because it had acquired

---

27. Brock, *Ephesians*, 126.

28. Jeremy Taylor (1613–1667) was a famous Anglican divine during the period of the Commonwealth. After the restoration of the monarchy, he became bishop of Down and Connor (to which was later added Dromore). He is buried in Dromore Cathedral.

29. *BCP* 2004, 532.

anti-episcopal connotations during the Commonwealth period." He also notes that, although the word "pastor" was removed, "the pastoral, shepherding metaphor is retained and driven home repeatedly."[30]

The Ordinal is very clear on the importance of the pastor-teacher relationship in ordained ministry. The question to the candidates, after the question on vocation, is about the foundation of teaching the Scriptures:

> Are you persuaded that the holy Scriptures contain sufficiently all doctrine required of necessity for eternal salvation through faith in Jesus Christ? And are you determined out of the said Scriptures to instruct the people committed to your charge, and to teach nothing as required of necessity to eternal salvation but that which you shall be persuaded may be concluded and proved by the Scripture? I am so persuaded and am so determined, by God's grace.[31]

Bishops, who have an additional pastoral responsibility to hand on the truth of the gospel unsullied to generations still to come, as implied by the fact that they have a teaching-chair (*cathedra*[32]), are asked this additional question:

> Will you then exercise yourself in the same holy Scriptures, and call upon God by prayer, for the true understanding of the same; so as you may be able, by them to teach and exhort with wholesome doctrine, and to withstand and convince the gainsayers? I will so do, by the help of God.[33]

The other thing we might note is that the exercise of the pastoral-teaching ministry is framed very often in the Ordinal in terms of eternal salvation. The sheep are cared for so that they may "be saved through Christ forever." The bishop is instructed, when given the Bible: "Take heed unto thyself, and to thy doctrine, and diligent in doing them, for by so doing thou shalt both save thyself and them that hear thee."[34] The

---

30. Atherstone, *Anglican Ordinal*, 15.
31. BCP 2004, 534.
32. Cathedrals are so-called because they have a *cathedra* or a teaching chair. And throne-like imagery about this chair is, in my view, unhelpful; for example, when the seating of a new bishop in the chair is called an "enthronement" or when the chair itself is described as a "throne." Of course, cathedrals in Scotland have retained the title "Cathedral" without the chair (*cathedra*) or the bishop!
33. BCP 2004, 538.
34. BCP 2004, 549.

Scriptures are there to lead us to eternal salvation. A dereliction of duty in pastoring and teaching is so serious that it can have eternal consequences.

5. The Pastor Needs to Model Christian Living and Relationships to the Flock. It is a Ministry of Example.

It often strikes me that St. Paul, on occasion, felt able to ask people to follow his example. He does so in the following verses: "Join together in following my example, brothers and sisters, and just as you have us as a model, keep your eyes on those who live as we do" (Phil 3:17 NIV); "Whatever you have learned, or received or heard from me, or seen in me—put it into practice" (Phil 4:9 NIV); "Therefore I urge you to imitate me" (1 Cor 4:16 NIV). And yet he is aware of his own weakness and human frailty, for example, when he says: "For I am the least of the apostles and do not even deserve to be called an apostle" (1 Cor 15:9 NIV); "I am less than the least of all the Lord's people" (Eph 3:8 NIV); and "Christ Jesus came into the world to save sinners—of whom I am the worst" (1 Tim 1:15b NIV). Perhaps his own weakness, honesty, and humility are also good examples for us.

What is critical with Paul is that our witness is seen, not only in words but in the example of our living. This is particularly true of those who are set aside to be ministers of the gospel. In a sense, the word used of the laying-on of hands for bishops—"consecration"—is also truly a requirement for all Christian ministry. In truth, all of the words can apply to each of the three orders. But the basic message here is that a pastor-teacher ministry requires the consecration of a whole life. It requires an exemplary, but not perfect, life to be lived. The whole being of the minister is to be illustrative of the teaching of Christ and his church.

One of the parts of the service that illustrates this well is the litany, with its suffrage: "That it may please thee to illuminate all bishops, priests and deacons, with true knowledge and understanding of thy Word; and that both by their preaching and living they may set it forth and show it accordingly."[35] This theme also appears in the two epistles set from 1 Tim 3. Verses 1–7 are applied to bishops, and verses 8–13 are applied to deacons. Bishops are to be

> blameless, the husband of one wife, vigilant, sober, of good behavior, given to hospitality, apt to teach, not given to wine, no

---

35. *BCP* 2004, 544.

> striker, not greedy of filthy lucre, but patient, not a brawler, not covetous; one that ruleth well his own house. (3:2–4 KJV)

And deacons are to be

> Grave, not double-tongued, not given to much wine, not greedy of filthy lucre; holding the mystery of the faith in a pure conscience. And let these also first be proved; then let them use the office of a deacon, being found blameless. Even so must their wives be grave, not slanderers, sober, faithful in all things. Let the deacons be the husbands of one wife, ruling their children and their own houses well. (3:8–12 KJV)

Nowadays, these readings may seem a little sexist and male-dominated, but they nevertheless express several aspects of what it is to be a lived example of faith in leadership. The lived example is in positive aspects of ministry: opening homes to others, teaching well, living holy lives, and passing the faith on in families. But Paul also speaks fearlessly of the areas that can destroy a ministry—not least money, sex, and power; and also the things we say. These passages show clearly that one of the most important aspects of a minister is character, which must be assessed and developed in a Christlike way.

The Ordinal also expresses these Pauline priorities in the questions the bishop asks of candidates. In the Making of Deacons and in the Ordering of Priests, "Will you apply all your diligence to frame and fashion your own lives and the lives of your families, according to the doctrine of Christ; and to make both yourselves and them wholesome examples of the flock of Christ?"[36] The importance of the pastor as a model to the flock cannot be overestimated. It is a question of integrity. It really matters that the ordained person is practicing what they preach.

6. Pastoral Care Means Knowing the Flock by Name. It is a Ministry of Presence.

In 2013 Pope Francis famously called on the priests of the world to be "shepherds, with the 'odour of the sheep.'"[37] Jesus says in John 10:3–4 that the shepherd "calls his own sheep by name and leads them out. When he has brought out all his own, he goes ahead of them, and his sheep follow

---

36. *BCP* 2004, 535.
37. Francis, "Homily."

him because they know his voice" (NIV); and in John 10:27, "My sheep listen to my voice: I know them, and they follow me" (NIV). Pastoral care is a ministry of presence. This was so for Paul, who begins his farewell charge to the Ephesian elders in Acts 20 with these words: "You know from the first day that I came into Asia, after what manner I have been with you at all seasons" (20:18 KJV). Knowing the sheep, and being with them at all seasons, is essential to pastoral care. Christian ministry is not a nine-to-five operation; it is not to be conducted from a desk in an office; it is not a formal or distant relationship. It means availability, closeness, and faithfulness to the flock of Christ. Now, that does not mean that the minister is to be worn out, meeting every demand immediately, nor does it mean that the minister is not to have holidays or a day off each week, but it is an orientation of the heart towards the sheep, a preparedness to be involved when the going is tough for those under the pastoral care of the shepherd, presence in the homes of people, and getting hands dirty.

There is another kind of sheep that expresses a different aspect of all of this: the one who strayed when the ninety-nine safely lay in the shelter of the fold. That one gives a starting-point for some of the most powerful words in the Ordinal, which are carried over into many of the newer ordination services. Presbyters, for example, "must always set the Good Shepherd before them as the pattern of their calling, caring for the people committed to their charge."[38] They are instructed, "Remember with thanksgiving that the treasure entrusted to you is Christ's own flock," and they are to "search for God's children in the wilderness of this world's temptations, and to guide them through its confusions."[39] All of this is the most wonderful privilege and a major challenge. For some who find it hard to remember names, it means very hard work. I knew one rector of a very large church who determinedly learnt five new names every Sunday before he sat down to lunch! Knowing the flock is vital to any meaningful pastoral care.

7. Pastoral Care of Necessity Involves the Discipline of the Church. It is a Ministry of Protection.

Discipline has, of course, the same root as "disciple." It is a key characteristic of the church, without which the church cannot flourish. It applies

---

38. *BCP* 2004, 565.
39. *BCP* 2004, 573.

to all in the church, not just lay people, and those who are being ordained place themselves under the godly authority of those who are over them in the Lord. So, the Ordinal speaks both of exercising discipline and of ministers being under godly authority. The latter is expressed in the contemporary order for the Ordination of Priests/Presbyters, and also for deacons, when the bishop asks the candidate, "Will you accept the discipline of this Church and give due respect to those set over you in the Lord," and the answer is, "By the help of God, I will." A bishop is asked, when consecrated, "Will you guard the faith, unity and discipline of the Church?"[40] Of course, bishops have also a specific role in exercising discipline. That can make for challenging situations when the role of *pastor pastorum*[41] requires both care and discipline to be exercised at the same time. Sometimes, it is hard to understand that discipline is actually an aspect of pastoring, not only for bishops but for other clergy. Because discipline is a very important aspect of *episcope*, more is said about it in the consecration of a bishop. For example, in the preface to the declarations:

> Bishops are called to lead in serving and caring for the people of God and to work with them in the oversight of the Church. As chief pastors they share with their fellow bishops a special responsibility to maintain and further the unity of the Church, to uphold its discipline.[42]

And it continues: "They are to be merciful, but with firmness, and to minister discipline, but with mercy." What a wonderful godly balance is expressed in those words. The ordination prayer continues the theme with these words: "Enable him as a true shepherd to feed and govern your flock."[43]

Discipline is, of course, intended to bless the sheep, not to destroy them. It is a necessary characteristic of a true church, practiced for the sake of love, enabling a person to come to true repentance and be restored. In the mid-nineteenth century, the Baptist theologian, John L. Dagg, said, "When discipline leaves a church, Christ leaves with it."[44] That is an interesting quotation to ponder. But discipline must never be

---

40. BCP 2004, 577.

41. Latin for "pastor of the pastors" or "shepherd of the shepherds"—in other words, the one who cares for their fellow-ministers, which is a traditional role of a bishop.

42. BCP 2004, 576.

43. BCP 2004, 577.

44. Dagg, *Treatise on Church Order*, 274.

practiced harshly or abusively, but rather, as in the Ordinal, gently but firmly.

8. Pastoral Care is a Ministry of Bringing the People Before the Lord. It is a Ministry of Prayer.

In James Montgomery's ordination hymn "Pour Out Thy Spirit from On High," the role of the ordained with regard to intercessory prayer is given beautiful expression when he writes, "To bear thy people in their heart, and love the souls whom thou dost love; To watch and pray, and never faint, by day and night their guard to keep."[45] The ordained minister has a priestly calling to bring God to the people and the people to God. This is a critical part of ministry. The question is asked, "Will you be diligent in prayer?"[46] In the Ordination of Presbyters, the charge by the bishop includes these words in relation to priests (or presbyters): "They are to lead God's people in prayer and worship, to intercede for them, to bless them in the name of the Lord."[47]

Ordination and ordained ministry are to be soaked in prayer. Ordination itself only happens by prayer and the laying-on of hands; the ordained presbyter prays for their people and absolves and blesses them in the name of the Lord in prayer. In the 1662 Ordinal another aspect is also expressed in the charge by the bishop:

> So that, as much as lieth in you, you will apply yourselves wholly to this one thing, and draw all your cares and studies this way; and that you will continually pray to God the Father, by the mediation of our only Savior Jesus Christ, for the heavenly assistance of the Holy Ghost.[48]

A prayerless ministry is nothing short of a tragedy. Pastoral care of the people of God needs to be steeped in prayer. It means praying for the sheep, praying with the sheep, and providing a model of a prayer-filled life which will pour out to them in blessing.

---

45. Montgomery, "Pour Out Thy Spirit."
46. *BCP* 2004, 567.
47. *BCP* 2004, 565.
48. *BCP* 2004, 533.

9. Pastoral Care is a Ministry of Seeking the Weak, Vulnerable, and Lost. It is a Ministry of Outreach and Evangelism.

A particular aspect of the life of the shepherd is to care for the sheep who are weak and vulnerable. Luke 15 and the parable of the lost sheep has already been mentioned. A good pastor will be sensitive to the sheep who are most in need of pastoral care. This will include those who have strayed from the fold, those who have challenges in their lives, those who are poor and needy, those who face addictions or mental illness, those who are sick and lonely, and housebound, and those who are dying. The Ordinal is sensitive to these things.

Deacons, of course, came into being with the choosing of the seven in Acts 6, specifically because of the practical and pastoral needs of the widows in the early church. Deacons are charged in the 1662 service to

> search for the sick, poor and [powerless] people of the parish, to intimate their estates, names and places where they dwell, unto the curate, that by his exhortation they may be relieved with the alms of the parishioners, or others.[49]

Clearly this was a pastoral system suited to the time, but at its heart lies care for those in need, a sense that there is a particular ministry of seeking needs out, and that the church should be engaging in practical help, as did the seven in the Acts of the Apostles.[50] Newer ordinals put the role of the deacon in words like these:

> Deacons have a special responsibility to ensure that those in need are cared for with compassion and humility. They are to strengthen the faithful, search out the careless and indifferent, and minister to the sick, the needy, the poor and those in trouble.[51]

---

49. *BCP* 2004, 524.

50. It should probably be noted that the seven in the Acts of the Apostles are never called "deacons," and also that their ministry in this role did not define them for the entirety of their lives. Clearly, Stephen went on to speak publicly, to perform miracles, and to be martyred. The whole question of whether the diaconate should be a more permanent office in the church, rather than a transitional one, has been very much to the fore in the last decades. Whatever is said about that, the old adage "once a deacon, always a deacon" clearly applies so that presbyters and bishops remain deacons (servants) for life.

51. *BCP* 2004, 555. The liturgical role of a deacon, giving expression to this, is the reading of the Gospel, the leading of the people in intercession, especially for the world, and the dismissal—sending the people out into the world to serve the Lord.

This emphasis, however, continues for priests, when they are asked the question "Will you be faithful in visiting the sick, in caring for the poor and needy, and in helping the oppressed?"; and for bishops, who are asked the same question, prefaced by "[Bishops] are to have special care for the sick and for the outcast and needy."[52]

Of course, in large parishes and dioceses the bishop or the incumbent will not be able to do all this on their own, nor should they try, but they will have oversight of it and are tasked to ensure that it is happening.

10. Pastoral Care is a Ministry that Must be Given Priority and Focus. It is a Ministry that God will Judge.

St. James gives a warning to any who may become teachers: "Not many of you should presume to be teachers, my brothers and sisters, because you know that we who teach will be judged more strictly" (Jas 3:1 NIV). St. Paul declares about his own ministry that "I do not run like someone running aimlessly; I do not fight like a boxer beating the air. No, I strike a blow to my body and make it my slave so that after I have preached to others, I myself will not be disqualified for the prize" (1 Cor 9:26–27 NIV). Ezekiel warns the bad shepherds, "As surely as I live . . . because my flock lacks a shepherd, and so has been plundered and has become food for all the wild animals, and because my shepherds did not search for my flock, but cared for themselves rather than for the flock, I will hold them accountable for my flock. I will remove them from tending the flock, so that the shepherds can no longer feed themselves" (34:8–10 NIV).

The privilege of pastoring and teaching the flock of Christ is a privilege above all other and a high calling indeed. Those who are ordained to this role will be strictly judged if they abuse the privilege. There is sometimes a danger when handling holy things, that the element of wonder and joy in the calling of God becomes simply normal and ordinary; or that the calling is abused and becomes a vehicle to serve our own purposes.

One of the helpful aspects of having a set liturgy is that it allows things to be said that we would never dare to say if we were making it up. So, in the Ordinal, there are warnings to pastors that they will be held accountable for the task that God has given them in ordination. For example,

---

52. *BCP* 2004, 567, 577.

> Have always printed in your remembrance, how great a treasure is committed to your charge. For they are the sheep of Christ, which he bought with his death and for whom he shed his blood. The Church and Congregation whom you must serve is his spouse and his body. And if it shall happen the same Church, or any member thereof, to take any hurt or hindrance by reason of your negligence, ye know the greatness of your fault, and also the horrible punishment which will ensue.[53]

Some of that language is probably considered very strong today, and the second part is omitted in many contemporary ordination services, but it does emphasize the weight of responsibility being placed on the shoulders of the ordained person and the reality that God himself will be the judge of our ministries. This is a salutary reminder. The warning resonates with that in Jas 3:1—"Not many of you should become teachers ... for you know that we who teach will be judged with greater strictness" (NIV).

The parable of the talents in Matt 25:14–30 is also a reminder of the importance of using what God gives us to fruit for the kingdom. The goal of all ministry is to receive the joyful commendation rather than the condemnation of our Lord Jesus Christ, our audience of one, who declares to those who have invested the talents well: "Well done, good and faithful servant! You have been faithful with a few things; I will put you in charge of many things. Come and share your master's happiness!" (25:21 NIV).

That hope and prayer is summed up in the very last words of the contemporary Ordinal of the Church of Ireland, just before the dismissal, when the newly ordained bishop is told, "Keep watch over the flock of which the Holy Spirit has appointed you shepherd. Encourage the faithful, restore the lost, build up the body of Christ; that when the Chief Shepherd shall appear, you may receive the unfading crown of glory."[54] That deserves a resounding "Amen!"

Conclusion

This chapter has essentially been an exposition of the Anglican Ordinal in relation to pastoral care. As we come to an end, it is important to note some wider considerations. First, Anglicanism in its self-understanding

---

53. *BCP* 2004, 532.
54. *BCP* 2004, 584.

considers itself simply as an expression, one among many of the one holy catholic and apostolic church. It is a particular expression that emerged in its present form at a particular time in the history of the church and in a particular place—England—which gave it its name, "Anglican." So, although there are ordinals and emphases in its liturgies, the ordination of a person is essentially to be a deacon/priest/ bishop in the church of God, rather than to a particular denomination.

Second, the sad truth is that issues of ordination have often been weaponized in the history of the church and caused great hurt and division. The non-acceptance of "Anglican" orders by the Roman Catholic Church has for many been neuralgic. This was made firmer by the letter *Apostolicae curae*, issued in 1896 by Pope Leo XIII, which saw Anglican orders as deficient because of the teaching of the Ordinal in *The Book of Common Prayer*.[55] Of course, Anglicans, especially Anglo-Catholics, often did the same thing to others, creating a fussiness about a particular understanding of apostolic succession[56] and almost negating the ministry of those ordained in other churches.

Third, we now live in a much more eirenical environment in which, while holding on to the value of the historic episcopate, Anglicans have generally become much more open to different understandings of what that might mean and how it might be expressed, as was put into words in the original form of the Chicago-Lambeth Quadrilateral.[57] This laid out the key things required for unity with other churches and declared that the fourth of those was the "Historic Episcopate, locally adapted in the methods of its administration to the varying needs of the nations and peoples called by God into the unity of His Church."[58] In recent years, that has led to a recognition of *episcope* differently expressed in different contexts.

And lastly, whatever the expression of church might be, the understandings of ministry espoused in the Anglican Ordinal can be a real blessing. No church can flourish without servant ministry based on the

---

55. In a sense, it was a correct assessment that Cranmer's Ordinal did not include a sacerdotal understanding of priesthood.

56. Often called the "pipeline" theory. The idea was that hands had been laid-on continuously back to Jesus Christ and the apostles. This was, of course, entirely unverifiable but held with great vigor at times.

57. Originally adopted by the bishops of the Protestant Episcopal Church in the United States in 1886. It had several subsequent formulations and became an important document in ecumenical relations.

58. "Chicago-Lambeth Quadrilateral," 1.

Servant King and expressed in that context. Indeed, no church will flourish unless that servant ministry is foundational. Equally, the leadership of elders who enable the church to experience good teaching and care, and to be held together and moved forward in the vision and purposes of God, is also vital. And the role of overseers, knitting and holding together the body of Christ in its wider context, if it were not there, would have to be invented. It is therefore good that the contemporary Ordinal starts from that wider perspective that all ministry is for the blessing of the whole church: "We are the body of Christ: By the one Spirit we were all baptized into one body. There is one Lord, one Faith one Baptism: One God and Father of all."[59]

---

59. *BCP* 2004, 553, 563, 574.

6

Discovering Resilience Within Pastoral Ministry

Maurice Elliott

Pastoral ministry is beset with ambivalence. To serve others in a full-time capacity is, on the one hand, a joyful privilege, and, in giving of themselves, pastors paradoxically find a deep measure of fulfilment. Against this, there are different factors which create what can only be described as a shadow side to the pastor's experience. Several recent studies evidence pastoral burnout, noting that a growing proportion of those who serve in ministry are liable to succumb to illness and citing stress due to excessive administration, congregational dissension, and cultural distancing away from the kind of values that pastors represent. Given these challenges, this chapter begins by exploring such inherent complexity. Beyond that, the discussion moves to considering three potential sources of remedy: self-care on the part of pastors themselves; care as expressed by the various support systems of the church; and the experience of being cared for that comes only through a living relationship with Christ. Each of these strands in turn is annexed to the metaphors of ministry as prescribed in the Anglican Ordinal,[1] with the goal being to identify the kind of practices that can enable those in pastoral ministry to discover a richer sense of flourishing and stronger resilience.

---

1. In the Ordinal these five metaphors are named as "servant," "shepherd," "sentinel," "messenger," and "steward."

The Preciousness and Precariousness of Ministry

In 2 Cor 4:7 Paul speaks of having "treasure in jars of clay" (NIV). In the first instance, the "treasure" in question is the gospel itself, and the wonder of how it is that human eyes are opened to understand the glory of God in the face of Jesus Christ (vv. 4–6). When this same phrase is set within the broader context of Paul's defense of his ministry against his Corinthian detractors, however, and especially as he relates his experience of opposition (being "hard pressed," "perplexed," "persecuted" and "struck down," vv. 8–9), the "treasure" could equally be applied to a more generic sense of what *gospel ministry* signifies. If this interpretation is followed, the "jars of clay" might then indicate the kind of vulnerability that pastors might feel when ministry becomes challenging. A contrast thus emerges between the desirability of the task and the frailty of those undertaking it. Pastoral ministry ought to be rewarding, yet it can on occasions lead to feeling drained and coming close to an emotional breaking-point.

In the past, to be ordained was sometimes likened to being "the mother of Moses": when ministry is fulfilling and fruitful, pastors flourish as they rejoice in being remunerated for doing the very thing that is closest to their hearts.[2] This positive sense historically of pastoral ministry is noted by Proeschold-Bell and Byassee. In their extensive survey of United Methodist ministers in North Carolina they record that in 2006 as many as 87 percent of interviewees disclosed a high level of job satisfaction by comparison with other professions.[3] Nevertheless, by current markers such favorable comparisons would be at best only "half the story."[4] The reality nowadays is that pastoral ministry generates highs and lows, with a significant majority reporting both satisfaction in their work and encountering "difficult situations on a routine basis."[5] The clergy surveyed felt under pressure because of criticism from parishioners, unpredictable routine, social isolation, and a sense of guilt brought on by not working enough.[6] Given that the strain induced by such factors can be accentuated by poor physical well-being, the authors conclude

---

2. See Exod 2:1–10.

3. The next nearest out of eleven other occupations were firefighters on a score of 80.1 percent. See Proeschold-Bell and Byassee, *Faithful and Fractured*, 18.

4. Proeschold-Bell and Byassee, *Faithful and Fractured*, 18.

5. Proeschold-Bell and Byassee, *Faithful and Fractured*, 18.

6. Proeschold-Bell and Byassee, *Faithful and Fractured*, 47.

that there now exists a "crisis" in clergy health.[7] In a comparison between Methodist ministers and the general population in North Carolina, for example, those in ministry outscored non-ordained counterparts across five primary markers of disease;[8] and episcopal priests were shown to struggle in areas such as self-acceptance, life-purpose, independent living skills, and social integration.[9] According to Proeschold-Bell and Byassee, such alarming trends overturn more than four hundred years of previous data[10] and point to an imbalance between positive and negative "affect" in pastors' lives.[11]

In the United Kingdom Leslie Francis has taken up this dichotomy between positive and negative affect among clergy. Since so much of the clergy's time is taken up with painful situations—dealing, for example, with sickness, bereavement, and loss—healthy functioning calls for the impact of negative experiences to be compensated with others that are more positive. He comments,

> The notion of balanced affect suggests that positive affect is able to offset some of the effects of negative affect. While it may not be easy for clergy to reduce their exposure to those factors that generate negative affect (emotional exhaustion in ministry), it may be somewhat easier for them to increase their exposure to those factors that generate positive affect (satisfaction in ministry).[12]

What is striking from Francis's research is that clergy appear more prone to negative emotions than what would be considered normal, and that this tendency derives from innate personality traits as much as from other sociological factors.[13] Pastors, for example, manifest heightened levels of both positive and negative affect by comparison with other professions, and they are more susceptible to burnout by virtue of an accentuated inclination towards introversion and neuroticism.[14] Little wonder

---

7. Proeschold-Bell and Byassee, *Faithful and Fractured*, xxi.

8. Specifically, angina, diabetes, asthma, joint failure, and obesity. See Proeschold-Bell and Byassee, *Faithful and Fractured*, 84.

9. Proeschold-Bell and Byassee, *Faithful and Fractured*, 106–12.

10. Proeschold-Bell and Byassee, *Faithful and Fractured*, 90.

11. Proeschold-Bell and Byassee, *Faithful and Fractured*, 99ff.

12. Francis, "Healthy Leadership," 23.

13. Francis, "Healthy Leadership," 10. See also Village and Francis: "Introducing the Index"; "Wellbeing and Perceptions"; and "Exploring Affect Balance."

14. Francis, "Healthy leadership," 13.

then that a substantial proportion of those who embark upon what ought to be a lifetime of rewarding pastoral ministry eventually find that its unrelenting demands result in feeling overwhelmed, perhaps doubting a sense of call, or even faced with giving up on ministry altogether. Christopher Ash records the startling statistic that in the United States fifteen hundred pastors quit their posts every month, and that "almost a half of pastors and their wives [sic] have experienced depression or burnout to the extent that they needed to take leave of absence from ministry."[15]

The Church of England recently conducted a major research project investigating clergy well-being before and since the onset of the COVID-19 pandemic. In the first report, *How Clergy Thrive*, Liz Graveling collates responses from clergy under five aspects of personal "thriving."[16] Across all age-groups the findings disclose pastors who are "managing" but feeling "stretched." The report documents a sense of "fulfilment that gifts, skills, and passions are being used," and yet that there remains "a relentless, overwhelming, and all-encompassing workload."[17] The reality of an ambivalent experience is more than simply hinted at. Notable sources of stress for clergy include periods of transition into a new parish, the blurring of personal boundaries, and church politics, while over one third cited loneliness as an ever-present cause of anxiety.[18] A more recent publication from the same project indicates that almost half of English clergy feel that navigating the global pandemic has accelerated a "deterioration of their mental well-being," with a majority craving "helpful spaces for prayer, mutual support, and accountability."[19] As Graveling concedes, since it is much easier to measure personal well-being than to assess the flourishing of a ministry, such research may be only scratching the surface of the true extent of the challenges being faced.

Applying the Anglican Metaphors of Ministry to Pastors

Ordained ministry is simultaneously a high privilege and a weighty responsibility. According to the Anglican Ordinal, those in ministry are

---

15. Ash, *Zeal Without Burnout*, 16.
16. The five areas are spiritual/vocational, physical/mental, relationships, financial/material, and participation. See Graveling, *How Clergy Thrive*, 8–51.
17. Graveling, *How Clergy Thrive*, 22.
18. Graveling, *How Clergy Thrive*, 29.
19. McFerran and Graveling, *Time of Covid*; Davies, "In the Dark."

called to act as "shepherds," "servants," "messengers," "watchers,"[20] and "stewards."[21] These metaphors describe the qualities that clergy are expected to demonstrate in their interactions with others. Nevertheless, against the backdrop of ambivalence that pastors experience, and with a need to rediscover a richer sense of flourishing, the contention of this chapter is that those in ministry should not only embody these metaphors, but that there must be a mirror-image expression of what those same metaphors represent which they receive. To sustain their vocation, in other words, pastors must find ways of allowing what the descriptors signify to be made real in their own lives.

As of first importance, for instance, pastors must attend to self-care. If they are to remain resilient in the face of difficulties that arise, they must shepherd their own souls, they must act as messengers to their own hearts, they need to steward their own well-being, and so forth. Secondly, pastors need to know that institutional church structures are functioning as intended in support of their ministry. Within many patterns of church governance, and not least Anglicanism, it is bishops who are called to act as shepherds, servants, messengers, sentinels, and stewards towards those under their care. Likewise, church resources must be managed, and, if need be, redirected, so that ordained foot soldiers are adequately provided for. This means not only appropriate financial assistance and adequate accommodation, but also networks of accountability, collegiality, and opportunities for professional development. Lastly, and arguably of most significance, pastors need to reinvest in rhythms of spiritual nourishment so that they minister out of a sense of genuine dependence upon God. The imperative is that they should become more diligent about personal discipleship, humbly seeing themselves as servants of the

20. In the Church of England Ordinal the term "watcher" (Church of Ireland Ordinal, *BCP* 2004, 566) is captured as "sentinel" (see Cottrell, *Priesthood*; Malone, *God's Mediators*; and Bennett, *Metaphors of Ministry*). This chapter uses these two terms interchangeably.

21. Although certain origins of the terms may be contested between local and itinerant emphases and other emerging purposes that undergird the writings of Paul and Peter, the theology behind these Anglican descriptors can be broadly captured under the three core areas of word ministry, loving service, and personal discipleship. Generically they can be applied to comparable pastoral offices across the various Christian traditions. Historically within Anglicanism, the thinking of Westcott, *Some Thoughts*; Moberly, *Ministerial Priesthood*; Dix, *Question of Anglican Orders*; Ramsey, *Christian Priest Today*; and Hanson, *Christian Priesthood Examined* have been influential; and in more recent scholarship, the voices of Bradshaw, *Anglican Ordinal*; Pickard, *Theological Foundations*; Percy, *Study of Ministry*; Chapman et al., *Anglican Studies*; and Gatiss, *Reach* are all significant.

Servant and as under-shepherds of the Chief Shepherd, and embracing devotional habits whereby the Holy Spirit can renew them inwardly.

Pastors Caring for Themselves

The principle of self-care for pastors derives from Paul's injunction to Ephesian elders to "watch over [themselves] and the flock over which Christ [had] made [them] overseers" (Acts 20:28 NIV). The dual nature of the apostle's command is inescapable: only a due sense of watching over self can ensure effective watching over others, and conversely, neglect of self-care will have detrimental consequences. In the nineteenth century the renowned Scottish pastor Robert Murray McCheyne, having graduated from university at the tender age of fourteen, found himself leading a large congregation of over a thousand people by the age of twenty-three. McCheyne worked tirelessly yet neglected his own physical well-being to the extent that within a few short years his health had broken down. Just before he died at the age of twenty-nine, he wrote in his journal, "God gave me a message to deliver and a horse to ride. Alas I have killed the horse and now I cannot deliver the message."[22]

The first assertion, then, is that pastors must apply the five ministerial metaphors to themselves. Given that the vows of ordination insist that presbyters "continually stir up the gift of God that is in [them],"[23] this has to involve self-care. As they offer themselves in service to others, clergy must minister to their own needs. As they steward the flock of Christ, they cannot ignore the precious gift of their own humanity. As they watch over others, they must identify the warning signs of an interior crisis. As they preach to others, they must speak the same message, as it were, to their own hearts. Resilience to cope with the vagaries of pastoral ministry will emerge only as those who are ordained watch appropriately over themselves, and yet, there can be no scope in this for self-indulgence. Kirsten Birkett cautions that an emphasis on self-care must not mean becoming "self-absorbed."[24] A focus on self-care is not an excuse for either pastoral detachment or personal obsession. It does,

---

22. Skoglund, *Burning Out for God*, 12.
23. *BCP* 2004, 567.
24. Birkett, *Resilience*, 41.

however, insist that those who serve as pastors become intentional about their own well-being, their own godliness, and their own physical needs.[25]

Writing to Timothy, Paul advises his protégé to "watch over [his] life and doctrine closely" (1 Tim 4:16 NIV), and in 2 Timothy he depicts pastoral ministry as the endurance of a soldier, the dedication of an athlete, and the labor of a farmer (2:3–6). The call to self-care could scarcely be more evident—what is needed is discipline, rigor, and hard work, with each of these deriving in the first instance from having the right frame of mind. Elsewhere the apostle names "self-control" as a manifestation of the fruit of the Spirit (Gal 5:23). The word used, *akrasia*, is typically read in terms of personal conduct and the avoidance of unwise choices. For those in pastoral ministry a broader sense of *akrasia* might include "self-regulation" and the ability for ministers to live in a way that allows them to address their own vulnerabilities.

I recall on one occasion listening to a senior pastor being asked by a group of enthusiastic younger ministers how he had kept himself through many decades of faithful service. The elderly minister replied that he had long since come to understand it was the exercise of ministry itself—his regular listening to Scripture, his weekly preaching to others, his faltering efforts to attend to his congregation, and so forth—which had served to remind him of his need of grace. His very role as a pastor had become the means whereby God enabled him to know sufficiency in the face of his own inadequacy. Such an honest perspective reinforces the necessity of self-care. Whereas the ministerial metaphors rightly invite those who are ordained to focus on the needs of others, they can equally fasten attention on the pastor's needs.

Distinguishing Between "Sacrifice" and "Burnout"

Closely related to self-care is the importance of differentiating between pastors expending themselves and ensuring that this does not come to resemble an act of self-harm. Ash notes that sacrifice and burnout are different and that any expression of sacrifice within ministry must be "sustainable."[26] Hence, "to neglect sleep, Sabbaths, friendships and inward renewal is not heroism but *hubris*."[27] In a similar vein, Proeschold-Bell

---

25. Birkett, *Resilience*, 39.
26. Ash, *Zeal Without Burnout*, 27.
27. Ash, *Zeal Without Burnout*, 78.

and Byassee suggest that many clergy disregard health concerns because they view pastoral work as "sacred,"[28] and they strongly encourage prioritizing "the big three of sleep, exercise and nutrition."[29] In her study of *Sacred Rest*, Saundra Dalton-Smith suggests that, from a biblical perspective, rest is the foundation of work, not the reward for it, and that "sabbath should [therefore] be embraced as the beginning of the week and not its end-point."[30] Dalton-Smith advises the need for rest, which is physical, mental, spiritual, emotional, social, sensory, and creative, and pastors would do well to heed her emphasis on the need for "joy [that points] in the direction of God's best," "making room for things that are enjoyable," and "seeking out time with life-giving individuals."[31]

A further impediment to self-care arises when pastors, whether subconsciously or otherwise, begin to believe that everything rests upon their own ability. If, for example, a minister becomes aware that their congregants may be starting to become dependent on them, the danger is that this can lead to a sense of indispensability, and this in turn will cause overworking and burnout. Several years ago, Catherine Marshall reflected on the premature death of her husband, Peter, who had been a chaplain to the US Senate:

> In Peter's case, she admitted, I am certain that it was not God's ideal for him to die of coronary occlusion at forty-six. After his first heart attack a friend asked him what he had learned through his illness [and this was his reply]—". . . that the kingdom of God can go on without Peter Marshall!"[32]

Writing in the *Church Times*, Angela Tilby observes a trend towards ordinands in the Church of England naming a desire to exercise "leadership" ahead of "pastoral care."[33] The difficulty for those who think like this, and who thereby misappropriate the nature of their vocation, is that such a mindset can lapse into an attitude of "everything depends on me," with the attendant risk that church members feel harangued by the leader's drivenness. In a devastating critique of the current preoccupation with leadership philosophy within church life, Justin Lewis-Anthony decries

---

28. Proeschold-Bell and Byassee, *Faithful and Fractured*, 33.
29. Proeschold-Bell and Byassee, *Faithful and Fractured*, 53.
30. Dalton-Smith, "What Sort of Rest."
31. Dalton-Smith, "What Sort of Rest."
32. Marshall, *Man Called Peter*, 30.
33. Tilby, "Pastors, Not Persuaders."

a false "Messiah complex,"[34] and in similarly salutary words, Ash insists, "God has already appointed his Messiah and it is not you [the pastor]."[35] Whereas there is undoubtedly a leadership aspect to the pastoral role, the shape of ministry ought to be led from a servant-heart and it must avoid any tendency towards either egocentricity or narcissism.

One major challenge in all of this is the disparity between what pastors consider expected of them and what are in fact the expectations of their parishioners. In an Australian context Peter Brain found that there was on average a difference of up to 25 percent between these two figures, with clergy invariably inclining towards a higher sense of expected workload than what was deemed necessary.[36] Such research indicates that those in ministry consistently overinterpret the requirements of their role, and, as noted earlier, depending on the psyche of the individual clergy concerned, this propensity can be accentuated. While to some extent lay congregational leaders may be able to help pastors in this regard, the chastening reality is that only pastors themselves can take responsibility for avoiding this pitfall.

Learning to Cope

Appropriate self-care for pastors involves not only evading negative affect; it also warrants being intentional about positive strategies that are able to make ministry more sustainable. Proeschold-Bell and Byassee recommend that pastors should be upskilled in withstanding criticism and in their ability to discern between competing demands. If clergy, for instance, can be more specific about how their particular vocation fits with their gifting, being able to say "Yes" to rewarding tasks should result in saying a forthright "No" elsewhere. Furthermore, they advise that any strategy concerned with emotional well-being must embrace flexible thinking, appropriate socializing, frequent "playfulness," physical activity, and creativity in identifying solutions.[37] Competency in all such areas will go a long way towards alleviating much of the stress that pastors encounter, enabling them to cope with stronger resilience. In her treatment of *Creative Repair*, Anne Holmes suggests that well-being can be restored

---

34. Lewis-Anthony, *You Are the Messiah*, 57ff.
35. Ash, *Zeal Without Burnout*, 63.
36. Brain, *Going the Distance*, 17.
37. Proeschold-Bell and Byassee, *Faithful and Fractured*, 112.

in learning to appreciate aestheticism, and she names the importance of making time for beauty, art, music, poetry, and even writing.[38] For those in pastoral ministry, John Pritchard suggests that self-care should engage the intellect,[39] and, in a similar vein, Gregory Mabry recommends that clergy stimulate their minds through reading "solid theology" along with secular biographies.[40] No other books, he notes, can provide such breadth of knowledge, and indeed the quieter months of the summer are ideally suited to this endeavor.[41] Mabry's conclusion is arresting: "It is a well-known fact that those who spend much time in small-talk and gossip [as many clergy are apt to do] are deficient in serious mental pursuits. Lack of study, then, may even be the incentive to sin"!form[42] In all such ways pastors can begin to realize positive affect, and, with wiser stewardship of their own humanity, it may even be possible to stave off the early warning signs of internal breakdown.

Pastors Being Cared for by Others

Pastoral ministry can be lonely, and those who serve must learn to work collaboratively, being accountable towards those with oversight and receiving support from colleagues. Within an Anglican system, priests serve under the authority of a bishop, whose role is primarily that of *pastor pastorum*.[43] In support of their clergy, bishops are charged with ensuring that adequate resources are made available for them to flourish. In relation to coping with stress, for example, Francis notes the importance of clergy being made aware of interventions that can result in "material benefit," and that those responsible for the ongoing development of pastors are best placed to help.[44] At this point, therefore, the application of the ministerial metaphors speaks to the roles of the episcopate and the institutional church respectively. Together, overseers and those who manage church systems must care for those on the pastoral frontline.

---

38. Holmes, *Creative Repair*, 6–26.
39. Pritchard, *Handbook of Christian Ministry*, 170–77.
40. Mabry, *Priest*, 127.
41. Mabry, *Priest*, 127.
42. Mabry, *Priest*, 125.
43. Standing and Goodliff, *Episkope*, 29.
44. Francis, "Healthy leadership," 13.

The Role of Overseers

Michael Ramsey's seminal work, *The Christian Priest Today*, ends with an entreaty concerning the role of bishops in which he draws from Gregory the Great's *Liber regulae pastoralis*. Bishops, he suggests, are called to "care intensely," acting as "missionary leaders" and "good listeners."[45] In relation to clergy well-being, Ramsey advises as follows:

> The bishop is still a priest, and unless he [sic] retains the heart and mind of a priest he will be a bad bishop. As man of theology, he will *teach the clergy* and *help them in their perplexities*. As man of prayer, he will *help the clergy . . . to see their vocation in prayer and to practise it*. As reconciler he will be . . . one who unites people and groups and conflicting tendencies in the common service of Christ. As man of liturgy, he fulfills his role not only in the Eucharist but in his distinctive office of laying-on of hands. . . . In all these ways *he will be the priest's priest* and the people's priest.[46]

The need for bishops to inhabit the ministerial metaphors vis-à-vis the priests under their charge could not be stated more plainly.

As community figureheads, it falls to bishops to set the tone of church life. In their survey of "credibility" within human organizations, James Kouzes and Barry Posner note how crucial it is for those in overall leadership to "create [the right] culture."[47] All the evidence suggests that workers thrive within an atmosphere of optimism and affirmation, and, conversely, that the absence of such values will undermine morale and drain motivation. Proeschold-Bell and Byassee suggest that "clergy need to be *given permission to care for themselves* over and over again,"[48] and within an episcopal system it is bishops who must therefore give a lead. While individual church members have a duty to encourage their pastors, the primary responsibility rests with those in oversight. On this matter of setting the tone, the example of St. Paul is noteworthy. In his Epistle to the Philippians, and despite knowing that his death is imminent, the apostle speaks of his desire to hear that the Philippian believers are flourishing as his partners in the gospel. Paul describes his attitude towards the church in Philippi being characterized by "joy," with cognates of this

---

45. Ramsey, *Christian Priest Today*, 96.
46. Ramsey, *Christian Priest Today*, 97; emphasis added.
47. Kouzes and Posner, *Credibility*, 88ff.
48. Proeschold-Bell and Byassee, *Faithful and Fractured*, 24; emphasis added.

word appearing as many as fourteen times in only four chapters. The apostle leaves little room for despondency, and his positivity must have inspired these recent converts. Bishops likewise ought to be those who hold a message of resilient hopefulness in front of their clergy.

In *Theological Foundations for Collaborative Ministry*, Stephen Pickard develops a paradigm of Anglican ministry framed by the Pauline description of the church as the body of Christ. Given some of the challenges to ongoing ecumenical endeavor, Pickard suggests a need to reassess the concept of "historic episcopate."[49] His inference is that many of the difficulties for Anglicans stem from "an episcopate that is trapped in a steel-hard casing of an inflexible ecclesiality,"[50] and his conclusion is that this aspect of theological heritage risks uncritical transmission. Pickard's contention is that there should be a deeper level of collaborative relationality across the various ministerial orders of Anglicanism so that a more authentic sense of church might be recaptured. One obvious consequence of this is his appeal for bishops to connect meaningfully with their clergy not only in offering support, but also by attuning themselves to ways in which either discouragement or sheer exhaustion may be taking hold. He dares to hope that Anglican bishops might become better at supporting their clergy, and to this end he even proposes smaller diocesan boundaries. In contrast to the prevailing managerial model and sometimes rather distant culture of episcopal oversight, Pickard's vision that goes to the very heart of shepherding, serving, and watching is refreshing. Were such goals even partially fulfilled, the pastoral care and flourishing of those under such oversight might be transformed.

Graveling's research documents that a significant number of respondents to the Church of England survey mentioned as problematic "a perceived lack of care and understanding received from senior diocesan figures."[51] In reality, the reason may be that bishops function as line-managers, and their potential role in disciplinary matters can act as an obstacle, at least in the mind of the clergy, to genuine pastoral support. This conflict of purpose invites revision of existing structures and the implementation of a more robustly collegial culture. Moreover, the development of such collegiality cannot to be limited solely to the role of bishops; of equal importance is the need for clergy to enjoy stronger networks of support among their peers as well as between themselves and

---

49. Pickard, *Theological Foundations*, 105.
50. Pickard, *Theological Foundations*, 180.
51. Graveling, *How Clergy Thrive*, 49.

their lay leaders.[52] Intriguingly, under the original Anglican reformation settlement, Thomas Cranmer's vision for churchwardens was that they should act as quasi-lay elders, sharing responsibility with their priest for the smooth running of the parish and also acting as a buttress to the priest's own needs. Is there perhaps something in this that latter-day Anglicanism could usefully revisit in the cause of clerical well-being?

The Place of the Institution

The institutional church must also play a role in enhancing clerical well-being. Simply put, administrative structures ought to represent an expression of church at its best towards those in pastoral ministry. Typically, this support will extend to housing, yet whereas this is rightly viewed as a generous provision, tied houses can be a cause of angst for clergy, and especially given the way in which such properties are managed. Since this normally involves local patronage, it can place incumbent ministers in the invidious position of chairing the very body of trustees that has responsibility for decisions affecting the material well-being of themselves and their families. It is reassuring that institutional systems appear to be increasingly aware of such pressures on ministerial life. In many contexts, the direction of travel is towards enhanced practical support, whether in the management of properties, advice about human resources and administrative processes, or the development of ancillary programs. Within the Church of Ireland, for example, the central trustee body has recently rolled out a major mental health initiative entitled Mind Matters.[53] This project aimed at alleviating stress and improving quality of life across all sectors of the church, including for clergy. The fact that such provision exists is indicative of heightened desire on the part of the institution to care for those in ministry who may be feeling under emotional pressure, and the preliminary feedback has been overwhelmingly positive. In these and other ways the institutional church must learn to serve, support, and steward appropriately.

---

52. Patterson, "Clergy Discipline."

53. See Mind Matters COI—The Church of Ireland Mental Health Promotion Initiative (mindmatters.ireland.anglican.org).

The Focus of Training

A major investment on the part of the institution comes at the point of initial ministerial education. In her exploration of resilience within pastoral ministry, Birkett notes the need for theological formation to ground students in the doctrines of God and of the church, and in the disciplines of personal and communal prayer. She posits that candidates for ordination will cope better with stress "by [being trained] to be Christian,"[54] and that, beyond the acquisition of skills, they should be firmly established in their understanding of the apostolic faith. "Transcendence and spirituality," Birkett asserts, "are directly linked to the most practical of skills in coping with the dirty and stressful circumstances of life."[55] To this end, staff with responsibility for training need to model authentic Christian spirituality "in one-to-one interactions, in tutorials and in casual encounters,"[56] and "corporate worship in chapel [should] be frequent and compulsory, not as an institutional disciplinary tool but as a genuine aid to developing student capacities."[57] Birkett laments the loss of biblical authority within mainstream church life as a significant contributory factor to the emotional plight of clergy, and she insists that "confident pastors [can] negotiate suffering, opposition and emotional hardship through a life based on the thoughts, actions and motivations that come from knowing Christ through his revealed word."[58]

From his survey of contemporary Anglican training methods David Heywood suggests that ministerial formation must prioritize three disciplines: ongoing theological reflection; deepening emotional intelligence; and continuing professional development after ordination.[59] When students are invited to reflect on their experience of theological training, invariably they identify the usefulness of theological reflection in providing them with a toolkit with which to sustain spiritual health and navigate congregational conflict. Moreover, programs of theological reflection within training can facilitate enhanced self-awareness and growth in emotional intelligence. Given the frequency with which

---

54. Birkett, *Resilience*, 38.
55. Birkett, *Resilience*, 34.
56. Birkett, *Resilience*, 38.
57. Birkett, *Resilience*, 38.
58. Birkett, *Resilience*, 42. This Christ-centered perspective will be further considered under the final section below.
59. Heywood, *Reimagining Ministerial Formation*, 14, 108.

difficulties encountered by clergy are triggered by an inability to read situations appropriately, neglect of emotional intelligence during training is merely storing up future problems. Related to this, Francis and Village suggest the usefulness of more rigorous psychological screening at the point of initial selection so that those who are weaker in emotional intelligence might be identified, and hence that the development of protective measures within the training process against a susceptibility to stress can be prioritized.[60] Heywood's final priority concerning professional development points to the importance of well-organized Continuing Ministerial Education (CME). Typically, CME has concentrated on years one through three of pastoral ministry post-ordination. Increasingly, however, both bishops and institutional systems are becoming aware of the need for such courses to spread across all stages of ministry life. Returning to some of the themes identified earlier, lifelong CME ought to deal not only with the acquisition of further knowledge and skills, but also, for instance, with deepening commitment to self-care, emotional affect, management of stress, physical well-being, material contentment, personal spirituality, and "creative repair."

Pastors Under the Care of Christ

The ordination liturgy emphasizes the inadequacy of those who undertake the task. Each of the vows bearing on aspects of the presbyteral role is predicated upon "the help of God,"[61] and, following the public declarations, the bishop solemnly reminds the candidates that "none of [them] can bear the weight of this ministry in [their] own strength, but only by the grace and power of God."[62] Such salutary words draw attention to a *sine qua non* of effectiveness within pastoral ministry, namely divine enabling, and hence that clergy must find ways whereby they can know themselves to be under the care of Christ. In the final analysis only as Christ himself is allowed to represent the perfection of each of the metaphors can ministry be fruitfully sustained. While this has been implicit in the various facets of self-care, episcopal oversight, and institutional provision (in that they, too, are expressions of Christ's gracious provision), the matter at hand is now to consider how Christ himself can act as

---

60. Francis, "Healthy leadership," 24.
61. *BCP* 2004, 566–67.
62. *BCP* 2004, 568.

shepherd, servant, steward, sentinel, and messenger to those who serve within his church.

Christ as Shepherd

In John 10 Jesus describes himself as the Good Shepherd. As the Good Shepherd he stands in contrast to the hired hand by his readiness to "fight the wolf," and he proves his commitment to the flock by "laying down his life" for their well-being (John 10:12–15). This role of shepherd-care is one that Jesus exercises towards all his disciples and not only to those who are ordained. As shepherd, he feeds, guides, leads, and protects, and, as Chief Shepherd, his sufficiency reminds all his would-be servants of their absolute dependence upon him for life and for ministry. This aspect of who Christ is bears on the need for pastors to attend to the healthiness of their own discipleship and how they express a sense of complete reliance and trust. Deeper flourishing within ministry is inextricably linked to the priority that pastors give to the intimacy of their own relationship with Christ, and again here the apostle Paul provides a telling example. In every circumstance, whether favorable or adverse, Paul kept his eye on what it meant to be in a relationship with the risen Christ. His identity was drawn from Christ; his longing was to know Christ; his resolve was to proclaim Christ; and his desire was to be at home with Christ. Paul's prayer life was anchored to the reality of who Christ is, and what Christ had accomplished, and for him this was the sole foundation upon which ministry could be built. Pastors would do well to emulate the pattern that Paul has left to them.

Addressing the magnitude of what is involved in making vows of ordination, Pickard offers a commentary that is at once salutary and hopeful. The sobering dimension derives from an insight of Paul Ricoeur, who suggests that the permanence of public vows, such as those of ordination, depends upon the twin coordinates of character and promise.[63] Building on this, he then cites Hannah Arendt's caution that such vows are fraught with risk because of the inconsistencies of human character—in her words, they are precarious because of "the darkness of the heart."[64] As a result of ordination, clergy take upon themselves pastoral responsibility for others, yet in so doing they must recognize that the stability of their

---

63. Pickard, *Theological Foundations*, 217.
64. Pickard, *Theological Foundations*, 217.

undertaking depends ultimately upon their own personal choices. The reminder is stark: unwillingness to deal appropriately with any persistent lack of integrity will undermine remaining steadfast to such vows. Defeat, however, need not be inevitable, and this is precisely where the ministry of Christ as shepherd must be emphasized. Pickard's final word draws from David Ford, who contends that for ministers to remain effective even despite their own shortcomings, they must cling to "worship,"[65] or in other words that they should stay close to the shepherd, and, moreover, that such worship should be led out of ongoing penitence. If pastors can train themselves to adopt a posture of subservience towards Christ through a life of prayer and a genuine commitment towards obedience, they can be confident that he will continue to keep them.

Christ as Servant

As servant, Christ offered himself supremely in his death and resurrection. Rebuking his disciples for their petty in-fighting over seats within his kingdom, Jesus declared, "The Son of Man did not come to be served but to serve, and to lay down his life as a ransom for many" (Mark 10:45 NIV). Ministry is not about jockeying for position, still less about interpersonal rivalries or trying to prove oneself. Instead, it must be grounded in grace, and ministers need to be reminded of this not least as an antidote to their frenetic busyness. Stanley Hauerwas tells the cautionary tale of a pastor who agreed to collect a parishioner's child from school and run him to a sports practice. Such a servant, Hauerwas observes, "is well on the way to becoming a quivering mass of availability,"[66] and, whereas most ministers may possess a well-intentioned aspiration to change lives, he suggests that they often end up "being nibbled to death by ducks."[67] Proeschold-Bell and Byassee reference an acquaintance of theirs whose obsession with relentless overworking made him "a martyr to bureaucracy,"[68] and, in view of this, they then ask perhaps the most significant question of all:

> What's the answer? A bigger gospel. One with a crucified Jew who rules the cosmos. One where resurrection changes all

---

65. Pickard, *Theological Foundations*, 219.
66. Hauerwas quoted in Proeschold-Bell and Byassee, *Faithful and Fractured*, 8.
67. Hauerwas quoted in Proeschold-Bell and Byassee, *Faithful and Fractured*, 8.
68. Proeschold-Bell and Byassee, *Faithful and Fractured*, 8.

our systems of power and glory. One where we ministers are profoundly secondary because Christ and his church are first. A gospel big enough to take up a cross and follow Jesus is the answer to every human challenge.[69]

If Christ is to act as servant, then it is only by his grace that ministry can be sustained, and as such it does not permit either drivenness or self-aggrandizement. In keeping with John Piper's proposition that Christ is most glorified in his followers when they are most satisfied in him,[70] perhaps it could be said that pastors must learn to find contentment in calling to mind that it is Christ who enables them to serve in the first place.

In one of his addresses to candidate-priests, Ramsey offers the following advice:

> Recapture the sense of wonder. Let the griefs, pains and humiliations which come to you help you to be a little nearer to Christ crucified. Think far more often about heaven. Thank God, often and always. Take care to confess your sins. Accept humiliations. Use your sense of humour. Our Lord will be there with the words, "Peace be unto you."[71]

What comes through these words is an insistence on the need for those in ministry to cling to a sense of divine equipping. In *The Reformed Pastor*, Richard Baxter likewise advises his colleagues to "see the work of saving grace to be thoroughly wrought upon [their] own souls."[72] In the final analysis, only a foundation of grace, deriving from the message of the cross and its suffering servant, can animate those who serve as pastors. After the manner of Paul who "resolved to know nothing except Jesus Christ and him crucified" (1 Cor 2:2 NIV), pastors must recognize that beyond the privilege of doing ministry there is the greater privilege of knowing grace. Ash notes that all ministry is conducted in "a messed-up world of sinful brokenness," and as such it emblematizes a crucified redeemer.[73] Hence, to cling to Christ as servant can be a source of great comfort to pastors, and especially when they may feel that they are expending their energies in a spirit of "apparent failure."[74]

69. Proeschold-Bell and Byassee, *Faithful and Fractured*, 8.
70. Piper, *Desiring God*, 127.
71. Ramsey, *Christian Priest Today*, 58ff.
72. Baxter, *Reformed Pastor*, 155.
73. Ash, *Zeal Without Burnout*, 99.
74. Ash, *Zeal Without Burnout*, 97.

Christ as Steward, Sentinel, and Messenger

Lastly, it comes as no surprise to realize that Christ must also act as steward, sentinel, and messenger towards pastors. As steward, it is he who enables them to have right judgment, to take a sober view of themselves, and to avoid any delusion of machismo.[75] Going back to the insights of Daulton-Smith, pastors can experience Christ's stewardship in his provision of the many things that bring them joy—hearing afresh the promises of the gospel; investing in times of quiet and retreat; appreciating art and beauty; enjoying physical exercise; watching sport; making conversation; listening to music; or even simply reading books.[76] Recognizing that "every good and perfect gift is from above" (Jas 1:17 NIV) can enable those who serve to realize that even God's smallest mercy may be a medicine to salve their wounds.

Christ the sentinel is the one who literally "sees" all things. He is Alpha and Omega, and he alone can watch over the full gamut of why and where and when and how both the blessings and the buffetings of ministry may unfold. Whereas pastors often struggle with the provisionality of their role and their limited capacity to know in reality all that is going on within their ministry, the essential thing is that they keep their focus on the one who is omniscient. This perspective is appositely captured in some words of Reinhold Niebuhr:

> Nothing that is worth doing can be achieved in our lifetime; therefore, we must be saved by hope. Nothing which is true or beautiful or good makes complete sense in any immediate context of history; therefore, we must be saved by faith. Nothing we do, however virtuous, can be accomplished alone; therefore, we must be saved by love.[77]

Only Jesus Christ sees everything, and, moreover, his seeing extends both to those heart-warming moments of encouragement, which every pastor may experience, and to the impending signs of imminent challenge or emotional crash. Moods swings, physical discomfiture, changes in circumstances, family worries, collegial angst, or even episcopal discipline all happen under Christ's all-seeing eye. Pastors can therefore find solace in taking to heart this assurance of his lordship.

---

75. Ash, *Zeal Without Burnout*, 77.
76. Ash, *Zeal Without Burnout*, 75. See also Dalton Smith, *Sacred Rest*.
77. Niebuhr, *Irony of American History*, 63.

Finally, as messenger, Christ declares himself to be the truth and the life, and he it is who voices his loving call into pastors' hearts and his gracious word into pastors' lives. In John 15, where Jesus discloses himself as the true vine, he reminds his disciples that "apart from [him] [they] can do nothing" (John 15:5 NIV). Mindful of this, Birkett draws attention to the danger of "self-efficacy" for those who serve in ministry, a mindset of determined positivity that is often put forward by secular voices as the key to resilience.[78] By contrast, Christ the messenger speaks of the need for "God-efficacy." His word brings pastors back again and again to quiet confidence in his sovereignty, and to a belief that in every circumstance he will work for the good of those who love him (Rom 8:28).[79] Rightly apprehended, adherence to Christ as messenger can generate strength in the face of adversity as pastors continue to know that, come what may, he will accomplish his eternal purpose.

Conclusion

Given the preciousness and precariousness of pastoral ministry, this chapter has sought to argue that the five ministerial metaphors of the Anglican Ordinal might make for an important point of reference. Those who serve as pastors enjoy a glorious sense of vocation as shepherds, servants, sentinels, messengers, and stewards—there could be no greater privilege, and the bar is set exceedingly high. Yet the "treasure" exists in "jars of clay," and this not least when measured against the challenges that pastors experience, the ambivalence that they encounter, and the vulnerability of their own humanity. To guard against the many ways in which those in ministry may be in danger of burnout, this chapter has advocated a need for the five metaphors to be applied in reverse. Stronger resilience and richer flourishing can be discovered through more robust commitment to self-care; in more targeted support from bishops and the institutional structures of the church; and out of the contentedness that is found only in a healthy relationship with Christ himself.

The clay jars may risk being either cracked or broken, but measures can be put in place to prevent this. Proeschold-Bell and Byassee suggest that "if a pastor's jar is broken, it is harder to fill it with the water about to be changed to wine. If the jar has integrity, however, it can hold God's

---

78. Birkett, *Resilience*, 36.
79. Birkett, *Resilience*, 36.

grace much better."[80] Hence, the pressing need is for pastors to identify workable ways in which they can address their own spiritual, emotional, and physical needs. The psalmist offers wise counsel when he declares, "For [the Lord] knows our frame; he remembers that we are dust" (Ps 103:14 ESV), and perhaps the most apposite final word might be given to Christopher Ash:

> When you and I surrendered to Jesus as Lord, we did not offer him the services of a divine, or even semi-divine creature to strengthen his kingdom: we offer him the fragile, temporal, mortal, frail life that he has first given to us. That is all we have to offer. God knows that.[81]

---

80. Proeschold-Bell and Byassee, *Faithful and Fractured*, xviii.
81. Ash, *Zeal Without Burnout*, 41.

7

Pastor pastorum: The Responsibility of a Bishop

Patricia Storey

Introduction

This chapter will seek to explore a number of important questions: What is the role of a bishop? What do bishops actually promise or understand to be their role as diocesan overseers, and what is their primary function? Is it, for example, to be a leader, and if so, should it be a prerequisite for a bishop to be skilled in strategic thinking; or, on the other hand, is a bishop's principal duty simply to look after their clergy? And whatever may have been the bishop's instinctive, and arguably idealistic, priorities to begin with, what kind of issues might divert them away from that path after they are in post? In truth there are many competing views on all such matters as these, and in what follows we will endeavor to do justice to an honest assessment of what it means for a bishop to be a *pastor pastorum*.

The Nature of the Episcopal Role

First, how shall we define what a bishop actually is? In Anglican theology, the threefold ministry of bishops, priests, and deacons has always been understood as a historic practice based on Scripture, with the bishop as lead-presbyter and diocesan overseer. As captured by Martin Davie, "Because bishops are elders, multiple roles are theirs as well. As elders, bishops are called to be the rulers and instructors of the churches, to be involved in prayer for healing, to implement pastoral discipline and to preside at the Eucharist."[1] Steven Croft helpfully sets this aspect of episcopal oversight in a broader context:

> Each denomination, as it has emerged, has discovered the need to develop its own expression of these three dimensions of ordained ministry ... the diaconal dimension of service lovingly given ... the presbyteral dimension of ministry centred around the ministry of preaching and of prayer and the sacraments in the local congregation, and the episcopal dimension of keeping watch over the life of both local churches and the wider church, and of commissioning and nurturing others in ministry.[2]

As is the case with a deacon or a priest, then, it is assumed that the office of a bishop is first and foremost a calling, and, moreover, after a bishop has been nominated by an electoral college, that nomination must also typically be ratified by a wider college of other bishops. In Anglican understanding, therefore, bishops are considered to be guardians of doctrine and unity, and they all, including those who are archbishops, function within a diocesan context. Unlike the Roman Catholic view, however, Anglican bishops do not possess the unilateral authority to move clergy to a new appointment without due consultation.

What then do the clergy primarily expect of their bishop? Elsewhere Croft also writes,

> The bishop's role is to be the chief pastor of the diocese, called to lead in serving and caring for the people of God. The work is richly varied: caring for the clergy; overseeing clerical appointments; encouraging vocations; ordaining priests and deacons; promoting ecumenical endeavour; conducting confirmations, and visiting parishes.[3]

Bishops also serve as patrons of church schools; they act as teachers of the faith; they further the unity of the church and promote its mission. In addition, bishops devote time to the work of the wider church, they share duties with other bishops, and they also represent the church

---

1. Davie, *Bishops*, 263.
2. Croft, *Ministry in Three Dimensions*, 40.
3. Croft, *Bishops*.

in civic society. If every bishop were to fulfil each of these functions diligently, the likelihood is that they would be permanently exhausted. While some duties are non-negotiable, it would be fair to say that every bishop is different, not only in their skill set and individual interests, but also in what they feel are their own personal priorities. Looking at the above list, it is probably fair to assert that all these activities happen to a greater or lesser degree in every bishop's life, yet where each one places their time and energy may greatly differ.

The key expectation of a bishop is often portrayed as being *pastor pastorum*. This phrase is thought to have originated in the writings of Gregory the Great, however there is debate as to whether in fact it remains definitively part of what a bishop actually promises in the context of a consecration service. On the one hand, whereas the liturgy clearly suggests that "bishops are called to lead in serving and caring for the people of God and to work with them in the oversight of the Church," and that they are "chief pastors,"[4] the words *pastor pastorum* are not made explicit. Nonetheless, every bishop, and probably every clergyperson, would understand that this "caring for the carers" is a key aspect of episcopal ministry. How this presents itself in each diocese may look vastly different, but it would be inaccurate to infer that it is not uniformly expected.

This being the case, what might a local cleric understand by the phrase? How "hands-on" do they want their bishop to be? In large dioceses it is not possible for the bishop to know the daily lives and concerns of their clergy, but in smaller areas this may be both achievable and even desirable. It would be safe to say that no clergyperson wants their bishop to actually interfere in their parish ministry unless, of course, they find themselves in a crisis or difficulty. In larger contexts there can sometimes be hundreds of clergy ministering within a single diocese, and a diocesan bishop would find it simply impossible to know in any depth what may be happening in an individual's life. While this is completely understandable, at the same time the distance that it causes between a bishop and his or her clergy warrants an even more urgent focus on ensuring that provision should be made for other avenues of pastoral and spiritual care. To this end, in certain contexts bishops have established panels of spiritual directors, counsellors, and coaches. This is a confidential arrangement that is not intended to replace the pastoral care of the bishop, but it can

---

4. *BCP*, 576.

certainly help in making available additional support outside the episcopal relationship.

The Multiple Duties of a Bishop

Delving further into the meaning of *pastor pastorum*, the list above envisages a range of the duties that a bishop ought to undertake in their professional life. For every bishop, the pastoral care of the clergy remains a vital priority, however in practice there are myriad obstacles that can often get in the way of implementing this. Like all clergy, for instance, bishops have to deal with a mountain of administration. Some of this may be undertaken by a bishop's secretary (if they have one), but much of it can only be processed by the bishop directly. In certain dioceses the patronage of schools can take up inordinate amounts of time, and it is not uncommon for a bishop to be patron of up to twenty schools. Whereas this gives wonderful access to schools—and most bishops genuinely enjoy doing assemblies and meeting with staff—the flipside is that there is an avalanche of paperwork regarding appointments, boards of management, and, not least, complaints. When a problem arises in a school, the patron is often the first port of call, and if patronage extends to many schools, it is easy to see how the workload will rapidly multiply, especially if the bishop is required to act as chair of the board. For the majority of bishops, fulfilling this role is unlikely to have been uppermost in their minds when responding to their sense of vocation!

A bishop must attend central church meetings, including with other bishops, they chair national and diocesan committees, they prepare candidates for ordination and other ministries, they confirm, and they make weekly visits to parishes, during which the normal expectation is that the bishop will both preside and preach. In addition to all of this, bishops have to deal with unanticipated emergencies, for which they may need to offer immediate attention and move aside all other commitments. The nature of a bishop's role is that very often such emergencies only come to their awareness when they have already become much more complex to resolve. Mediation can be an option, and most bishops do seek to use this method in order to stave off a crisis, however if both parties are entrenched before it ever reaches the bishop in question, this is not always achievable. Many bishops find that a great deal of time and energy is spent on trying to resolve such difficulties, whether in a school or in a parish. They find their time usurped by firefighting, problem-solving, and managing people much more frequently than they would choose. The net result here is that even though the perception of needing to act as *pastor pastorum* remains widely held, much of the bishop's time may be spent on a plethora of issues that essentially prevent proper concentration on fulfilling this, and moreover, it cannot be forgotten that bishops themselves are still human—they forget, they falter, and they fail. When the care of those in pastoral ministry is operating well within a diocese, whether delivered by the bishop or other allocated persons, it can bring great comfort to the clergy concerned, however it must also be acknowledged that the provision of such support varies enormously across every diocese.

One anomaly that all parties find difficult is that as an overseer the bishop is effectively both the pastor and the line-manager for the clergy. Anglicanism is inherently hierarchical, and those who suggest otherwise ought to listen to the people who feel themselves to be at the bottom of the structure. While it is true to say that clergy are "self-employed," and hence that the bishop cannot technically act as their "boss," the reality is that most clergy and most laypersons do perceive the bishop to be precisely that, which is why again bishops in turn receive so many complaints. Whereas clergy have statutory independence and are not managed as in other organizations with weekly time sheets and monthly reports, it still remains the case that the cleric in trouble or the layperson who is angry at their clergy will invariably revert to the bishop. How then might it be possible both to pastor and to professionally manage at the same time? This is a notoriously difficult path that bishops have to navigate, and it is made even more challenging when a bishop both cares deeply for the individual and yet at the same time sees ways in which that person could be aided. One matter that many churches are beginning to explore is the requirement for supervision or coaching. If this were to become mandatory (and indeed starting with bishops themselves), there would most likely be many fewer crises arriving into the bishop's inbox. An issue may well be resolved much earlier in the process and thus avoid escalation and intractability. After all, anyone now in training for other pastoral professions is automatically required to undertake supervision as part of their ongoing development, and perhaps the church has some significant catching-up to do in this regard.

When a situation becomes severely strained, for instance between an incumbent and a parish, the *pastor pastorum* has limited options.

Mediation is typically the first recommended port of call in the hope of avoiding an official complaint, but this will depend upon both parties being willing to undertake a mediation process. Sometimes this can help and will begin to set the parish on a better trajectory; at other times it resolves nothing and simply delays the inevitable, which can vary from a formal complaint to a resignation, or someone simply remaining in-post and everyone then feeling unhappy. When a dispute escalates, there are not many easy options for either a congregation or a pastor to explore. Furthermore, the hands of the bishop are tied, and while they would very much want to see things satisfactorily resolved, they are also bound to consider the wellbeing of all sides. On occasions, if there is not going to be a resolution locally, the best (and slower) option may be to persuade the clergyperson that it is in their own best interests to make a fresh start somewhere else. When this happens, both sides can then avail of a clean sheet and hopefully learn from their painful experience.

Whereas the bishop remains *pastor pastorum* throughout such a mediation process, they may also have to rely on the support of a senior clerical colleague to intervene, and within Anglican polity this would usually be an archdeacon. As diocesan overseer, the bishop has to act as advocate for both the clergyperson and the parish, and hence the role of the archdeacon is vital. They are often the person who stands in the gap between clergy and the bishop, and who have an "ear to the ground." Clergy often feel that the archdeacon is there to be a sounding board and a support to them as incumbents, and this is true; however, the archdeacon sometimes also takes on the difficult role of being the person who communicates from the bishop to the clergy. From the perspective of the bishop, a good archdeacon is worth their weight in gold.

The Bishop and Leadership

There is a variety of views around the wider church about whether or not the bishop should be a "leader." Management-speak and business practices are welcomed by some and yet disregarded as inappropriate for the church by others. Nevertheless, in my view it is incumbent upon a bishop to "lead" the diocese to which they have been called. If a bishop wishes a diocese to move forward, it will take leadership of one kind or another. In the Western context, society is changing so rapidly that clergy can feel disorientated and unprepared for the new voyage that future ministry and church-life may require. As life evolves, everybody may need to learn new skills and shed certain presuppositions. Given this, consideration of the issue of leadership need not be binary—some business approaches may indeed be irrelevant, but others may prove useful. The church can learn from secular innovations about how to embrace efficiency and a culture of personal development alongside its responsibility to pastor and to preach. Since nowadays there are so many other calls on pastors' time and energy, the traditional role of simply conducting worship and doing visiting has not held sway for some time. In turn, this raises the thorny matter of statutory compliance in areas such as safeguarding, data protection, and charities' legislation, all of which have come to play such a significant role in recent years. For the most part, even if there is a recognition of the worthiness of these issues, clergy themselves are feeling utterly swamped by these new requirements. Some may be able to delegate responsibility for this compliance to administratively gifted volunteers in their parish, but many feel completely overwhelmed. The vast majority of local clergy work alone and can have to manage an avalanche of paperwork. Like bishops, they find themselves heavily involved in administrative duties that were not a part of their original vocation—yet it has to be done. While some dioceses are seeking to employ dedicated compliance officers, it is the individual cleric who has to take responsibility for filling out lengthy and complex forms. This is not something that can be hastily improved, but without doubt it is the heartfelt complaint that is heard most often by bishops, and sometimes from those who are in abject despair.

A Bishop's Workload

While acting as *pastor pastorum* takes up the bulk of a bishop's time, there may be many other tasks equally suited to a particular bishop's skill set. When it comes to the division of episcopal labor and the distribution of committee chairs, for instance, it is wise to consider the specific interests of each individual bishop so that someone does not get burdened with a role for which they have neither interest nor aptitude. A retired bishop once advised me not to agree to anything for six months, and this was exceedingly helpful. Speaking personally, I found it essential to have a concentrated period of "finding my feet" before taking on any specialisms. If a bishop is careful, he or she can play to their strengths and avoid aspects of work that could frustrate both them and their committee members. Likewise, within a diocese it is undoubtedly best practice to hire or volunteer someone other than the bishop for the areas in which they themselves may be least well-equipped.

In relation to the matter of overall workload, bishops, like all ordained clergy, do get overwhelmed and exhausted. As aptly captured by George,

> Many leaders go through a crucible when they have an experience at work that dramatically tests their sense of self, their values, or their assumptions about their future or career. I call this "hitting the wall," because the experience resembles a fast-moving race car hitting the wall of the track, something most rising leaders experience at least once in their careers.[5]

Bishops are not immune from this "hitting the wall," and it often happens precisely because they have had to focus on areas in which they feel incompetent and under-resourced, or which simply drain them of the joy of ministry. All clergy, whether in curacy, incumbency, or episcopacy, will experience highs and lows. However, again in the words of George, there is some reassuring good news: "These journeys illustrate that . . . in truth, it is the difficult experiences that prepare you to lead your organization through the challenges you will face."[6] In other words, the hard times are character-building!

Perhaps we also need to look further back into appointment processes and recognize that the church has not always been adept at role-induction. This may vary from one context to another, but in many instances it is virtually non-existent. Most business organizations will prepare someone for stepping into a new position, and especially someone who is transitioning into senior leadership for the first time. In the church, however, there is stubborn reluctance to embrace any such formal induction procedures. One of the first things I initiated after my first year as a bishop was to prepare a folder of information for other incoming bishops who might feel just as much at sea as I had. Local pastors too often begin their first charge with an insufficient sense of direction, and for this reason it is refreshing to see at least the emergence of some teaching seminars that are seeking to address such a deficit.

History records that when Susannah Wesley's life became busier, she insisted on praying for longer, and this in my opinion offers a superb example for hard-pressed clergy. I love the title of the book by John Mark Cromer, *The Ruthless Elimination of Hurry*, and I take it with me on most

---

5. George, *True North*, 23.
6. George, *True North*, 23.

retreats. It is hardly a positive thing that all of us as clergy, both rectors and bishops, are known best for being busy. Given that the main focus here is to look specifically at the role of bishops, and given the astonishing plethora of tasks that bishops undertake, the question that must be asked is what might then be the first casualty? Being honest, sometimes it is the very things that at our peril we should not neglect, namely, prayer and the study of the Scriptures. If there is something bothering me, it is tempting to ruminate, or to fret, and only eventually to pray. Whereas it can be difficult to get the mind to settle into prayer, or even into sleep, the essential thing for a bishop is that they should be asking God for wisdom. Even when bishops do not feel equal to the task, they must remind themselves of the sufficiency of divine grace.

The Loneliness of Episcopal Ministry

One issue that becomes recurrent in this discussion of episcopal ministry is the absence within church-life of ongoing professional development. As soon as someone has finished their time as an assistant pastor, they are effectively left on their own. Whether it is a coaching arrangement, or the opportunity for further study, or a stronger emphasis in a local network on caring for one another, it should be expected that those who serve in pastoral ministry ought to be growing deeper in their role. With regard to this, there is much more that institutional systems might do to enable those who want to invest in lifelong learning to do so. What if the tables were to be turned, and it was those who do *not* engage in ongoing professional development who were regarded as the exception? Again, at this point, those of us who are involved within the church can learn from the secular world. There, the idea of putting someone into a position, leaving them alone, and not seeking either to resource or develop them would be unthinkable.

In his exploration of "team dysfunctionality," Patrick Lencioni offers the following observation: "If you could get all the people in an organization rowing in the same direction, you could dominate any industry, in any market, against any competition, at any time."[7] Sometimes it has to be noted that the main underlying cause of loneliness is a straightforward lack of collegiality among those who serve, and this can apply to both clergy and bishops. The temptation to become overly territorial and even competitive is an ever-present one. At clergy meetings, for example, there

---

7. Lencioni, *Five Dysfunctions*, 8.

can be discussion about who is the busiest, who can never get a day-off, who has the most members. Such attitudes may be symptomatic of insecurity and the fear of failure, and it could hardly be asserted that they are indicative of rowing in the same direction. Those in pastoral ministry will also flourish to a greater extent if they can train themselves to focus on that which is most urgent—the priority of mission, the centrality of preaching, the importance of empathy, and the goal of joyfully reversing church decline. A popular metaphor in the world of organizational change is that of "the burning platform," and it is precisely here that the churches of the West need to concentrate their thinking in a post-pandemic world—the reality now is that the church's task is in need of urgent renewal, and it is essential that new insights be allowed to sit alongside treasured ancient truths.

Ultimately, the business of ministry must be concentrated on God himself. Those who serve have responded to his call as he has placed his hand on their lives and invited them into ministry. Given the magnitude of what this actually means, it is completely normal to feel inadequate, and yet there is also the abiding promise of God's equipping. This is helpfully expressed in the following words of Ken Costa:

> The point is that God comes alongside us in our callings. He works with us in relationship. Clearly sometimes God breaks into our lives in a big way ... but other times it is much gentler—a beckoning and a whispering. Sometimes God places roadblocks if we are going in the wrong direction. And sometimes it may well be up to us to decide the way ahead. Whatever the circumstances, we have a God who walks beside us, helping us keep a sure footing when the path ahead seems uncertain.[8]

While this assurance is an immense antidote to loneliness, those in pastoral ministry also need fellow human beings. And yet, whereas the various networks of church-life ought to help them feel less isolated, again, here the reality is that most clergy do not work collaboratively. Aloneness is not the same as loneliness, but anyone who works consistently on their own will inevitably face moments when they feel that the burden is simply too much to bear. There are ways in which clergy can support one another in a non-judgmental and uncompetitive manner. Speaking personally once again, I have chosen to be part of a support group that has met consistently ever since I was first ordained. All of us would say that, were it not for each other, none of us would still be

---

8. Costa, *Know Your Why*, 23.

in ministry. I realize that having such a group is dependent on an individual's ability to be proactive, but it genuinely pays dividends in offering support—feeling isolated can never be God's best for those who serve him.

That being said, where then might a bishop go for pastoral care? Unless bishops are intentional in establishing support systems for themselves, the likelihood is that this will not happen organically. Bishops need to be resolute about the importance of self-care. If they are to be effective in giving care to others, they must stay well themselves. By nature someone serving in episcopal ministry will be an inherent giver, and perhaps not necessarily good at spotting the signs of personal burnout. It is essential that the church should advocate for, and resource, clerical self-care, and likewise that bishops should ensure that the care that they provide for others does not come at a detrimental cost to themselves. For all who serve in pastoral ministry the diary is never empty, and at the end of any given week there are always more things still needing to be done. The nature of ministry is such that the job is never fully accomplished, and equally, there are no instant results and no rewards for performance. Both clergy and bishops are fortunate if they enjoy the support of a spouse and family. However, ministry can be a very lonely journey for unmarried clergy—they may have plenty of friends and colleagues, but coming home at the end of a difficult church meeting to an empty house is far from ideal. The reality is that single clergy probably need even more of a support network than those who do not live alone.

A Bishop's Capacity to Listen

As *pastor pastorum* the bishop needs to stay in touch with the issues that clergy face. Bad things do happen to good people, and hence the family lives of clergy will include both joys and sorrows, as normal families do. From the perspective of clerical family life, there are particular complications that have to be navigated over and above what is normally the case for other professions—working every weekend, constant evening work, tied housing, financial worries, housing requirements at retirement, the complications of moving to a new charge when a spouse is working or children are in school, to mention but a few. Those whose job it is to care for the carers need to be acquainted with what the individual pastors are facing. As already mentioned, whereas this may to some extent depend on the size of the diocesan area, what matters most of all for the bishop is the ability to empathize with sound emotional intelligence, and sometimes all that is needed is simply to sit and listen. That goes to the very heart of what it means to be *pastor pastorum*.

For many clergy a particular challenge now is coming to terms with the effects of the COVID-19 pandemic. Many churches have not recovered, either numerically or financially, and are struggling to re-engage younger generations after two years of Sunday mornings when families realized it was much more appealing to watch their Sunday service online from home. In many places, the rise of Sunday sports has also dealt a substantial blow to church attendance. Clergy who have been ordained for some time again find themselves living in an atmosphere for which they feel untrained. In the words of Steven Croft, they feel "unprepared" and, as it were, "left naked in a situation of great change in society and in the churches."[9]

Many national churches are actively experimenting with new missional initiatives such as pioneer ministry and fresh expressions, and without doubt these projects may help to reinvigorate and replenish. If clergy want to flourish and thrive, they will need to find fresh hope and vision for the future, and while this may not be easy, it nevertheless remains that the church as such has always found itself in the business of realizing the impossible. Within the life of the church, change is inevitable, and it is essential that bishops are able to give a lead in this regard. As aptly put by Beaumont,

> It is much easier to be the kind of leader that strives to restore what was, the leader who makes people feel safe and happy. But that leader rarely takes the organization any place meaningful in a liminal era. That kind of leader often drags an organisation back into its preliminal state, so that no adaptation takes place.[10]

Conclusion

In conclusion, it is clearly the case that for bishops, ordained clergy, and church-members alike, the expectation is that a diocesan bishop ought to function as *pastor pastorum*, and, in addition, they must also exercise

---

9. Croft, *Ministry in Three Dimensions*, 154.
10. Beaumont, *How to Lead*, 20.

pastoral diligence towards other ministry staff such as youth officers, diocesan officials, honorary secretaries, and pioneers (whether ordained or not). An important consideration here is the reasonable size and extent of how many others any individual bishop may be expected to look after. Regardless of whether or not pastoral care is being provided, it is certainly *expected*, and, while there may be other ancillary support programs for clergy, bishops cannot neglect this, their primary duty.

Equally, it is evident that bishops have myriad other matters with which they need to deal at any given time. Some of these are simple to resolve and resource; others of them will require much time and further advice. The frustrations which people sometimes have in relation to how long certain issues can take to reach resolution is invariably matched by the exasperation of the bishop, and clearly there is no such thing as a completely flawless system. Ultimately, bishops are expected to be pastorally sensitive and available to their clergy. Yet, in another sense such responsibility ought also to be mutual and reciprocal—within the church of God we are all actually meant to be responsible for one another. Hence, not only might bishops help others by being pastorally available, but equally they too could be assisted by the clergy having an ear to their needs. Ministry is far from an easy choice or lifestyle. It takes dogged commitment, resilience, and endless patience. It can be demanding and will bring disappointment, but it is also both a delight and a joy. When the former outweighs the latter, it is almost impossible not to become fractious, and with that the soul suffers. As *pastor pastorum* a bishop is expected to be mindful of both the joys and sorrows of local church ministry, recalling it from their own experience, wanting to be what is needed, but also being aware that sometimes this is simply unfeasible. MacDonald gives wise advice when he says,

> Who are the people who populate [our] inner circle, that, presumably, will walk through life with each of us, and who will make an inestimable contribution to the development of our resilient life?[11]

These are the relationships that we should seek to nurture as of first importance.

---

11. MacDonald, *Resilient Life*, 211.

Pastoral Skills

8

"Rejoice with Those who Rejoice, Weep with Those Who Weep": Reflections on Pastoral Visiting

Robin Stockitt

THE STORIES AND OBSERVATIONS expressed in this chapter are the fruit of many years of engagement in pastoral situations. I spent the early part of my working life as a teacher, both in England and in Nigeria. Later, in mid-life, I was ordained in the Anglican Church and worked in parishes in England, Germany, and Northern Ireland. I am now retired. It is my conviction that theological insights and their practical implications often emerge from, and are shaped by, the experiences of life. Unavoidably, we inhabit a storied world and so it is narratives that offer us the chance to derive meaning and purpose. Stories never remain simply as stories. They are always interpreted. Christian discipleship takes place within the unpredictable ups and downs of life, often requiring an improvised response. There is no easy step-by-step approach to pastoral engagement; pastoral visiting is not a painting-by-numbers exercise. It requires the audacity to respond with a nimble gentleness.

Perhaps the most outrageous biblical narrative of dramatic improvisation is contained in the story of Nathan as he visits King David in the aftermath of his adultery with Bathsheba, recounted in 2 Sam 12. Nathan is anxious to avoid being the target of David's ire, yet he knows it is his role as a prophet to confront the king with his own misdemeanors. He does so by weaving a clever tale about two sheep farmers. In the tale, a late-night visitor arrives at the home of the wealthy farmer, needing accommodation. The farmer chooses to go to his neighbor's farm and seizes his only lamb in order to cook a meal. King David is outraged by this wanton act of theft. It is precisely at this point, when he is fully immersed in the narrative, that Nathan is able to declare "you are the man [who has taken what did not belong to you]" (2 Sam 12:7 NIV). It is the narrative that contains the prophetic message and brings David to a point of self-awareness and conviction. Much of biblical theology is contained within such narrative structures. I make no apologies therefore for sprinkling this chapter with narratives from my own experience and the reflections that flow from them.

The Late-Night Phone Call

The need to improvise was brought home to me very vividly when I once received a very distressed late-night phone call. The man who spoke to me explained that his four-year-old son had seen a ghost in their home and was so terrified that he was refusing to go upstairs to bed. The caller was not a member of the church where I was a curate, but he had contacted every other local church minister without finding anyone prepared to visit his home. The phone call to me was his last resort. I agreed to go, not knowing what I would find. Upon entering the house, I found a dozen adults clustered around the small boy. The situation had been ongoing for several hours. Everyone looked terrified and expressed some relief that I, as a priest, would know what to do. Of course I did not know what to do. I asked the little boy if I could hold him close to my chest, to which he nodded. Taking him in my arms we went from room to room looking for "the bad people." In each room I asked him if he could see any bad people and each time, he shook his head. Following me around the house there was a trail of frightened adults. Finally, we came to the boy's bedroom, and I suggested that he should lie on the top bunk of his bed. I then told him that I was going to say a special prayer that would protect him from any bad people. After the prayer I asked him to think of a happy time. He told me about making sandcastles on a beach. I suggested that he simply remember that happy time and within a few minutes he was fast asleep. The adults were utterly astonished and felt that I had some kind of magical power. In reality I was simply making things up as I went along.

Or was I? In his book entitled *Improvisation*, Sam Wells claims that Christian ethical behavior is intrinsically improvisatory.[1] This does not mean that it is loose, free, and entirely without structure. Rather it is more like the performance of a jazz musician who has been trained in musical theory and practice and now is able, within certain parameters, to create new and innovative music. Wells draws upon the work of N. T. Wright in offering a model in which to understand the trajectory of the gospel story.[2] He offers a five-act-play theory. Act one is creation, act two is covenant, act three is cross and resurrection, act four is the period of improvisation and act five is the eschaton. We live in between acts three and five. The major interventions of God have already taken place in the first three acts, and the final consummation is yet to happen. The period we inhabit therefore is one of improvisation upon the great stories and events of God in Christ. Each new event or context is by its very nature, utterly unique and therefore demands a response that draws upon the biblical parameters while making decisions that are pertinent to the particularity that faces us. Improvisation is thus fully informed by biblical narrative while also being free to "perform" in the present moment.

This is surely what was happening on the day of Pentecost recorded in the book of Acts. The frightened huddle of disciples in an upper room are depicted as being overwhelmed by an outpouring of the Holy Spirit with surprising and entirely novel manifestations. Foreign tongues, fire, wind, joy, exuberance, and divinely given confidence emanate from those fearful disciples. Within minutes the city center is filled with astonished onlookers. Someone needs to step up and explain what is happening. It is Peter, the unpredictable, unreliable disciple who stands before the crowd and, seemingly with no preparation, is able to draw upon a lifetime of scriptural study and preach a sermon that draws together a plethora of biblical narratives. It is his compelling storytelling that is so convincing, so apt, so pertinent to this moment that the crowd are brought to a point of deep conviction and faith. How was he able to improvise in this extraordinary manner? Surely it was because he knew his Torah, he was familiar with the hope of Israel, and he could interpret the signs of the times. His improvisation was no fluke. It drew upon a lifetime of faith.

When I was called upon to visit that house late at night, what the frightened family needed from me above all was a sense of presence.

---

1. Wells, *Improvisation*.
2. Wright, *New Testament*.

They needed the physical presence of another who would understand their fear and not minimize it, who would step into that place of terror and bring a sense of surety. But it was not any human presence that they wanted. They wanted the presence of God in human form and thus only an ordained priest would suffice. Whether I realized it or not, my presence ushered into the room a sense of the sacred.

At times in the biblical narratives a sense of presence is what fundamentally changes the dynamic of a situation. The presence of the risen Christ in the upper room did just that. Those terrified disciples could not face the prospect of daring to venture outside. After this encounter with Jesus and the experience of his breath upon them, everything changed. When Elijah hid himself in the cleft of the rock and could only hear the faintest whisper, that sense of presence empowered him once more (1 Kgs 19). The phone call late at night catapulted me into unknown territory as far as pastoral visiting was concerned. It was also one of my greatest times of learning.

The Man at the Back Door

Many years after this story I was rector in a small, Northern Ireland parish. I was in the utility room at the rear of the rectory when suddenly an unknown stranger appeared at the window. He was breathless, urgent, desperate. I asked him what was the matter and he explained that two or three days earlier he had rashly and inexplicably had an affair with another woman. He was so distraught about this that he had immediately rushed home to confess to his wife. She, in turn, was so distressed that, as an act of revenge, she had done the same thing on the same day. She paid for the services of a male sex worker. The man who stood before me was so desperate to repair his marriage that he had asked the local Catholic priest to help but he had declined. As he was not a member of any church, he did not know where to turn and eventually stumbled across the Church of Ireland rectory where he found me.

After hearing his story, I felt somewhat wary. Could I trust this man? Should I get involved? Should I invite him into the rectory? I decided that I would meet with him, provided he brought his wife along. We agreed to meet at the door of the church in half an hour. I was again placed in a position in which I had little idea what I should do. I asked the couple to sit in the front row of the church and told them that we were going to do three things. To begin with, I gave them a copy of *The Book of Common Prayer* and asked them to turn to the page where together we would read out the confession. They were reluctant to do so and asked me to read the confession instead, and they would repeat after me. It then became apparent that neither of them could read. I explained that the confession was a way of turning back to God, expressing remorse, and then, having done that, I would declare that they could know God's forgiveness. They readily and gratefully participated in this. The next stage, I explained, would involve them standing before each other, looking at each other in the eyes and saying sorry to one another. This they were also ready to do. The last stage, I explained, was the most difficult and could take months or even years. They needed not only to accept the forgiveness of God and the forgiveness of one another, but also they needed to forgive themselves. Without this last stage they would live with a burden of regret and shame for many years. Having explained all three stages, I suggested that they might like to embrace each other, which they did. The whole encounter in the church took no more than thirty minutes and the couple left to return home hand-in-hand and were profoundly grateful to me. I was left somewhat dazed and bewildered at the speed of this encounter but glad to have been of some assistance.

Was I improvising? Most certainly yes. But on reflection I think I was sufficiently aware of biblical patterns of repairing human relationships. One of the petitions in the Lord's Prayer asks God to forgive us our sins as we forgive those who sin against us. Here is a twofold reciprocity in the repair of relationships. Our sense of being forgiven by God is paired with our capacity to extend that same forgiveness to others. Elsewhere in the New Testament when Jesus is asked about the greatest commandments, he replies, "Love God with all your heart and soul and mind and strength and love your neighbor *as yourself*."[3] Our love for our neighbor is paired here with the kind of love that we extend to ourselves. Knowing these biblical parameters was perhaps the background to the improvisation that I was compelled to adopt in this strange story.

The Confession

With considerable trepidation, Margaret (not her real name) approached me in the kitchen of the church hall and asked if I would be willing to

---

3. See Matt 22:37–40.

come to her house. She wore a burdened expression on her face and appeared tense as she spoke, explaining that she wanted to make a confession to me. I had only been the rector of the small rural parish for a few months, so her use of the word "confession" was surprising given that this was a predominantly Protestant part of Northern Ireland, and such a word was loaded with Roman Catholic connotations. A few days later I sat in her living room with her husband and listened to her story.

Some thirty years earlier her first husband had worked as a delivery driver and received an instruction to go to a particular address in a nearby town. It was during the height of "the Troubles," a term used to describe the turbulent, violent period of time when paramilitary atrocities had become commonplace. Unknown to her husband, the Irish Republican Army had used an address as a base to ambush him solely because he was a member of the volunteer police force. As soon as he arrived at the house he was gunned down. At the time, Margaret had two teenage children, and one evening her grief was so overwhelming that in a moment of intense despair she went into the kitchen and tried to take her own life. Her young son, noticing that she had left the room, followed her and managed to remove the tablets from her mouth.

Ever since that one defining moment, Margaret lived with an unresolved and unbearable sense of both guilt and shame. How could she have contemplated leaving her children as orphans? She wanted to confess this incident in the hope that through my intervention she might experience a sense of forgiveness and peace with God. Once I heard this story we sat in silence for several minutes. I then asked Margaret to stand before me, I laid my hands on her head and together we read the general confession from *The Book of Common Prayer*. I then pronounced the absolution and assured her of God's acceptance of her, his welcome, and his unconditional love. For me this was a truly sacred, beautiful moment. It was a privilege to be entrusted with her story and to be asked to be a conduit of God's grace. I have often ruminated over this experience and wondered if it could be possible to discern what took place.

Each pastoral visit takes place within a cultural context. In my case, the context was the shadow of the Troubles that persist to this day in Northern Ireland, even though the Good Friday Peace Agreement was signed in 1998. There is a lingering trauma in the hearts of many people, for everyone knows someone who was killed or injured during those thirty years. All pastoral visits, whether in Northern Ireland or Chicago, need to be sensitive to the particularity of each culture. Even a cursory reading of the ministry of Jesus illustrates how deeply aware he was of the sensitivities of Middle Eastern culture. Kenneth Bailey, in works such as *Jesus Through Middle Eastern Eyes* and *Poet and Peasant*, has amply demonstrated that all the random human encounters depicted in the Gospels alongside his parables are thoroughly imbued with cultural emblems and expectations, which, to the modern Western reader, may be lost.[4] The parable of the friend at midnight, for example, illustrates how the Middle Eastern cultural emphasis on showing hospitality to anyone who visits is paramount.[5] It would have been unthinkable to refuse hospitality to anyone who visits, however inconvenient the time. The meaning of the parable turns around this commonly accepted cultural practice. If the grumpy householder could extend hospitality to the surprise visitor at an unwelcome hour, then how much more will God attend to us.

Each culture tells stories about itself, and the meaning of these stories gives purpose. Such narratives evolve over time. Their perpetuation is buttressed by repeated storytelling and symbolic actions. What might appear to be a simple pastoral visit is in reality a complex cultural encounter, and those who engage in pastoral visits in the name of the local church need to be able to discern the locally accepted norms, expectations, and hopes that lie, often unacknowledged, beneath the surface.

The transaction that took place in Margaret's living room also highlights the way in which both of us had a different constellation of need. Margaret needed above all to feel safe. She needed to feel that her story would be truly heard at its deepest level and that the telling of her story would be treated with the utmost respect and gentleness. The need to feel safely attached to someone is a primal, existential necessity. This has been most powerfully demonstrated by the work of John Bowlby and Mary Ainsworth who asserted that the need for a secure bond, initially with an early caregiver, remains with all of us throughout our lives.[6] Their work developed into what is now more formally recognized as Attachment Theory. This theory states that each of us forms attachments at an early stage of development. For some, such attachments are secure and unconditional. For others the attachment style can be more anxious or dismissive and convoluted by a variety of conditions. And these early patterns of attachment often remain imprinted in us into adulthood and shape every encounter and relationship that we form.

4. See also Bailey, *Jacob and the Prodigal*.
5. See Luke 11:5–8.
6. See Bowlby, *Attachment*; and Ainsworth, *Patterns of Attachment*.

Although Attachment Theory has only emerged in recent decades, the patterns it illustrates are clearly visible in Scripture. The need to feel safe is a repeated cry in Psalms where the psalmist is often depicted as one whose safety is in doubt. The frequent images of being overwhelmed or needing a rock on which to stand are all poetic expressions of the cry for security. And in response to such heartfelt cries the reassurance from Yahweh is reiterated time and time again. His *hesed* (loving faithfulness) remains unchanged. It is unchangeably secure.

So, when Margaret approached me in the kitchen with her request, her voice, her expression, her demeanor were all asking me this one question: "Are you a safe person?" And underneath that one question lay multiple other unspoken questions—"Will you truly hear me? Will you see me as I am? Will you hold my story without judgment? Will you try to fix me? Will you respect me? Will you weep with me?" I hope I was sufficiently aware of this. That is why I have headed this chapter with the citation from Rom 12:15—"Rejoice with those who rejoice, mourn with those who mourn."[7]

In addition to being thoroughly attuned and attentive to Margaret, I needed to be similarly attuned and attentive to what was going on in my heart. There is a seemingly innocuous phrase a few verses earlier, "Love must be sincere" (Rom 12:9). I wonder why Paul felt the need to say this? The implication is that some expressions of love may not in reality be genuine. The Greek word used in this verse is *anupokritos*, which means "unfeigned," the negative of, *hupokrinomai*, from which the English word "hypocrite" is derived, meaning "to speak or act falsely." In my experience as an ordained minister, I recognize that this is always a possibility. Churches can sometimes be places of competing agendas with awkward, stubborn personalities. The minister, and indeed the pastoral visiting team (if there is one), must find a way to navigate such potentially stormy waters. One way in which this is sometimes dealt with is to employ "strategic visiting" or even "pre-emptive visiting." I have heard ministerial colleagues talking in this way. This means engaging in pastoral visiting in order to prevent a crisis later on, in order to smooth a tricky agenda item in a forthcoming committee meeting, or even to prove to the keen eyed that visiting is actually taking place. Pastoral visiting done for such motives can be less than truly sincere with other unspoken agendas in play.

---

7. All Scripture quotations in chapter 8 are taken from the NIV.

The sensitive member of the church who is being visited may quickly sense that such expressions of "love" are in fact fake.

Recognizing one's own agenda is fraught with danger and requires ruthless honesty. For the minister or the pastoral visitor, searching questions need to be asked. What is my own agenda in this situation? Is this visit actually about meeting my own need for validation? Am I here in order to prove a point? Am I here in this home in order to recruit? If so, that needs to be made clear at the outset. Am I here in an to attempt to evangelize? If that is the purpose of the visit, that, too, needs to be made explicit. Awareness of these hidden agendas can prevent an expression of love from being feigned.

The House Blessing

The issue of learning to be culturally sensitive has occurred on numerous occasions in my experience. Margaret's story took place in the relatively familiar territory of Northern Ireland. On another occasion while living in Germany and working as the minister of an international English-speaking church, I was asked by a Nigerian family who were members of the church to visit them in their new apartment. They wanted me to bless the house. I readily agreed and said that I would call round early one Saturday morning. In my mind, this visit was likely to last half an hour at most, allowing for some chat to begin with, a look around the house, followed by some prayers. How wrong I was!

When they opened the door upon my arrival they looked at me in disbelief. "Where is your wife?" they asked. The blessing ceremony they had in mind could not possibly take place without my wife being present as well. I called my wife and explained the situation. She hurriedly got ready, walked to the nearby railway station, and eventually arrived at the house about one hour after my arrival. Then followed a prolonged process of blessing each room separately, then a blessing on the whole house, then a blessing for the family. This was followed by a lengthy wait while the wife prepared a Nigerian meal for us all to share. We returned home in the afternoon. Clearly my expectations of a pastoral visit were completely wrong.

The Two Sisters

A member of the church was a widower with two adult daughters, each of whom had their own families in towns some distance away from where I was living. I had never met the daughters, but both contacted me on separate occasions to ask if I could speak to their father whom I had got to know reasonably well. Their problem was a tricky one. Their relationship with their father had completely broken down and they had both asked him not to try and visit in order to see his grandchildren any longer. He had refused to agree to this request and had tried to visit the primary schools of his grandchildren secretly. These covert visits eventually became the cause of a police injunction against him in which he was not permitted to visit the schools again. Both daughters asked me to visit their father and to try and effect some kind of reconciliation. I was reluctant to do so but agreed to try on the condition that they inform their father that they had requested me to get involved. My subsequent visit to him was very tense. He brought out a pen and paper and started making notes about what exactly I had been told and what I intended to do. I explained that I had merely responded to his daughters' request and was here to listen.

It soon became apparent that my presence was extremely unwelcome and after a while I returned home. The man left the church soon after that visit. With the benefit of hindsight, I wished I had not agreed to make the visit, as I had unwittingly become collateral damage in a family dispute. This experience highlighted for me the necessity of recognizing my own limitations. Here was a complex, broken family dynamic that had no doubt been years in the making. I did not have the skills to enter such a complex web of relationships, accusations, and counter accusations and should have instead realized that this situation went beyond the limits of my capability. Recognizing limitations is, I believe, a vital component of pastoral visiting. It is a way of recognizing the role that visitation has and also what it is not equipped to do. When a situation has reached the point of limit, then it is time to refer to a different sphere of competence.

The Sheep Market

Not every pastoral encounter is of such an intense kind. The majority, in my experience, are much more mundane. The occasional encounter in the local supermarket or the chat over the garden wall about the minutiae of life can all communicate something of the incarnational nature of Christian vocation. In the village where I used to live, there was a sheep market every Saturday morning. Large numbers of tractors and trucks would queue up to deliver their sheep, and in the auctioneer's ring incomprehensible numbers were called out at high speed. I attended this weekly spectacle from time to time, both out of curiosity and out of a desire to enter the world of the farming community that surrounded where I lived. I do not claim to have understood what was going on but did understand how important this event was to those men present.

The prologue in John's Gospel speaks of the Word becoming flesh and dwelling among us (John 1:14). The Greek word translated as "dwelling" means "to pitch one's tent" or "to camp." It is the kind of word used to describe nomadic people travelling from place to place and stopping to spend the night. The incarnation of Christ is likened to this kind of journey. Christ who travels with us, who enters our day-to-day life, who pitches his tent right where we are. It is a statement both of identification and belonging. The incarnate Christ fully identifies with the human condition and chooses to fully belong within the communities where we reside. This beautiful depiction of the immanence of God speaks of the value that God places on the ordinary, the unspectacular, the humdrum aspects of human existence. It is right here in the mess and muddle of life, that God chooses to dwell and where he can be found. Frederick Buechner writes eloquently about discovering the grace of God in such places:

> Listen to your life. See it for the fathomless mystery it is. In the boredom and pain of it, no less than in the excitement and gladness: touch, taste, smell your way to the holy and hidden heart of it, because in the last analysis all moments are key moments, and life itself is grace.[8]

The Ignatian tradition places great emphasis on this very aspect of Christian spirituality. The daily examen is a practice that asks this question at the end of each day: "Where have I been able to detect the presence of God in the ordinariness of the day that has just ended? Can I look at the experiences of this day and discern their meaning?" It is a way of learning to perceive the sacred wherever the experiences of life take us, and this is especially pertinent within the context of pastoral visiting. A conversation that centers around the price of lambs at the local sheep market may not sound particularly "spiritual," but to the sheep farmer

---

8. Buechner, *Now and Then*, 2.

who is being visited it is absolutely paramount and filled with both anticipation and fear. While such emotions may not be articulated verbally, they are hidden within the factual statements about recent events at the market. The pastoral visitor needs to be attentive to what is being said and also to what remains unsaid.

The Email

In the years of my pastoral experience, not every visit to a home ends happily. One day I received an email from a female member of the church where I was the minister in which she claimed that another church member, a man, had met with her and had spent the entire time speaking ill of me. By temperament, I would tend to be conflict avoidant, but this was clearly something that needed to be faced. It was a disturbing email, and I decided that I would arrange a visit together with my church warden, who was a member of the leadership team. At the outset of the visit, I showed the man the email that I had received in which there were serious allegations of his slanderous speech against me. At first, he denied all knowledge of this. Later he admitted to some of the allegations and finally he broke down in tears and confessed that for the previous two years he had indeed systematically tried to destroy my character and ministry by targeting every new family or visitor who turned up at the church. He explained that he would invite the visitors to the church out for a meal and advise them strongly not to consider joining the church. Having confessed this, he asked for my forgiveness to which I agreed. I left his home after the visit amazed at the outcome and grateful to God for what appeared to be divine intervention. The following Sunday he and his wife claimed that I was the one who had besmirched his character. They said they were outraged and disgusted at my every word and felt that my visit was intended to humiliate and shame. The couple promptly left the church and were never seen again.

This whole episode left me bruised and confused. I had tried to follow appropriate protocols, I had taken a witness with me, I had listened attentively and had given time for a response, I had witnessed what appeared to be a sudden conviction of sin. And yet the outcome was deeply unsatisfactory and troubling. Perhaps the words of Paul are most apposite here: "If it is possible, as far as it depends on you, live at peace with everyone" (Rom 12:18). Sometimes it is simply not possible.

Gathering the Threads Together

The stories that I have told illustrate, I hope, a range of issues that lie beneath the surface of the apparently simple practice of pastoral visiting. Let me list them.

1. *Safety*. The visitor must be, above all, a safe person. This means being able to stay with another as they tell their story without being overwhelmed, distracted, or triggered by the conversation. Being a safe person is a quality that comes from within. It stems from the deep conviction of being held and loved unconditionally within the embrace of the Father, Son, and Holy Spirit. I do not believe it is possible to truly get to know someone unless you meet them in their own context, that is, at their home. If that encounter is a safe one, then doors may open for entry into people's hearts.

2. *Listening*. Listening to another requires attentiveness to the clues, the hints, the suggestions, and the body language of the one who is being visited. Such deep listening demands concentration and empathy. There is a big difference between listening to understand and listening to fix.

3. *Culture*. All pastoral care takes place within a cultural context, and the person who engages in visiting needs to be sensitive to its norms and expectations. Culture may be defined in a number of ways including historical antecedents, geography, language, and ethnicity. Furthermore, each individual church may also have developed its own micro-culture, which differs from the church down the road. The Puritan pastor Richard Baxter used to spend two full days a week visiting his congregation in order to catechize. This may have been entirely appropriate for a seventeenth-century English church in Baxter's tradition. It may not be appropriate elsewhere. Some churches place a very high emphasis on the absolute necessity for ministers to be engaged in visiting; other churches do not share this expectation.

4. *Authenticity*. The injunction in Rom 12—love must be genuine—is the only defining driver for pastoral visitation. This is how the early church is described in Acts 2, where we witness the early converts going from house to house, sharing bread, and meeting the needs of the poorest. Unless there is an authenticity about the pastoral care being offered, the church risks being a sham. This requires

attentiveness to the balance between remaining in a professional role and simply being a fellow human. The two are not mutually exclusive but there must be an authentic relationship between the two. Those people who met the late Pope Francis all testify to his ability to remain truly papal and a man of the ordinary people at the same time.

5. **Limit**. All pastoral care has its limitations. It cannot deal with every crisis that emerges in a church and the visitor must not attempt to overreach beyond their capability. The ability to know when to refer onwards is essential. The Gospels testify to some occasions when Jesus recognized that there were limitations to his own ministry. "A prophet is not without honor except in his own town" (Mark 6:4) And as I have intimated in my stories, some pastoral visitation simply does not lead to a happy ending.

6. **Presence**. Finding God in surprising places is a thoroughly Ignatian form of spirituality. It asserts that the presence of God is not confined to the pulpit or the communion table but can be discerned in the ordinary situations of life. It is predicated on the conviction that the mission of Jesus to "seek and to save" is an expression of the character of God who continually reaches outwards towards humanity in unmerited grace. The movement of God is both centrifugal in that it never ceases to extend outwards and centripetal in drawing us back to where we truly belong. The Holy Spirit is present therefore within those who are engaged in pastoral visitation as well as those being visited.

7. **Improvisation**. Pastoral care often requires the capacity to improvise, for improvisation is the hallmark of the action of the Spirit. Those biblical narratives that depict the prompting and intervention of the Spirit all illustrate the way in which the Holy Spirit communicates grace within the particularity of each unique situation. In pastoral visitation there is no handbook that provides a step-by-step solution to each and every human dilemma. Improvisation in a pastoral setting emerges as a result of the coming together of biblical knowledge, psychological awareness, sensitivity to culture, and years of life experience. The astonishing improvised sermon that the apostle Peter preached on the day of Pentecost was clearly imbued with the power of the Holy Spirit. Who knows whether our stuttering attempts at improvised responses to critical human dilemmas are likewise filled with the Spirit's presence?

Concluding Metaphors

It may be helpful to bring this collection of stories and reflections to a conclusion by recourse to metaphor. Any form of speech about God has no other choice but to resort to metaphor. Metaphor is a fluid, poetic form of speech that defies precise definition. How else can we know something of the nature and character of God without reference to metaphor? Sometimes God is depicted as a rock and a fortress and at other times as a mother hen. Jesus describes himself as the light of the world as well as the lamb. All of these different metaphors convey something different—a nuance, a shade, a hint perhaps—each of which elicits an image of the divine in our minds and in our hearts. When Moses asks God his name, the enigmatic answer comes, "I am who I am" (Exod 3:14). God as the eternal "I am" has the potential for multiple meanings.

No less is true when we need to find a way to make sense of who we are. We are sometimes depicted in the New Testament as the light of the world and at other times as a living stone or even as a sheep. These metaphors shape our sense of identity as disciples of Christ. So, I wonder if it would be useful for those engaged in pastoral visiting to consider what kind of metaphor adequately conveys what they are about. Here are some, which, in my view, may be unhelpful—doctor, psychotherapist, handyman, coach, lawyer. Each of these metaphors imply that the one doing the visiting has some expertise to offer and the one being visited is merely the recipient. It sets up an unequal, asymmetrical dynamic in which there is the "professional" and the "amateur." There may of course be occasions when the visitor is an ordained person and is asked to perform a "priestly" function, such as an absolution, a funeral, a baptism visit, marriage preparation, or the distribution of Holy Communion. I have already alluded to this in some of my stories. These are indeed professional functions and usually require the ordained minister to take on such a role. If, however, the minister only remains "in role" at all times, I believe something vital is lost. At a deeper level the most powerful form of human encounter will always be the "I-Thou" connection that Martin Buber wrote about.[9] "I-Thou" relationships are about knowing who we are in the presence of another. It is the person-to-person communication that touches hearts and sometimes changes minds too. They describe mutuality and reciprocity and, perhaps, the creation of a fertile environment for growth.

9. Buber, *I Thou*.

My suggestion therefore is that the metaphor of "fellow pilgrim" might be a useful way in which to approach pastoral visiting. We are all sojourners on the journey of faith and need one another to plot a course through the vagaries of life. Pastoral visiting is a venue for two or more pilgrims to meet together and to discover how the mysterious transformation of broken, wounded people can happen as we journey through life together. For me the metaphor of "pilgrim" contains something of the sense of being available towards others and being willing to offer an appropriate vulnerability towards those we encounter. It admits that none of us have "arrived" and that our own transformation into the likeness of Christ is an ongoing process.

For me, Ps 84:6 captures this encounter perfectly:

> As they pass through the Valley of Baka, they make it a place of springs; the autumn rains also cover it with pools.

The valley of Baka, a desert in the Holy Land, is a synonym for utter desolation. The word "Baka" means tears, which suggests that this forbidding landscape can become, for pilgrims, a fruitful place. I bring this chapter to a conclusion with a poem that I have written inspired by this psalm.

The Vale of Tears

> Our journey took us to the valley.
> "The vale of tears" they called it,
> by those who had once plodded through.
> A place of dusty desolation
> where no path, no plant, no signs of life
> interrupt its monotonous emptiness.
> There was no other way that we could see
> but through.
>
> Through the deadening silence,
> and crushing absence,
> picking out a lonely trail
> amid the jagged stones.
>
> But as we travelled a gentle mist descended,
> softly,
> O so softly at first as if heaven was weeping
> for lives lived in quiet desperation.

The dew caressed the barren ground
and tiny shoots appeared demanding our attention.
We bent down to slake our thirst from one small pool
that had collected, surprisingly,
amongst the rocks where our feet had trodden.

This vale of tears
this beautiful vale.

9

Pastoral Care in Christian Marriage

Drew Gibson

Introduction

IN THIS SHORT ESSAY, we shall look at three general areas that go together to form a coherent approach to the pastoral care of Christian marriage. First, we shall look at the context in which Christian marriage is lived out in the contemporary world. Second, we shall outline some general principles that underlie how marriages can be supported in the ordinariness of life. Third, we shall think of a general approach to responding pastorally to marriages that are experiencing relational difficulties. It will be impossible to do more than offer broad principles in a short chapter, but the resources listed at the end can give some more specific help.[1]

Marriage does not exist in a vacuum. It is formed by patterns that have been inherited from the past and it is strongly influenced by the culture in which it exists. In many places today it "tends to be viewed as a form of mere emotional satisfaction that can be constructed in any way or modified at will."[2] We will consider the traditional Christian understanding of marriage as a covenant, the influence of contemporary Western culture in general, and the importance of valuing the network

---

1. While some of the works in this bibliography contain comments on marriage with which I disagree, this merely illustrates the value of reading widely and not, as I promised at my ordination, "to refuse light from any quarter."

2. Francis, *Evangelii gaudium*, 66.

of relationships within which any given marriage exists. This will lead naturally into taking a relational approach to pastoral care.

Covenant Love

The traditional Christian understanding of marriage is that it is a covenant of love, made between a man and a woman in which they commit themselves to each other for life. It is a covenant, not a contract. A contract is a legally binding arrangement, made on the assumption that the partners cannot necessarily trust each other, whereas a covenant is a legally binding arrangement made on the basis that the partners *can* trust each other . . . but cannot necessarily trust themselves! In other words, in a contract the person holds the other accountable for *their* actions, but in a covenant, the partners hold themselves accountable for how they treat the other. Similarly, love is not warm feelings towards another because that other makes life good for them; it is a step of loving commitment that both partners believe will be reciprocated. It is a prioritizing of the other's welfare and flourishing over a selfish desire for one's own gratification. In a healthy marriage this commitment to mutual care leads to self-giving, as husband and wife do all that they can to help the other to flourish.[3]

Culture

While we are primarily thinking about marriage as historically understood by Christians, it is important to recognize that many people today live in relationships that are similar to marriage and that contemporary culture is not necessarily supportive of Christian marriage. A proactive response to contemporary culture can challenge destructive assumptions about marriage, including those that are based on an inappropriately patriarchal view; those that spring from a "rom-com" informed fantasy and those that buy into a consumerist mindset that has few expectations of the "consumer" and that expects that, when one is done with a spouse, they can be ditched or exchanged for a newer, updated model.

Intercultural marriages often have particular problems because expectations can vary hugely and patterns of what is deemed acceptable

---

3. See further Keller, *Each*, 67–85; Thomas, *Sacred Marriage*, 39–51. Bonhoeffer's comment is stark: "Christian marriage is marked by discipline and self-denial." *Discipleship*, 84.

in a marriage can even include things against which we ought to take a strong stand. It is tempting to think of intercultural marriages as those which take place across racial, ethnic, sectarian, or social class divides, but differences between rural and urban, between levels of education, or between geographical location can be just as telling. We might even go so far as to recognize that every marriage is intercultural to some extent. Clergy should help a couple to see that all relationships have their strengths and weaknesses, and each particular marriage should develop its own wholesome pattern.

Some people live in broadly committed relationships, sometimes for many years, without a formal marriage commitment. Others live in much looser arrangements with the expectation that the current relationship is unlikely to be their only one in future years. Still others live in same-sex partnerships either with or without the formal recognition of the secular state. Much of what follows might well apply to these relationships and, however we regard them theologically, those forming and breaking these relationships may well go through the joys and traumas of traditional marriage and therefore will benefit from good pastoral care.

A Network of Relationships

Marriage is only one of a network of relationships in which a couple lives. Most couples will have children and each spouse may have their own siblings, parents and grandparents, and wider family circle. There may also be children from a previous relationship. They will probably have a circle of friends, work colleagues, and neighbors, all of whom are important in their lives and for whom they may carry significant responsibilities. These relationships flow into the marriage relationship between husband and wife, hopefully supporting the couple but sometimes bringing tensions and divided loyalties. Not least, we must remember that it can be appropriate for a spouse to look for specific kinds of support from someone other than their wife or husband. For example, whereas I rejoice in going to watch rugby regularly with my friends, I would not dream of asking my wife to go. More seriously, my wife was able to share the pressures of pregnancy and menopause with her female friends in a way that I could not hope to understand fully! Increasingly, no sooner have parents waved farewell to children who have flown the nest, than the need to care for aging parents brings a new set of pressures to the marriage. So, it is imperative therefore to invest in these wider relationships.[4]

A Relational Approach to Pastoral Care

One of the key characteristics of congregation-based pastoral care is that it is normally offered in the context of longer lasting relationships within the local Christian community. It is in the very ordinariness of life, then, that clergy and other pastoral carers should seek to develop strong relationships with those who may one day need specific pastoral care. It is important to understand that what constitutes a strong or healthy relationship will not be the same in all situations. For example, some relationships are between equals who laugh easily together and open up to each other at deeper levels regularly and with some abandon. In contrast, other healthy relationships can be paternal or maternal, in the context of mentoring, or some more structured teaching or ministerial role. All such relationships will allow the person seeking care to know that they will be treated with respect, will be loved and honored, and what they say will be treated in confidence.[5]

No doubt this will be examined elsewhere, but a reminder here is apposite. We should only offer pastoral care that is consistent with our ongoing relationship with Jesus Christ. We do not offer care by simply following a manual or in a vacuum. It is a spiritual endeavor in which our relationship with Christ is the vehicle through which the Holy Spirit works, so we are unafraid to use Christian vocabulary and theologically rooted wisdom. However, this must never descend into simplistic thinking in which the impression is given that the Christian approach to relationship difficulties offers quick-fix answers with a religious gloss.

Consistency is also a watchword when we consider our own relationships. While it is clear that our marriages ought to model what a good marriage should be, this must be tempered by affirming that those who are unmarried can also model what it means to develop healthy relationships such as the ones noted above. Moreover, any of us who have been through personal difficulties that give us insight into the experience of others can speak with greater authority, while also recognizing that each

---

4. See further Moore, *Puzzle*, 42–59.

5. This must always happen within the normal legal and moral constraints. The British Association for Counselling and Psychotherapy (BACP) has guidelines. See BACP, *Managing Confidentiality*.

individual's experience is unique and that a simplistic transfer of "solutions" from one context to another can be very dangerous.

General Principles for Pastoral Care in Marriage

Building a Healthy Marriage

One of the key principles that operates in virtually every area of life is that it is better to prevent problems from arising than wait until they do arise and then try to deal with them. This can be called "preventative care" and good pastoral care takes it very seriously.[6] The guiding principle is that, in the ordinariness of life, patterns of living should be adopted that support, rather than militate against a healthy marriage. Some examples of such patterns include: maintaining a healthy work–rest balance; developing the ability to address issues of disagreement early and safely (including how to have a healthy "row"!); appropriate and equitable division of family responsibilities (including childcare, responsibility for finances, housework, etc.); management of stress and maintaining supportive relationships with family, neighbors, and friends. There is no set formula for an overall pattern of family life, but each family should develop patterns that reflect the natural talents and divinely given gifts that husband and wife possess. The patterns will develop through the years, fluctuating with such things as illness, unemployment, wider family responsibilities or social disruption.

One aspect of a healthy pattern of living that deserves special attention is that such a pattern will prioritize the holistic development of both spouses. A pattern that allows one to flourish, while the other withers is to be rejected. It is important that a Christian understanding of what it is to flourish does not necessarily mean that each individual's dreams and aspirations will be fulfilled. Developing a healthy pattern may well lead to difficult choices having to be made. One spouse's career may have to be prioritized to the detriment of the other's; one spouse's leisure activities may need to be significantly curtailed while another's involvement in church activities may not be all that they (or the parish leadership) might like it to be. Perhaps both will have to accept that not reaching what they

---

6. Having said this, there is precious little literature on this from a pastoral care perspective. Parrot and Parrot, *Complete Guide*, is helpful although they deal with structured mentoring. Perhaps best to consult books written for couples such as Chappell and Chappell, *Each*; Lee and Lee, *Marriage Book*.

could have made of themselves if they had had a personal assistant rather than a husband or wife is a sacrifice that is well worth making.

One area in which personal development does not normally require an extensive amount of give and take is spiritual development. Growing together in Christ is mutually supportive and complementary, rather than a zero-sum game. The simple fact that marriage is a covenant of love demands that mutual maturing is to be the norm. In passing, it is worth mentioning that theological understanding and time spent in Christian activities are not necessarily a sign of spiritual health and maturity. An honest relationship between husband and wife allows prayer together to be helpful and upbuilding; it also means that exploring the Bible together need have no questions that are deemed out of bounds. Areas of service within and through the local church will be embraced according to each spouse's gifts and talents. Some will be done together while others that are done separately will provide much material for conversation, encouragement, support . . . even for questioning or correction, when seen from the other's perspective.

Healthy Habits

Healthy patterns can be developed across the whole spectrum of married life including work and leisure, spending and saving, spiritual development . . . everything really. It is important to remember that we are creatures of habit, so thoughtfully developing good habits in every aspect of family life is necessary because the only alternative is the heedless development of bad habits! Obviously, it is best to cultivate wholesome patterns in the early stages of a marriage although, as the years go by and circumstances change, these may well develop to meet changing circumstances. Healthy patterns can be supported by good pastoral care in which clergy (along with other parish leaders and mature, wise Christians in general) can provide a sounding board for couples, offer appropriate guidance, and point to specialist support from those who are professionally trained to offer it.[7]

---

7. See further Gottman, *Seven Principles*.

A Healthy Church

Patterns of living and the development of healthy habits are important, not only in individual families but in local congregations. Pastoral leaders must carefully nurture patterns of congregational life that support marriages. While we greatly appreciate those who volunteer readily and are involved in a range of church activities, wise leaders are not afraid to call an individual's attention to over-involvement and to enable such a person to withdraw from some activities. While we all like to keep historically important activities going, this is not always wise as times change, leaders grow older, and committed people have to juggle many responsibilities. Some congregations might need to consider ending some activities or postponing them until overstressed leaders can be replaced. There is something very wrong when a man's or woman's commitment to Christian organizations or activities actually brings pressure and conflict into his or her marriage. Wise leaders who suspect that this might be the case should be proactive, facilitating the overcommitted person's withdrawal from some activities without them experiencing embarrassment or regret.

Healthy Patterns for Children to Learn From

It is beyond the scope of this essay to look at raising children, but a brief comment is appropriate. The ordinariness of family life is where children learn most about the relationship between husband and wife. They daily observe their parents and unconsciously imbibe patterns of relating that they see as being natural and "just the way life is." Boys see how their father treats their mother and assume that this is how a woman should be treated. Girls see how their mother treats their father and accept this as the norm for how a wife should act. Positively, this passes on wholesome patterns and gives children a wonderful starting point for their own marriages. Tragically, young children are not able to discern what is unwholesome in their parents' marriage. They will unconsciously assume that parents treating each other with contempt, absentee fathers, lazy mothers, verbally abusive fathers, violent mothers, emotionally volatile fathers, or alcoholic mothers are simply how life is. Even as they grow up into teenage years, their ability to discern what is wholesome and what is not is compromised; they know that they are in anguish but do not know why or what to do about it.

Growing up in an unstable, dysfunctional or tragic marriage with experiences of abuse, divorce, serious illness, or bereavement can be devastating. If wise grandparents or other members of the wider family are around, this damage can be, to some degree, mitigated. In addition, the patterns that children see in all of the other marriages that they interact with in a local congregation can also play a part, allowing children to see that a marriage does not have to be as toxic as their parents'. Church life, especially youth and children's organizations and organizations that encourage intergenerational mixing, brings new light into some children's lives, showing them positive role models that will help mold better patterns for them to adopt in the future.

Another aspect of support for marriage in the ordinariness of life arrives when children grow up, develop adult relationships with the opposite sex and one of these relationships becomes so special that it leads to marriage. Couples who wish to be married in church (or perhaps by a minister in a hotel or other setting) give two sorts of opportunity to ministers. First, clergy have wonderful opportunities to develop positive relationships with couples whose weddings they conduct. This is particularly important for couples who have little or no living relationship to the local congregation. Meeting such couples before they marry, during their wedding day, and in a follow-up visit allows at least some seed to be sown. This seed may be simply that the couple find that the minister is a good person who has wisdom, whom they can ask for guidance or help further down the line. It might also be that the gentle but clear presentation of the gospel through the wedding service can bear fruit quickly or as an early part of a longer process.

Another opportunity for preventative care for marriages is through pre-marriage counselling. Normally this happens in one of two ways. First, couples can take part in a course, along with other couples. This may be a course devised and run by the local minister or a group of local clergy, working together. It might also be a more generally available course, such as *The Marriage Course*,[8] organized and run in-person or online by local clergy. Other courses are available from Christian agencies such as those run by Christian Guidelines,[9] Accord,[10] or Care for the Family.[11]

8. Themarriagecourse.org.
9. Christianguidelines.org/marriage.
10. Accord.ie/marriage-preparation.
11. Careforthefamily.org.uk/product/pre-marriage-sessions-pack.

A second alternative is that a minister can meet with each couple individually to explore a Christian understanding of marriage in general and of the full range of areas that a couple should think through before they marry. This one-to-one approach has many advantages, including privacy and being able to move at a speed that is comfortable for everyone. It also allows the minister to get to know the couple better and to develop a relationship that might be of long-term significance.

Central to marriage preparation is the enabling of honest conversation between the couple. If they are silently saying to themselves, "We'll not talk about this until we're married" or "Let's not risk a fall-out now," then they are only storing up heartache for the future. Better for a minister to encourage and facilitate a discussion that will get things sorted out beforehand, even if this means that the couple realize that their visions of the future are not compatible and the marriage does not go ahead.

There is some evidence[12] that continuing a marriage preparation course *after* the wedding can be beneficial, so arranging a further meeting (e.g., a month or two following the wedding) could be valuable, especially if the couple are not regularly involved in the life of the local church. In more general terms, the early months and years of marriage are times of learning and reorientation for two individuals who have now become one couple. It is not surprising that ongoing support from clergy or other mentors in the local congregation is very valuable. Here, also, courses such as those referenced above are helpful. Of course, in a healthy local church informal "mentoring" of young couples can develop naturally in the ebb and flow of church life and should be positively encouraged, even facilitated by the church leadership. Then again, why restrict this support to newly married or young couples? With the passage of time, all marriages go through different stages, so learning from others who have gone through struggles with children, caring for elderly parents, financial pressures or the challenge of retirement, and walking through life with supportive peers is invaluable. To develop a healthy, multi-generational Christian community is, by definition, to support married couples.[13]

---

12. See further Beeson, *Counseling*; and Stevens, *Preparing Couples*.
13. See further Body, *Introduction to Marriage Preparation*.

Healthy Caution

Clergy and other congregational leaders are wise to recognize their limitations. We are not marriage counsellors and should not attempt to do more than we are gifted or trained to do. Good pastoral care is to walk with people going through difficulties, rather than necessarily to be the major professional resource. We do well to recognize the complexity of the difficulties that married couples encounter and that many of these difficulties require specialist support or intervention. Difficulties related to money require solid financial advice; health issues require medical advice; addictive or violent behavior cannot be dealt with by a "keen amateur." On recognizing that a specific issue needs to be addressed, good pastoral care brings the couple together with the most appropriate source of specialized support. Sometimes this support will be available within the church community, but, especially in particularly sensitive situations, some outside help can avoid developing unnecessarily strained relationships or the breaking of confidentiality. While it may be instinctive for clergy to look for support from specifically Christian groups or individuals, some non-churched individuals and certain secular agencies can be very helpful. Christian leaders ought to avoid the danger of over-spiritualizing problems and be encouraged to seek out advice from a wide range of possible sources.

The final observation to make is that, regretfully, we sometimes have to look for a "least worst option"; in other words we have to accept an outcome to the relational difficulties we encounter that is not what we would hope for. Sometimes the best that we can do is to walk with a couple through the dissolution and final breakdown of their marriage. We will consider this in more detail below, but it is appropriate to state clearly that any situation in which a husband or wife is in any sort of physical or psychological danger must be treated with the utmost seriousness and pastoral carers must be careful not to "allow the historic teachings of Christianity . . . to obstruct their immediate response to those in need."[14] A victim should never be encouraged to return to an abusive situation, and, if social services need to be involved or the police need to be called, we should not hesitate to do so.

---

14. Post, *Lasting Unions*, 2.

A Pastoral Response to a Marriage in Difficulty

Hurt and Hope

In a short chapter like this it is impossible to offer extensive commentary on all of the wide range of issues that can bring couples into a level of conflict that threatens the future of their marriage.

Living in a fallen world, marriages can come under stress for a huge variety of reasons. For our purposes, we can divide them into two. First, we recognize "no-fault" stresses. These are brought about by things that lie beyond the control of the couple, things in which both are innocent victims of circumstances. For example, illness can strike out of the blue, unemployment can come without warning, a hurricane can arrive in the middle of the night, or triplets can be born! None of these happen because one partner or the other did something wrong, they are simply life events that bring stress. Stress can bring couples closer together, but this is not always the case. For example, nursing a loved one through a long-term illness is very arduous, leading one partner to feel hard done by because of all the limitations placed on their own life. Equally, the other partner can feel ashamed of what their illness has done to their loved one's quality of life. Inappropriate anger and shame are deeply destructive and pastoral carers can help by enabling both partners to be completely honest in the safe place that they provide. Honesty before God and each other allows the incursions of human fallenness to be seen as common enemies to be fought together, with the enabling power of the Holy Spirit.

Secondly, marriages can be profoundly impacted because of foolish or sinful attitudes or actions on the part of one partner or other. These may be small sins that eat away at a relationship over time, destroying what was good and replacing it with a toxicity that comes on so slowly that it appears to be completely normal. Then there are the more dramatic sins: adultery, addiction, abuse (of many sorts), and so forth, which bring great pain and sorrow into a marriage, and make separation and divorce significantly more likely. On occasion, such an outcome seems to be almost inevitable, but our faith insists that healing and restoration are possible and that the destructiveness of sin has been overcome by the life-giving power of the resurrection. Following theologians like Moltmann,[15] we can affirm that because Christ has been raised from the dead, there is no situation in which hope is entirely absent. We may not know exactly

---

15. Moltmann, *Theology of Hope*.

what the solution will look like or how it is to be achieved, but we can continue to believe that God may provide a way forward that will be beneficial for everyone.

Helping in Times of Hurt

Pastoral carers of all sorts want to help. They want to make things better, to make the hurt go away. This is most commendable but is open to the danger that "fools rush in where angels fear to tread."[16] The wise pastoral carer may become involved quickly but should make haste slowly. In addition, offering "prepackaged" solutions is always dangerous and may well make a painful situation unbearable. The following is a four-step approach that enables pastoral carers to slow down, look and listen well, reflect thoughtfully, then build a response based on solid biblical foundations. It is based on the pastoral cycle that itself has many forerunners and fellow travelers.[17] It should go without saying that each of the four steps is to be taken prayerfully, maintaining an openness to the whispering of the Holy Spirit at all times.

Observation

When we become aware of, and are invited to become pastorally involved in, a marriage that is in trouble, the first step is to learn the truth of all that is actually happening. Each spouse will have their particular "take" on the "facts" and their own interpretation of events, words, looks, and silences. Some facts are relatively easy to establish, either immediately or with a little investigation, such as how long he spends at work, how much she spends on clothes, or who spends more time with the children. Other "facts" are much more difficult to determine: Is she selfish, is he lazy, are both or either of them more interested in their hobbies than their family? The line between hard facts and subjective interpretation of those facts is very rapidly crossed, so that a simple statement—"six o'clock"—becomes "late," "lazy," or "rushed" in the mind of the speaker and "early enough," "disciplined," or "in plenty of time" in the mind of the listener.

---

16. Pope, "Essay on Criticism."
17. See Green, *Let's Do Theology*. Also most helpful is Osmer, *Practical Theology*.

We need to listen well[18] and thereby to see the actual situation clearly, remembering, of course, that our observation may not always be completely accurate and that we are not just hearers but interpreters. We must also remember that people are not always truthful.

There are two overlapping characteristics of any valuable account of a pastoral situation: breadth and detail. The whole story needs to be told, including things that may not, at first sight, appear to be relevant. Of course, as a pastoral carer, and possibly a family friend, the minister may not be welcome into the details of the relationship, so as soon as things become too tense or it is sensed that one may be treading on very thin ice, suggesting professional counsel is appropriate. So long as the couple are happy that the minister continues to walk with them, one can continue to ask good questions and make accurate observations, until as accurate a picture as possible has been arrived at. Remember that telling this fraught story will be very emotional for the couple, so do not rush. Telling their version of the story may allow each to vent their frustration, pain, or anger and the minister's presence will allow this to be done safely. Even more positively, the questions and responses may allow each partner to listen to the other in a new way and thereby to begin the healing process.

> *Listen well, take notes if appropriate; write an account afterwards and keep everything confidential, with the usual legal limitations to this confidentiality.*

Interpretation

It will already be clear that the most important question that immediately follows any statement of fact is, "Why?" "Why did you do that?" "Why didn't you say something?" "Why do you seem to be so critical?" We need to aim for a thorough understanding of the situation. It must also involve seeing that an action may be the result of hugely differing motivations and unless motivations are teased out, misunderstandings are inevitable. One partner may act out of fear or anxiety, but this may

---

18. See further Babb, *Nurturing Hope*, 127-148; and Pembroke, *Foundations*, 70-87. For interesting ideas on listening, see Treasure, "5 Ways to Listen."

be totally misinterpreted because the other partner might have taken the same action, but in their case this would have been motivated by anger or ambition. Teasing this out allows for what is sometimes called a "meeting of meaning,"[19] where each understands, for the first time, what the action meant for the other.

Bearing this in mind, it is unsurprising that each partner is likely to question the motivation of the other, and, of course, each may not be completely honest in sharing why they have done or said something. No-one likes to admit to unworthy motives and shame can be a strong factor in tempting people to lie or, at least, to varnish the truth. The pastoral carer should do their best to communicate that they are not there to be judgmental, but that they are open to accepting whatever is said. This is not to say that sin is to be whitewashed or ignored, but condemnation must not be the first response to anything. Allowing a speaker to know that what they have said has been clearly heard and that they remain fully loved is of immense value. It allows honesty and openness to grow and, thereby, communication between the couple to develop into a more authentic channel of communication. Further, when one speaks openly about their inner life, they become vulnerable. This invites a husband or wife to respond with love and grace but obviously this can be dangerous. The minister's presence as a pastoral carer gives some security as they will be able to intervene if one partner's vulnerability is abused by the other. Damage can then be limited and the direction of travel be reset towards healing.

Time will be needed for the minister, as a carer, to reflect on what has been heard and seen in this pastoral encounter. This is for two reasons. First, the experience may have been very emotionally draining and the carer will need to recover. Make sure that there is a positive and effective way of doing this (and that there is no danger of falling into unhelpful, destructive coping mechanisms). Second, the carer will need to understand more deeply what they have heard. They were not trained as a psychologist, psychiatrist, or behavioral scientist, and, as Alexander Pope said, "a little learning is a dangerous thing."[20] The important thing is to read around the issues involved in the problem, talk (without

---

19. A term, possibly originally from Reuel Howe, that means ensuring that what a preacher intends to say when he preaches is what the congregation understands as they listen. The speaker must be aware that what he or she says may not be what the listener hears.

20. Pope, "Essay on Criticism."

breaking confidences) with those who are professionally trained,[21] and aim to develop valuable insight.

> *Look at and understand yourself. Gut reactions and emotions need to be acknowledged because they can cloud our vision or bias our judgments.*[22]

Theological Reflection

If understanding what is going wrong is important, having a sense of where things should be going is equally important. Theological reflection takes a step back and looks at what God would say into the situation. This is not, first, what God would say into the specific situation but what God says about the general themes that have emerged in the carer's listening and interpretation. Most obviously, a solid, biblically well-grounded understanding of the nature of marriage is crucial. Scripture clearly is the place to start with texts such as Gen 2, 1 Cor 13 and Eph 5 being foundational. But do not rely only on personal interpretation as there is good, helpful literature available on all biblical texts. When reading the supporting literature, remember that it is all written in a specific cultural context, so it is colored by that context and may not be directly transferable to the context of the couple.

Biblical teaching on marriage is not the only topic to be explored. If the couple have children, then biblical teaching on parenting must be explored. If finance is a contributing factor, then what God has to say about money and possessions is relevant. The same can be said about work, ethnic differences, extended family responsibilities, politics, health, and in fact any aspect of life at all. Remember that this part of the process is our attempt to understand God's perspective on the presenting situation, so we must not drift too quickly into thinking about what action we might take on any issue. For example, before thinking how best to handle

---

21. There are many Christian and secular agencies that can give support to pastoral carers but do check carefully any that do not have a long history and a strong reputation.

22. Moore, *Puzzle*, 102–7.

a family's finances, we should help a couple to build a biblically authentic attitude to money as a precursor to taking any action.

It is worth a reminder at this point that a regular practical teaching ministry that explores all areas of life helps people to avoid drifting into circumstances that will lead to serious relational problems. Also, a regular, structured teaching ministry in which the full range of topics come up within this structure avoids the accusation that the pastor is preaching "at" someone if they address a topic such as marriage, when everyone knows that a particular couple's marriage is in trouble. Thirdly, a regular teaching ministry will sow wholesome ideas and thoughts into minds that are regularly bombarded by a culture that is ignorant of, or hostile to, biblical teaching. Nowhere is this truer than with respect to human, interpersonal relationships, which have been deeply harmed by a combination of strident demands for one's rights, a consumer mentality, and a rampant individualism that puts one's own ego at the center of all things. If this is the world in which Christians must live, it is incumbent on all Christian teachers to equip them so to do. We are to critique contemporary culture courageously but also to be realistic in what we can expect from our congregation, many of whom have to live in an everyday world that clergy may know little about. A dialogical approach to enabling people to navigate through their daily experience should be built into all Christian teaching. This is as true of marriage as of any other aspect of life.

Action

A marriage that is in trouble will have developed patterns of relating that are the result of the attitudes that have led to the problems in the first place. These become entrenched and a downward spiral is almost inevitable. When we talk of taking action at an early stage, we do not mean "quick-fix" solutions, that is, actions that will swiftly solve the problem. Rather, we mean chipping away at the destructive patterns and starting to build new ones. Even very small changes can have dramatic effects. Saying "thank you"; doing the dishes; taking care of one's appearance; being open about spending patterns; stopping avoiding the in-laws or being more emotionally responsive when having sex all only deal with one aspect of a marriage, but being willing to address any one issue can show a willingness to change and can begin a positive feedback loop. Of course, even a cursory look at that short list will be enough to make any pastoral carer baulk and wonder how one can ever have enough insight to address these various issues. Wisdom dictates that you heed your cautionary thoughts, and, if your early impressions suggest that the marriage is in significant trouble, then pointing the couple to professional help, rather than trying to "make it up as you go along" is definitely the most appropriate "action" for the pastoral carer to take.

Thinking about actions that the couple might take, any simple, little initial action should at least show willingness to change and give a little feel-good experience to show that negative feelings are not the only ones possible. A useful tool to help think through actions is the popular SMART analysis[23] or, in this context, the SMARTER version:

a. Specific or concrete action, not just woolly ideas
b. Measurable, that is, open to being judged as successful or otherwise
c. Achievable within the constraints of money and other resources
d. Relevant, in that it actually addresses the situation, rather than just looking good
e. Time bound so that things do not drag on indefinitely without being reviewed
f. Easy, at least as easy as possible; better to take small steps and build momentum rather than reach too high and fail
g. Renewable, because this is a cycle and we assume that the first response will not be the final answer[24]

If the couple does engage with a marriage guidance counsellor, the pastoral carer's role is not thereby set aside. They can still meet regularly with them, talk through as much of what they are dealing with as they are comfortably willing to share, pray for them, or pray together and show concern for children, parents, or any others who have been affected. As we have already noted, the carer should always bring hope, selecting and sharing appropriate biblical readings or themes.

Each time a pastoral carer meets with the couple they will go through the four steps in their mind: listening for new information, including confirming or correcting what they already know; noting anything that

---

23. For example, see Bell, "SMART Goals." Another version of SMARTER is Meadows, "How to Set SMARTER."
24. Massey, 47–117, has some helpful guidance about developing action plans.

they need to understand in greater depth, that they will investigate later; bringing biblical wisdom to bear as they share Scripture with them in a little devotional time or as they introduce biblical wisdom at any appropriate point; and encouraging the couple to take further "confidence building" actions.

Sadly, some marriages will not be able to be rescued and the "least worst option" is to part company. If this is the case, sensitive legal advice should be sought, but the pastoral carer can walk with the couple as they go through the pain of becoming two single people again. It is unlikely that pastoral contact will be retained with both partners, so offering to put one or both in contact with a trustworthy minister in another parish or a trustworthy pastoral carer in your own context could be helpful. If this is done, be open about it and about the value and limitations of ministerial colleagues being in contact as caregivers.

Finally, remember that pastoral responsibility extends beyond the couple. Children need to be cared for and allowing the couple to talk through future arrangements will help them work through the best way forward and how the various legal obligations can be combined with the best way forward for the children. Further, a minister may well have contact with the parents of the couple, or other family members or friends, as members of their parish. The minister must get the couple's permission before contacting anyone, or, if anyone should come to the minister, they must be cautious about what they say so that they don't break confidences or make public things that the couple want kept private. A good rule of thumb is "do not tell anyone anything they do not already know!" To deflect awkward questions, it is always better to say, "I can't talk about that," which is true, rather than "I don't know," which may not be literally true.

Conclusion

The Christian understanding of marriage is that it is a covenant relationship between a man and a woman, both of whom are made in the image of God and both of whom are fallen creatures. This means that marriage reflects something of the nature of God himself but it is also open to all of the pressures, weakness, and follies of its location in this fallen world. Therefore, we encourage all couples to look to God himself for wisdom and power as they aim for the highest in their marriage, but we accept that, in practice, this will always be tempered by the reality of our fallen state.

The New Testament's use of marriage as a metaphor for the relationship of Christ and his church (2 Cor 11:2; Eph 5:21–33) adds to it a further dignity and gives us some further direction for our pastoral care. Jesus' self-sacrificial love (Phil 2:5–8) sets the pattern for all marriages. He gave himself fully and unreservedly for the benefit of his bride and looks for a response of loving commitment in return. This is the attitude to which all married couples are called: self-giving that looks for a response in kind. Both partners bring to their marriage a range of gifts, talents, strengths, and abilities. Following Christ's example means offering these freely to their spouse so that the spouse can flourish. But each partner also brings their weaknesses, follies, ignorance, and inexperience, so, like the bride of Christ, both partners look to the other to meet some of their deepest needs. Christian pastoral carers take this a step further by commending to married couples a relationship with Christ that meets their very deepest need and provides a solid foundation on which a marriage can be built . . . or rebuilt.

Pastoral carers act as "interpretive guides."[25] While each married couple walks its own unique path, pastoral carers understand the general terrain of marriage, its weather patterns, its hills and valleys, its sure paths, and its treacherous cliffs. Like experienced orienteers or hill-walkers, they can spot danger signs, avoid marshy ground, or help couples navigate back to safety. As pastoral carers, we walk alongside married couples to help them come as close as possible to God's ideal, encouraging them in their weakness and, for those of us who are married, by God's grace, by being a model from which they can learn.

---

25. Gerkin, *Introduction*, 116.

10

With Hearts That See:[1] Ministry in a Healthcare Setting

COLUMBA TOMAN OP

Introduction

THIS CHAPTER IS WRITTEN with some very specific themes in mind. Beginning with the "theoretical," it moves on to ask questions about what precisely the chaplain is seeking to do and what should their perspective be on the individuals to whom they minister and for whom they care. The ultimate guide in regard to these questions is Jesus himself, the Divine Healer. What was present in his ministry that should also drive our own faltering attempts at ministering to the sick? A second related emphasis that weaves its way through the whole chapter is that of the Roman Catholic perspective on healthcare ministry,[2] and how it is that the mystery of Christ animates every facet of a truly Christian response to healthcare, not least in the value or dignity placed on those who are cared for.[3] Although this question is highly academic at one level, it also speaks to the vital role of the healthcare team members who are charged with helping preserve *human dignity* in situations where that dignity is in danger of being lost. Finally, at the close of the chapter, I will deal concretely with one of the most challenging themes of healthcare ministry,

---

1. See Congregation for the Doctrine of Faith, "Samaritanus bonus," 3.
2. The sacramental ministry *per se* will not be reviewed.
3. Kalib, "Lessons."

end-of-life care. Here I explore what Jesus is asking of the chaplain or healthcare worker involved in this taxing but rewarding area of ministry. My hope is that the chapter will offer insights, not only to those seeking to communicate the healing love and compassion of God in the healthcare context but to others engaging in ministry outside the rarefied world of the hospital and other healthcare settings.

The Experience of a Chaplain

The ministry of the healthcare chaplain provides a myriad of the most profound, humbling, challenging, and inspiring experiences. It provides the opportunity of spending quality time with fellow human beings who are sick, and accompanying them, their families, friends, and healthcare colleagues, as they experience the effects of their illness, and for some, their final moments of life prior to death. The role encompasses the privilege of hearing someone's story and welcoming new life into the world; *alongside* witnessing at first hand the emotional and spiritual vicissitudes that come with caring for severely ill and dying people. Chaplains observe the extremes of death from serenely peaceful through to angst-filled and medically shocking; they are given the privilege of holding the hands of a dying patient and looking into their eyes with compassion and solidarity as the patient faces their final journey; and on occasion they experience awe-filled moments of admiration as they watch nursing staff perform the "last office" on the mortal remains of the dead person, very often in hushed tones and with the dignity they recognized and upheld in the living person moments before.

The chaplain has the privilege of simply being present. These profoundly moving experiences are, of course, in juxtaposition with other moments of negativity and conflict that take place in the healthcare setting. However, for the chaplain, each of these moments is embraced in the presence of our Lord Jesus Christ—the Divine Healer and Savior. Each moment becomes an opportunity to bear witness to the divine through the care of the other; an expression of ministry that testifies powerfully to God's grace and love.

"Seeing as Jesus Wants Us to See"

As already intimated in the introduction, all ministry in this area is predicated on the example of Jesus' life[4] and the call he extended to his followers.[5] Three times in the Synoptic Gospels Jesus refers to himself as "Physician."[6] The early fathers of the church use the image to draw out further understandings of the church and salvation. Origen, for example, identifies the church as Christ's infirmary and the sacred Scriptures as medicine. He lists the incarnation, the crucifixion, the resurrection, baptism, and the forgiveness of sins as remedies of the "Divine Physician."[7] Hence, the church has always prioritized taking care of those who are afflicted.[8] This was expressed in its practical care of the sick but also its ministering of a deeper healing that reflected God's eschatological purpose for human beings and the world.[9]

At the heart of this pastoral response is the profound recognition of the divinely given dignity of the human person made in the image and likeness of God. Guided by this profound understanding of the human person and their destiny in God's plan, the church over the centuries has made the service of the sick and suffering an "integral part of her mission."[10] This is a mission in which the healthcare worker is invited to look upon the one for whom they care with the heart of the good Samaritan, a "heart that sees."[11] This "seeing," when it takes place, is marked by compassion and a striving to convey God's love in the encounter.[12] The healthcare setting provides the chaplain multiple opportunities to participate, in a complementary manner, in the pursuit of the health of the whole person—body and soul.

---

4. Matt 8:1–4; 9:27–31; Luke 5:17–26.

5. Matt 25:34–40; Luke 10:8–9; Matt 8:16.

6. Luke 5:31–32; Matt 9:12–13; Mark 2:17.

7. Origen, *Homilies on Leviticus*. See also Thomas, "Christ the Physician" for a comprehensive introduction to the concept.

8. See Ferngren, *Medicine and Healthcare*, for a comprehensive account of the historical development of healthcare and the early church.

9. United States Catholic Conference, *Health and Healthcare*, 4.

10. John Paul II, *Dolentium hominum*, 1-2.

11. The Congregation for the Doctrine of Faith, "Samaritanus bonus."

12. John Paul II, "Address."

The One Seen

Before focusing on the related issue of human dignity (perhaps the umbrella theme of the chapter), let us spend a little more time reflecting on the nature of the person to whom we are called to minister. Some of the sources I draw on will be more academic than popular, but I encourage you to bear with me as we wrestle with a complex but rewarding perspective on human personhood.

John Crosby, a Christian ethicist from the Franciscan University of Steubenville, describes the human person as *unique, unrepeatable,* and *loveable.* His concern is to stress that human value is not fundamentally dependent on the person possessing traits that other human beings possess. Their value is based on something much more distinct than that. As Crosby notes,

> It is not only because I share in the rational nature common to us all that I have dignity, but because I am the unrepeatable person that I am. This unrepeatable person has value, for it awakens love when glimpsed by others. But it is not a value achieved only by some and not by others, for it goes with existing as a person.[13]

To interact with the patient in a way that really "sees" them involves appreciating that they are unrepeatable.[14] Unlike the daily newspaper or a plastic cup, which have shareable properties with every other newspaper or plastic cup of the same type, the human person is not simply replaceable. They have a unique identity given them by God and there will never be another person who is simply the same as them. Their "unrepeatability" is a God-given trait that can inspire and nurture our own regard for them. The discovery of the uniqueness of the individual and the value of their own "life stories" was brought to the fore by Anton Boisen, the founder of Clinical Pastoral Education (CPE). Boisen found himself in a psychiatric hospital in 1920s Boston. His experience was that he was never listened to, and out of that experience he developed a model of pastoral care based on the premise that every individual is a "living human document," worthy of the study of those offering pastoral care. For him, a central pastoral task became willingness to hear the voices of those whom others did not listen to. And while this may be familiar territory to us, it is difficult to underestimate the significance and influence of Boisen's

---

13. Crosby, "Why Persons Have Dignity," 88.
14. Crosby, "Two-Fold Source," 300.

work—it is out of his insights that a model of pastoral care developed (CPE), which became a key paradigm for pastoral training. Although not directly influenced by the Catholic theology of the person, he found within his own experience of crisis an ability to see himself and others as worthy of radical empathy. He saw through the Samaritan's eyes.

What is Man [sic] That You are Mindful of Him?[15]

There is a sense that the above question of the psalmist sets before us the overall purpose of this book. Drawing upon the *Pastoral Constitution of the Second Vatican Council, Gaudium et spes*, we find that answers to questions about human identity and how we should value human beings coalesce around three important and related concepts—*dignity*, *community*, and *vocation*.[16] Put simply, when the human is considered, these three ideas must remain central. I would further add that, even in the pastoral care of the sick person, these same three elements provide the framework for an understanding of how ministry should be understood. Each element helps us to gain an insightful and practical response to the challenges of that sector; responses that have the capacity to be worked out beyond the boundaries of the chaplaincy team. We shall examine them in turn.

Dignity

A recent magisterial document on the subject of dignity, published in 2024, ascribes a superlative value to the dignity possessed by humans; one emphasizing the intrinsic and infinite worth of every human being. This is reflected in its title, "Dignitas infinitas":[17]

> Every human person possesses an infinite dignity, inalienably grounded in his or her very being. . . . In the light of Revelation, the Church resolutely reiterates and confirms the ontological

---

15. See Ps 8:5–7.

16. See Second Vatican Council, *Gaudium et spes* for an insight to the question and response; the foundation for the relationship and dialogue between the church and the world.

17. Dicastery for the Doctrine of the Faith (DDF), "Dignitas infinitas."

dignity of the human person, created in the image and likeness of God and redeemed in Jesus Christ.[18]

Although the Judeo-Christian Scriptures do not refer to dignity directly, there are references to positions of honor and respect especially associated with those of rank. An extended understanding of such honor was that given to God, for which the Hebrew word *kavod* (glory) was used (Exod 24:16–17). It is suggested that *kavod* can be translated as "dignity" as well as "glory."[19] Three references in the Book of Genesis (1:26–27; 5:1–3; 9:5–7) to the *imago Dei* (image of God) speak of this divine glory/dignity, *kavod*, being shared with human beings and hence provides the foundations for the biblical concept of human dignity. Fundamentally, for Christians and Jews the human person is made in the image and likeness of God and is capable of entering into relationship or communion with God. For the Bible, the *imago Dei* provides an important understanding of the definition of what it is to be human. One might say that the mystery of who we are cannot be grasped apart from the mystery of God. This divine image is not just a superficial covering of the human being but rather an inherent part of their created nature. Intriguingly, our secular culture, which is still profoundly influenced by the Christian patrimony, in many ways maintains this elevated understanding of the human person, according them the sort of dignity presumed by the church's tradition. An examination of this reality in the contemporary world highlights the important role the healthcare worker plays in ensuring the Christian understanding of dignity continues to define care in the hospital context.

"Dignity" in the Context of Healthcare

At the very heart of the practice of healthcare is the recognition of the *intrinsic dignity* of the human being as manifested in and through their bodies. The notion of "dignity" is often presumed and its application is expected by all involved, but it is rarely defined or at least the definition can lack clarity.[20] Its usefulness is often as a kind of placeholder for the upholding of the value of the person in healthcare documents and protocols.

---

18. DDF, *Dignitas infinitas*, 1.
19. Arieli, "On the Necessary," 10.
20. Jacob, "Respect for Human Dignity," 17–35.

However, the lack of definition raises questions over what makes for an appropriate regard for patient dignity. Indeed, a situation arose in the nursing profession that highlighted the need to recognize the importance of this concept in every aspect of healthcare. In response to media reports about a lack of dignity in hospital care, more than two thousand nurses, nursing students, and healthcare assistants responded to a survey conducted by the Royal College of Nursing (RCN) in 2008. The results of this survey were published and were followed by the "rolling out" of the "Dignity: At the Heart of All We Do" campaign.

The RCN dignity survey had many outcomes, but it particularly highlighted a need to understand what dignity means and therefore help the provision of a dignified service. The promotion of dignity and the development of "dignity-promoting" leaders became important responses to the said survey and campaign. We note the warning that "without clarity on how to achieve or maintain dignity within the context of care, people are more likely to feel devalued; they are more likely to sense that they lack control and comfort."[21] The following may help contextualize this issue and highlight the church's role in maintaining dignity.

Two Types of Dignity

Fundamentally there are two ways of understanding what dignity is. The first (we might call this the theological or ontological one) highlights that there is a particular type of dignity that cannot be lost, and another, which is dependent on the existence of the first, that can be lost.

The first is referred to as intrinsic, inherent, and basic. This is the understanding of dignity that Ashcroft refers to "as a metaphysical property possessed by all and only human beings, and which serves as a foundation for moral philosophy and human rights."[22] Aquinas, Crosby, Lebech, and Sulmasy go further in understanding this definition. It is not only a metaphysical property possessed by human beings but rather it is a constitutive property; it is the fundamental value of the human person. It is therefore the inviolable value of the unique and unrepeatable human being.

Secondly, the subjective understanding of dignity refers to *attributed* dignity. It is with this second understanding of dignity that contemporary

---

21. Johnston and Chochinov, *Therapeutic Implications*, 696.
22. Ashcroft, "Making Sense of Dignity," 680.

scholars take issue. It is also in relation to the second definition that the sense of loss with the patient and others is manifested. Attributed dignity basically describes how we treat one another. It is to this type of dignity that the notion of a loss of dignity can be traced. Furthermore, it is from this concept that the terms "autonomy" and "respect" receive the basis of their meanings. Both these words have been offered, by others, as suitable replacements for the term "dignity." However, they are not true cognates of "dignity," but rather they form part of our understanding and response to the dignity of the sick person. By recognizing that every human being has a fundamental value of worth that has been referred to as human or intrinsic or basic dignity, then it is our duty to actualize this dignity through respect for the sick person. This understanding of respect is found in many of the national and international human rights and healthcare documents. In them, we can recognize the Kantian and Christian insistence that the person is treated as an end and not just as a means to an end. We now proceed to the second of those central themes highlighted in *Gaudium et spes*—community, the context in which issues around human dignity are played out. Here we will have the opportunity to understand better how the healthcare worker can play their part in protecting and conserving dignity. At this juncture in the chapter, I will draw on some of my own observations and experiences as a chaplain.

Community

No one fully understands another human being; the lived experience of each individual plays a critical role in their understanding of themselves and their own dignity, as well as that of others. This is not a failure but rather a clarion call to discover more about the nature of human beings, individually, and their relationship to the broader human community. Wojtyła acknowledges this challenge and refers to our ability to comprehend the dignity of the human being as "always more of a call and demand than an already accomplished fact, or rather it is a fact worked out by human beings, both in the collective and individual sense."[23]

Although many aspects can be known of what it is to be a human being, and therefore a human person, there are still elements that are yet to be discovered. Although we may not know every aspect of another person, we engage with them as a whole person. The chaplain has a crucial

---

23. Wojtyła, *Person and Community*, 179.

role in helping the healthcare team to engage in the question of the whole person, not just the ailment that they may present; as to do so is to discover and to acknowledge that they have an inherent worth, value, or dignity. An experience that helped illustrate this for me was the day in the hospital dining room when I heard a shout from a table of young medics: "Padre, have you seen the leg in ward eleven?" I replied, "I saw a lot of legs on ward eleven but all of them attached to various people. However, I did meet a lovely person who had a particular issue with one of their legs." The medics kindly invited me to join them at their table where we talked about the concept of whole person care and their role in it.

It is at the experiential level of engagement that the sense of loss is to be found. This is at the level of attributed dignity. It is at this level that the patient, or indeed family members and healthcare personnel, can have the profound sense of loss of dignity. Chaplains often finds themselves in a delicate advocacy role trying to resolve this noticeable sense of loss. By vocation, they must be watchful advocates for anyone whose dignity is threatened, compromised, or violated. There are other healthcare system factors that can lead to violation of the dignity of all involved. These include the way people are addressed, the undermining of personal privacy and space, and the environments in which a dying person and their family and friends find themselves, especially when death is imminent.

In light of this understanding, one is left with the question: Whom does this "call and demand" impress upon? Returning to the intrinsic nature of the term "dignity," the answer is simply this: each human being. There is also the recognition that this "call and demand" is the responsibility of the community. Fundamentally, the community is called to understand that *all* human beings have intrinsic dignity, which can never be taken from them, and that all human beings to some degree have attributed dignity granted to them by others. The chaplain helps embody concretely the presence of the community to the patient, loved ones, and healthcare colleagues. In the quiet of the night or the busyness of the ward, the chaplain can bring a still, calming presence that recognizes the profound dignity of the person before them and the people around them. The whole hospital community becomes the community of the chaplain, their village, congregation, or parish; every person comes under their caring gaze. This insight in faith can help the chaplain to move beyond simply being in emergency mode—waiting for the pager. There is something profoundly uplifting and impactful when members of the hospital staff stop you and ask for a personal request for prayers or share with you a personal aspect of their family life. The humble recognition of each person and the ability to spend time in conversation is important to the pastoral community under the care of the chaplaincy team. All are included. The chaplain is a signpost to a greater sense of what it means to be part of that particular community in the context of a much bigger set of communities. They bear witness to a further dimension and invite others to discover it.[24] This can be seen in the many roles the chaplain fulfills: pastoral carer, leader of prayer, advocate, guide, mediator, spiritual counsellor, and compassionate listener, to mention but a few. With their colleagues they offer themselves "as a gift to their patients by engaging in relationships characterized by caring and sensitivity, extending their knowledge and expertise to promote healing"[25] while recognizing the gift of the other whom they serve.

A Vocational Response

In this final section of the chapter we reflect on the role of the chaplain in the specialized ministry of end-of-life care. This is a key context in which chaplains live out their vocation to have "hearts that see," that is, understanding where love is needed and responding accordingly. In doing so, they will obviously be concerned with the dignity (inherent and attributed) of the sick and dying person and all the associated issues related to that reality, but most of all their ministry will be one of radical presence. Here, the vocational response of presence, listening, and divine entrustment come to the fore, and the healthcare chaplain is recognized as both a sign and a servant of divine love.[26]

As noted in the earlier discussion of Boisen, individuals above all need to feel that they have been truly listened to, truly seen. This idea was wonderfully explored in a novel by Taylor Caldwell entitled *The Man Who Listens*.[27] The premise of her novel is that a series of troubled souls speak about their difficulties and travails to an anonymous figure standing behind a curtain. Their attitude is one of railing against the universe until that moment when the curtain is pulled back and they see this

---

24. At the heart of this response is a profound understanding of the most holy Trinity, especially the concept of *koinonia* (communion).

25. Kalib, "Lessons."

26. Kalib, "Lessons."

27. This novel and the worldview of Miss Caldwell were drawn to my attention by Lake, *Clinical Theology*, 3–4.

mysterious figure nailed to a cross. It is at this point that their whole attitude to life is radically transformed. The novel is a metaphor for the power of empathetic listening and its capacity to impact radically a life. Caldwell's comments in the foreword of the book resonate deeply with the ministry style we have been advocating in this chapter:

> [Man's] real need, his most terrible need, is for someone to listen to him, not as a "patient," but as a human soul. He needs to tell someone of what he thinks, of the bewilderment he encounters when he tries to discover why he was born, how he must live, and where his destiny lies. . . . Our Pastors would listen—if we gave them the time to listen to us.[28]

The pastoral responsiveness that can engage with such a profound need is not merely the product of technique but the fruit of a deep spirituality nurtured and honed over time. In Frank Lake's publication, *Clinical Theology*, he cites an example of the kind of listening posture that elicits human openness. It is drawn from a book by Jewish psychiatrist Karl Stern who describes his journey to Christian faith after the horror of the Holocaust. One of the pivotal discussions that helped him deal with his suffering and search for meaning was with the Catholic philosopher Jacques Maritain. Lake highlights Stern's impression of the kind of listener Maritain was:

> He asked me the most personal questions about my spiritual life, but there was not for a moment the feeling of obtrusiveness or indiscretion. I had from the first moment that deeper impression of a strange and pleasant form of personal directness which was the result of a great charity and humility.[29]

Lake concludes that "when those who represent Christ can listen in this way to disclosures at this abysmal depth, the transformation of personality that results exists not only in the ontological but in the theological order."[30] These latter examples have highlighted the profound pastoral impact listening can have when viewed through the lens of a novelist or a Holocaust survivor. The general ministry of the healthcare chaplain may be more low-key in its effects, but in exercising that ministry the chaplain purposes to engage deeply with the "person" behind the terminal diagnosis. Using all the skills and training that are available to them,

---

28. Caldwell, *Man Who Listens*, 11–12.
29. Karl Stern, *Pillar of Fire*, 226–27.
30. Lake, *Clinical Theology*, 7.

they harness these to their own innate knowledge of Christ and his work in their lives. The section closes with some pointers to what must be uppermost in the mind of the chaplain.

Things to Bear in Mind

First, the immediate task of the healthcare chaplain and colleagues is to "listen to the patient to the point of discerning the personal center out of which [they] live."[31] This involves the awareness that the patient is not a thing, an object to be treated, but rather they are the subject of their illness. They are a unique "I" reaching out and engaging with another unique and equally unrepeatable "I." It is the relationship with this unique "I" that challenges us to respond to them in a particular manner. For example, there are number of useful tools relating to spiritual history taking that can prove to be very useful in the initial stages of this kind of pastoral conversation.[32] This can be reinforced by drawing on the paradigm-changing approach of Chochinov's "Dignity Therapy," which states in regard to the dying person, "You are a whole person and deserve my time, my respect and my care."[33] Linked to this dignity response is the asking of a very simple yet profound question: "What should I know about you as a person that will help me take the best care of you that I can?"[34]

The Dignity Therapy response offered by Chochinov and his colleagues includes the application of the "A B C and D" approach to dignity-conserving care.[35] The core elements of this approach are Attitude, Behavior, Compassion, and Dialogue, each describing a core competency that a healthcare provider must have when dealing with the dying person. Each of the elements are related to the attributed sense of dignity and a "whole person" approach to care. The application of these insights provides for a groundbreaking basis to treating people at the end of life in a manner that upholds their dignity. Practiced well, and integrated within

---

31. Crosby, *Patients as Persons*, 159.

32. Examples of spiritual history tools include the following: the FICA Spiritual History Tool, HOPE, AMEN, Brief Serenity Scale, SCNI, SNAP, SNI, SpNQ, SNS, and SpIRIT.

33. Chochinov, *Dignity Therapy*, 41.

34. Chochinov, *Dignity Therapy*, 31.

35. Chochinov, "Dignity and Essence."

the chaplain's own personal faith, they facilitate sick people having a good sense about their dignity being respected.

A second essential element is the need for open discussions with the dying person about the reality of their situation, the trajectory of their conditions, their existential issues, and a multitude of others, uniquely asked by this particular individual at a particular time. This process is crucial in recognizing and upholding their sense of dignity. One is reminded of the often quoted inspirational and definitional words of Dame Cicely Saunders, the founder of the modern palliative care movement:

> You matter because you are you, and you matter to the last moment of your life. We will do all we can, not only to help you die peacefully, but also to live until you die.[36]

Interestingly, this person-centered approach may mean that at times the healthcare professional has to take a "step back," so as to give the sick person the opportunity to express themselves fully. This reveals the crucial understanding of dignity as a relational term, which calls the community to respond to the needs of the other; forming the basis of why we care for the other and make provision for end-of-life care in a way that the purely utilitarian thinker may see as being wasteful—i.e., not because they have a particular social value but simply because they are human.

Finally, and not surprisingly, listening will be a core element in the dignity afforded the patient in end-of-life care; the formation of such skills will be crucial in all the various specialties associated with providing a truly person-centered palliative care response to the dying person.

Conclusion

How might we sum up what has been said over the course of the chapter? In healthcare terms, there must be a "duty of care" towards *all* human beings. This duty of care is not diminished by being a particular type of human being, e.g. sick, old, infirm, dying, but rather it applies without reduction to all involved. In taking account of the dignity of the sick person, the healthcare professional or policymaker is called to understand them as a unique, incommunicable, and unrepeatable human being, that their fundamental dignity is acknowledged as intrinsic and cannot be removed from them. They are called to be guardians of human dignity,

---

36. Saunders. *Cicely Saunders*, xxiii.

and, as such, they must work collaboratively to alter those social structures that undermine health and wellbeing by fostering a way of life that guarantees everyone has access to medical care that upholds their dignity from the time of conception until natural death.

Furthermore, it would involve recognizing that the individual sick person is also in relationship with others, which includes their families and friends and the healthcare professionals who are present to them. There is a responsibility on the healthcare professionals to recognize the fundamental worth of the person in their care, no matter what their condition is. It challenges us to recognize the dignity of everyone involved, a dignity that cannot be removed from them no matter what the change in circumstance. At the same time, it allows us to acknowledge that people experience the sense of loss of dignity and that we have a responsibility, in consultation with the sick person, to endeavor to uphold the many facets of their dignity and to help lessen the trauma involved when it is not fully possible. There may be undignified moments in the care of a sick person but at no stage must there be a loss of the recognition of the intrinsic worth of the other.

The "calls and demands" placed upon those who care for the sick truly reveal the ongoing apostolate of care commanded by the Lord Jesus. Returning to the question of the psalmist, we realize that it is because we are made in the image and likeness of God that we are unique, unrepeatable, and eternally loved by the one who created us, cares for us through others, and calls/invites us to be fulfilled in our vocation and ultimately be with him in the community of the heavenly realm. We pray for the work of the hospital chaplains and teams; through their prayerful presence may they bear witness to the Savior, the Divine *Medicus*, and to the inestimable value of the human being, upholding the divinely revealed dignity of all to whom they minister.

11

Bereavement Care: Pastoral Presence and Meaningful Hope

Daniel Nuzum

Bereavement is the lived response to the universal experiences of grief and loss. It is a complex and evolving human phenomenon that is multidimensional in nature and unique to the individual experiencing it. In this regard, bereavement is both universal as a shared human experience, yet uniquely experienced by each individual at the same time. The etymology of the word "bereavement" is of something (someone) being "torn" or "ripped" apart from us.[1] This ancient Germanic/English root captures the visceral and sensed meaning that so many describe when faced with the loss of someone or something close to them. Coupled with the one certainty that we will all die is the reality that we will all experience loss and grief in our life. Death is an inescapable reality.

At the core of a pastoral response to death is meaningful pastoral accompaniment and care that seeks to connect with the reality of the experience of loss. This is spiritual care at its best and conveys a compassionate presence of support, hope, acknowledgment, and care. Pastoral care has the capacity to embody all that evidence-based grief theory demonstrates as important in the acknowledgment, processing, and recovery from loss. How pastoral care is provided and experienced should be fully congruent with well-evidenced bereavement care.

1. Etymonline, "Bereavement."

This chapter seeks to explore the multidimensional experience of grief and contemporary pastoral care responses to bereavement as part of a wider integrated public health response. It does so primarily from the perspective of Christian pastoral ministry and seeks to situate this within the broader milieu of care with transferrable principles beyond a faith-based approach. It also seeks to establish that good pastoral care is congruent with known evidence in bereavement studies and care.

The Impact of Bereavement

Death is the most common loss associated with the term "bereavement"; however, the experience of bereavement can be associated with any significant loss with the same felt experiences and symptoms. As a phenomenon, loss is influenced by the level of attachment to the person, experience, or reality that one is separated from.

In addition to being a deeply personal experience, bereavement is also a societal reality and has a considerable social and community dimension and impact. In recent years there has been a growing awareness of the impact of bereavement on both individuals and on wider society, and a 2024 Lancet Commission called for investment in bereavement care as a public health issue.[2] There has also been much emphasis in how we prepare for death, how we speak about grief, and how we respond to grief both in wider society and in our local communities and networks. However, for many, grief remains a silent and isolating reality, and the lack of public discourse further isolates those who experience loss. This is particularly the case where grief is at the beginning of life or following particularly sensitive loss.[3]

The response to death is invariably marked by a community as loved ones and the wider community gather to mourn and to offer and receive mutual support. Indeed, there are recognized cultural and religious norms that shape the overall process of grieving and mourning. These traditions and cultural norms vary widely but have at their heart a practical and spiritual expression of love, attachment, and loss associated with the death of a loved one as well as embodying rituals to mark the

---

2. Lichtenthal et al., "Investing in Bereavement Care," 270–74.
3. Nuzum et al., "Impact of Stillbirth"; Nuzum et al., "Pregnancy Loss," 133–45; Marek and Oexle, "Supportive and Non-Supportive," 1190.

end of life and to facilitate the final care of a human body through burial or cremation.

Attachment

Attachment is core to our understanding of grief and loss. In attachment we develop strong bonds of connection, affection, and meaning, and through these we become close to self, others, experiences, roles, places, and things.[4] Indeed, attachments can be formed with anything that gives us meaning, value, and purpose in life. Attachment is therefore a significant spiritual reality and aligns closely with the widely used definition of spirituality as understood in palliative care in terms of the significance of connection "to self, to others, to nature, to the significant." Attachment theory gives us a deeper understanding of the significance of our relationships and how we as human beings are relational beings who naturally form close bonds with others from our prenatal existence *in utero* and throughout our lives, and that these bonds continue after our physical death for those who are bereaved. This has influenced what we know as "continuing bonds." In a spiritual sense, many world faith and belief traditions have a spiritual understanding of continuing bonds as a form of ongoing connection with those who have died. These spiritual approaches emphasize a sense of transformation from physical life to a spiritual reality after death. For the Christian, Scripture points in a number of places to the ongoing sense of "communion" with those who have died and an affirmation that those who have died are with God: "The dead will hear the voice of the Son of God, and those who hear will live" (John 5:25 NRSV). Those who see physical life as the only form of life, while remaining clear in there not being an "afterlife," nonetheless at a human level often continue to be inspired by the lives of loved ones after death.

A pertinent question for the professional in pastoral ministry, therefore, might be: What does it mean to feel attachment or to develop a relationship of significance? What does attachment mean to me? What does attachment feel like—emotionally, physically, socially, spiritually? What might the meaning be in a particular relationship? This meaning

---

4. Bowlby: "Making and Breaking," 201–10; "Attachment Theory" 5–33; "Attachment and Loss," 664–78.

may be positive, negative, or ambivalent, and in each case will texture the experience of grief and bereavement when the relationship ceases.

To ponder these questions aids us as carers to come close to what the experience of loss might be like for the person who is grieving. It brings us closer to the lived experience of the person we are caring for in grief and thereby fosters a deeper connection and capacity to be present in the midst of what is for many a bewildering and unfamiliar landscape without a loved one. In turn, having a deeper sense of the lived experience of loss fosters a more meaningful response as we seek to accompany someone in grief and in pastoral ministry to shape our care and the provision of appropriate ritual and expression.

The Impact of Grief

Although grief is a universal experience and one that is challenging, it is a "normal" and expected part of life that for most people will be processed as part of their daily life experiences with good support. This is not to say that it is not challenging or without impact—quite the reverse! It is well documented that grief impacts us in many different ways, not least physically impacting on our immune, endocrine, neurological, and cardiovascular functioning.[5] Grief is tough and painful, and the experience is often referred to as the "work of grieving." However, most people do recover and integrate their experience of loss without enduring negative impact. These experiences of grief are supported significantly by good personal, social, and community supports. The role of faith communities in this regard should not be underestimated as there is a particular intersection between faith/belief communities and the rituals associated with dying, death, funerals, and post-bereavement care. The role of personal and community support has a particularly supportive role in the grieving process of most people. This support is restorative and essential in the healthy processing and recovery from grief and is a low intensity intervention. The Irish Hospice Foundation developed the "Adult Bereavement Care Pyramid" in 2020 following stakeholder engagement and consultation and developed from the previously published "Childhood Bereavement Care Pyramid."[6] This model helpfully recognizes the appropriate levels of care and intervention to support people in their grieving. In this regard,

---

5. Neimeyer et al., "Measurement of Grief," 133–61; O'Connor "Grief."
6. Irish Hospice Foundation, "Adult Bereavement Care Pyramid."

it provides a helpful approach that is transferable to pastoral ministry and care in how faith communities can tailor support from a pastoral perspective. It also highlights the importance of working in collaboration with other stakeholders in the overall support of those who are grieving and in important signposting to appropriate professional services where that is indicated.[7]

It is recognized in clinical practice and in the published literature that up to 10 percent of adults will experience prolonged grief disorder (PGD) following bereavement with significant emotional, spiritual, and physical impact.[8] Therefore, up to 90 percent of those who are grieving are unlikely to experience PGD or "complicated grief," which highlights the invaluable role of supportive communities and it is within this space that pastoral care and support has an important role.

Pastoral Response to Loss

Pastoral support has much to contribute to the overall tapestry of grief support. As highlighted above, most people are appropriately supported without specialist therapeutic intervention in their grief. Pastoral support and care should ideally commence from when the experience of loss is anticipated or experienced. Community support has been a reliable source of bereavement care in what could be described as the "ordinary" (but nonetheless painful) process of grieving following the death of a loved one. During the COVID-19 pandemic the absence of hitherto community supportive processes such as funerals, gatherings, memorials etc. highlighted just how important these events were in the provision of grief support in wider society. These supports of course transcend any religious boundaries and have as much of a community dimension as they do a liturgical one. Research on grief support during the pandemic has highlighted the negative impact of the absence of these community supportive processes on grief and recovery following bereavement.[9] There have, however, been some positives as well. The increased appreciation of other ways to connect with those who are grieving has been a positive and can be a useful adjunct to in-person pastoral care as well as providing

---

7. Bates et al., "Implementation and Evaluation," 296–302.
8. Lobb et al., "Predictors of Complicated Grief," 673–98.
9. Bates et al., "Implementation and Evaluation," 296–302.

meaningful opportunities for families/friends to participate in care and ritual from afar.[10]

The approach to pastoral care, support, ritual, belief, and post-bereavement care may be seen as naturally intuitive to the experienced pastoral minister and faith community, however it emphasizes the natural and lived congruence of practice built up over many centuries that continues to be congruent with the latest published literature and knowledge in bereavement studies.[11] Good pastoral care is good bereavement care!

There are many areas where what we do pastorally and liturgically as faith communities is fully congruent with well documented approaches to bereavement care such as meaning making—where we seek to find meaning in the life and death of our loved one;[12] attachment—where we honor the significance of the relationship we had with the deceased;[13] continuing bonds—where we continue to feel an enduring connection with our loved one after death;[14] dual process—where we acknowledge the reality of the experience(s) of loss that can feel like a pendulum swing between feeling stronger and acutely feeling loss;[15] mourning—where we take time to process the experience of loss;[16] ritual—where through gesture, symbol, ritual, and prayer we express our love and loss; disenfranchised grief—where we acknowledge the complexities of grief that is not widely appreciated or recognized;[17] presence—where our pastoral care is humanized and embodied by pastoral carers/ clergy (Quinlan);[18] pediatric grief—where we recognize the distinctive experiences and approaches to grief for children;[19] and dignity—where we affirm the innate dignity of each person and the value of her/his life which continues after death; and so forth.

---

10. Byrne and Nuzum, "Pastoral Closeness," 206–17.

11. Nuzum, "Pastoral Care" 74–82; Newitt, "Chaplaincy Support to Bereaved Parents" 179–194; Kelly, "Marking Short Lives"; Doehring, "The Practice of Pastoral Care"; Schulz, Boerner and Hebert, "Caregiving and Bereavement."

12. Neimeyer et al., "Measurement of Grief."

13. Bowlby, *Attachment*.

14. Klass, "Continuing Bonds."

15. Stroebe and Schut, "Dual Process."

16. Worden, *Grief Counselling*.

17. Doka, "Disenfranchised Grief."

18. Quinlan, *Pastoral Relatedness*. See also Byrne and Nuzum, "Pastoral Closeness"; Doehring, *Practice of Pastoral Care*.

19. Carroll, *Survey of Childhood Bereavement*.

Role of Ritual

Ritual as applied in bereavement care is the expression of the multifaceted dimensions of loss that is textured by what we believe, understand, and hope for in our spiritual/religious or values-based beliefs. For the person of faith, ritual embodies what we experience at a human level in our relationship to the person who has died, an engagement with our belief(s) in connection with God, as well as our belief in what happens following death as we seek to make sense of and find meaning in the experience. For those who have non-religious beliefs or worldviews, ritual is also an important vehicle to express and process their loss. Ritual, therefore, is a universal way for us to express beyond words what we experience, and what we believe as a way to process and express the reality of loss. This is what a funeral does in a very concrete way. The rituals used by faith communities provide a meaningful way to confront the reality of death. The broad liturgical principles and actions associated with a funeral service such as preparation, gathering, reflection on mortality of self, forgiveness, reconciliation, tribute, eulogy, supportive Scripture, prayer, reflection, remembrance, hope, enduring connection, commendation, burial, cremation all provide a meaningful process to engage with the multidimensional aspects of loss both for the grieving family and also for the wider community.

David Jones died aged thirty-six following a long journey with leukaemia. He was married to Jane and they had three young children: Harry aged eleven, Isobel aged nine, and Josh aged six. David and Jane had been preparing their children for their dad's death, and they felt very much part of the journey in his final weeks as he was cared for at home with the support of the palliative care team. David and Jane had also discussed his funeral plans with their priest who had been visiting them at home and providing spiritual support. Following David's death, his funeral was held in his local church where the wider parish community gathered to support Jane and their children. Their children had an active part in the funeral of their dad. Harry was keen to assist with carrying the coffin, Isobel read a Scripture passage from John's Gospel, and Josh offered a special picture that he had drawn to celebrate his dad's love of football. The structure of the funeral service helped David's family to accept the reality of his death and also to acknowledge the value of their lives and mortality. The burial afterwards, although difficult, was a concrete expression of the finality of David's physical end yet textured by the hope and belief in a "new heaven and a new earth" (Rev 21). In the weeks after the funeral, their priest and the wider parish community continued to care for Jane, Harry, Isobel, and Josh and they were also invited to remember David at the annual time of remembrance in the parish in November.

Funeral liturgies are concrete, they should avoid euphemisms, and be supportive and multisensory in so far as they help mourners to engage with the reality of death with the presence of a coffin, final disposition by burial or cremation, and acknowledgment of death. These processes align well with Worden's "Tasks of Mourning."[20] The best liturgical expressions do not shy away from the challenges of life experiences—and grief is one such challenge. In the preparation of funeral and memorial liturgies, the pastoral minister is well placed to draw on the riches of the particular tradition he/she represents to craft and cocreate a ritual/liturgy appropriate to the particular needs of the bereaved person or family. Particular care should be taken to be inclusive of children and those with particular needs and cultural sensitivities so that the experience is accessible and supportive in the grieving process. An awareness of the therapeutic dimensions of ritual and liturgy is important in how it is crafted and led. An example of this from the vignette above was how Josh, aged six, was able to offer a personalized picture he had drawn as an age-appropriate prayer in celebration of his dad as part of the funeral liturgy. Likewise, Harry was supported to carry his father's coffin that was helpful in his being able to play a meaningful non-verbal role and perhaps as an expression of his love—in both cases, tangible and felt experiences supported naturally by the liturgy of the funeral service.

Grief can be messy, and therefore our liturgical expressions and experiences should reflect the messiness of the pain and sometimes disorienting dimensions of grief while at the same time encompassing the supportive care and hope of the particular family/community. There are many instances in Scripture where the "messiness" of the human experience of grief are vividly recorded and in doing so they give visibility to the rawness and pain of loss alongside the hope of recovery, support, and connection. These experiences are perhaps most poignantly expressed in Job, Psalms, and of course in the ministry of Jesus who expressed his own grief at the death of Lazarus his friend. Those who mourn are also recognized in various scriptural texts as having a special place in the care

---

20. Worden, *Grief Counselling*.

of the faith community. In this way, a supportive connection is fostered where the reality of grief is acknowledged and normalized. Ritual also provides a safe place to offer and receive support when death is particularly difficult or traumatic (for example, suicide, murder, natural disaster, terrorism) and in this regard provides a pastoral "holding" space by an intentionally gathered supportive community.[21] In these situations, pastoral care and liturgy are especially important in the wider community care of all involved and should also be provided in collaboration with other agencies with expertise.

Post-Bereavement Care

The role of community support following bereavement has been increasingly recognized in recent years as part of a wider public health initiative to reduce the negative effects of bereavement in society.[22] Compassionate communities are a growing global movement to provide a broad supportive culture of compassion for those who experience loss and a recent all-Ireland initiative and position paper seeks to promote "Compassionate Communities" as a meaningful way to support grief in the community.[23] The Compassionate Communities movement should be a natural synergy for all groups to be part of and in particular faith/belief communities as compassionate communities in themselves in the wider community. Good pastoral care following bereavement is a natural extension of the care that for many pastoral ministers begins when someone comes to prepare a funeral. Bereavement care should continue for as long as the person needs it and should be tailored to their particular needs and preferences. For those who are bereaved following a time of caregiving—for example during a prolonged illness—there can be a considerable (re)adjustment to a new life without their loved one. There is variable evidence in the published literature concerning the long-term impacts of bereavement in this cohort.[24] For example, caregivers of those with a progressive illness tend to have experienced anticipatory grief from the time of diagnosis.[25]

21. Marek and Oexle, "Supportive and Non-Supportive," 1190.
22. Lichtenthal et al., "Investing in Bereavement Care," 270–74; Sallnow et al., "Report," 837–44.
23. Graham-Wisener et al., "Fostering Compassionate Communities."
24. Schulz et al., "Caregiving and Bereavement."
25. Garand et al., "Anticipatory Grief," 159–65; Cheng et al., "Pilot Study," 261–69; Holley and Mast, "Impact of Anticipatory Grief" 388–96; Rando, "Clinical Dimensions."

In fact, the change of role can in itself evoke a grief response separate to the grief associated with the death of their loved one. There is no correct "way" or timeline in grief. Therefore, pastoral sensitivity and intuition should guide the support that is offered. There are particular touchpoints though that can be tender times following death. These include (but are not limited to) anniversaries, significant milestones, family/community events, festive occasions, and so forth. It is also true to say that these particular touch points continue after the first year. A pastoral example to illustrate this care is how a parish community might be mindful of bereaved members when celebrating particular events in the life of a parish community, e.g., Mothering Sunday or Christmas. Those who are bereaved rarely want the focus to be on them *per se* but rather a sense that their community is holding them during what can be a challenging time.

How we remember those who have died in our liturgical celebrations can bring much meaning and support to families. Included in this is how we also include grief, which is not always widely acknowledged, such as perinatal death, suicide, disenfranchised loss (for example, particular friendships, unacknowledged relationships, termination of pregnancy, etc.), and so forth. In situations where grief is textured with moral or ethical complexity it is important, above all, to provide a pastoral response to the grieving need(s) of the person being cared for. Pastoral support and the planning of a funeral in these contexts can be challenging when the nature of a death is sensitive. For example, following suicide it is important that the funeral and the language used is sensitive, compassionate, pastoral, and yet textured with the hope of the belief(s) of those who are mourning. In the case of suicide, it is important to be guided by public health guidelines on language and terminology used (or not used) so that families are not exposed to secondary trauma or potential shame. In these situations, clergy and pastoral ministers should also avail of pastoral supervision and guidance.

It is important to remember that in sensitive or complex situations those who are grieving are vulnerable, and it is imperative that the providers of pastoral care and support are mindful of the importance of their ethical behavior and practice and the safeguarding of the wellbeing of those in their care. This applies to how pastoral support is provided, being judgment-aware, and practicing to the highest ethical standards so that the care provided is supportive, restorative, and compassionate.

Self-Care

Bereavement care is demanding care, and it is well recognized that the provision of pastoral care in the midst of distress and loss takes a toll on the caregiver. It is therefore important that those who provide such care avail of appropriate support, pastoral supervision, and have access to and avail of spiritual/existential care themselves. Despite the evidence, there continues to be institutional avoidance of this important area for many in pastoral ministry. Good care of those who provide pastoral care translates to good care for those who receive their care: it is as simple as that. Pastoral care by virtue of being involved in relationally and spiritually demanding care requires intentional and proactive self-care. This is an essential ingredient in meaningful care.

Conclusion

This chapter has sought to evidence the principles and practices of pastoral care following bereavement as being congruent with the latest evidence in bereavement studies. It highlights how meaningful pastoral care in the context of bereavement provides an essential approach in the support of those who experience loss and, from a faith perspective, to access the riches of belief, expression, care, compassion, and hope. As a universal human experience, how we care for those who are bereaved is a core activity of a supportive faith/belief community.

12

Establishing Collaborative Pastoral Ministry

John Alderdice

THIS CHAPTER WILL EXPLORE the challenges and opportunities related to establishing models of collaborative pastoral ministry. It will concentrate on the Methodist Church in Ireland as a case study. Methodism emerged initially in England in the eighteenth century as a renewal movement within the Church of England. Led primarily by figures such as John Wesley, it soon spread to other places, including Ireland, where it saw significant growth, particularly during the nineteenth century. Beyond the horizon of its founders, Methodism evolved from being a mission movement to developing the familiar features of a denominational church. The chapter will survey the early Methodist approach to pastoral ministry and the ways in which John Wesley approached pastoral care matters; consider the development of ordained ministry in Methodism; outline the contextual difficulties that are faced in inherited models of church and ministry today; and finally, offer an approach to servant leadership that offers a template for developing collaborative pastoral ministry in the church today. The chapter will demonstrate that deploying servant leadership characteristics is in some ways a return to the early Methodist approach to pastoral ministry.

Application to My Own Setting

In 1998 I was appointed as a probationer minister in a semirural commuter village where the local Methodist church had undergone a significant season of growth over the previous decade. This was largely due to new affordable housing within a reasonable distance of larger urban centers of employment. Having attended theological college for ministerial training and having grown up in a ministry family where I witnessed firsthand how a presbyteral minister lived out their vocation day by day, I set about deploying that inherited and familiar model for which I had been trained. I was determined that I would visit every household within a few months, because, as I understood it, what better way was there to minister to and build up the congregation? Within those first months, however, I learnt that this was not going to be as straightforward a process as I had thought. Faced with the reality of a majority of households where the adults had full time occupations, the task of finding a suitable time to "visit" and to get to know the congregation and offer pastoral care was well-nigh impossible. Visiting the older, retired, but active generation was only a marginally more successful venture.

A further question began to arise in my thinking and reflection. Given the number of families and households for which I was pastorally responsible, how could I ensure a depth of pastoral relationship which extended beyond a transactional understanding of ministry in which the single clergy person was expected to "check-in" on each congregant. What I realized was that to be truly effective in pastoral ministry in the local church and to help people grow in their relationship with Jesus required a team approach.

The Early Methodist Model

John Wesley, the founder of Methodism, did not intend to form a denomination separate to the Church of England. He viewed Methodism as an evangelistic movement consisting initially of itinerating preachers not called to remain located in one place. The Methodist societies that developed became the context for the development of discipleship, fellowship, and pastoral accountability even though Wesley expected the early Methodists to continue to attend the parish church for holy communion.

At an early stage, this growth presented Wesley with a significant practical problem, and his solution demonstrated his adaptability.

Among his group of trusted friends and associates there were not enough ordained priests to oversee and lead the growing demands of the societies. The Wesley brothers moved around those societies that aligned themselves with them, but more leaders were required. David Hempton notes that Wesley appropriated ideas from Moravians, Quakers, and others involved in the revival, but he asserts this concerning Wesley in particular:

> What gave him his preponderance were energy, mobility, perseverance, and sheer force of will. What gave Methodism its preponderance over other early evangelistic associations was its ability to bestow an element of coherence and order on the disparate and often bizarre religiosity it encountered.[1]

The logical solution to the question of leadership was for Wesley to appoint lay leaders and soon the model became an effective means of ensuring the continued spiritual vitality of the societies. As Baker notes,

> It was a close-knit family system which made so many demands and maintained so many checks on deed and word and even thought that it is remarkable that most Methodists had time not only for normal parish activities but in fact attended them more faithfully than did the non-Methodists.[2]

Wesley organized small groups or "bands" within each society. In December 1738, he wrote his own rules for the "bands" involving a set of questions to be used during their meetings. The purpose of the band/group was to create a more intimate setting where questions could be asked of members to encourage continued spiritual vitality. Numerically, "bands" contained no more than four or five people, they were single-sex, and all members would have had the same marital status.[3] Rupert Davies maintains that Wesley did not merely copy what others were doing, but always sought to adapt what he saw as effective strategies for the benefit of his own movement:

> It is not hard to account for and trace the origin and growth of Wesley's Methodist societies, so long as it is remembered that he never adopted the practices of others, or his own earlier ones, without strict scrutiny or without modification for his purposes. He was certainly a pragmatist, in the sense that he was always

---

1. Hempton, *Methodism*, 16.
2. Baker, *John Wesley*, 78.
3. Baker, *John Wesley*, 79.

open to consider and use what was suggested to him in the form of ideas and activities. But he did not fail to put his own stamp on anything he proceeded to borrow.[4]

Later the "class" layer of organization was added to the local society, initially in the Bristol society in 1742, and then adopted more widely as societies grew. This was a bigger group of approximately twelve members, with mixed-sex and different marital statuses. The purpose of the "class" developed as a means of gathering a weekly collection and of providing pastoral care to growing societies. Baker describes the class as a "weekly meeting for fellowship of a somewhat less searching kind than that of bands."[5] "Classes" and "bands" were steered by lay leaders appointed initially by Wesley.

For the purposes of this chapter, what we can learn is that early Methodism was a movement that empowered and released people of faith to serve in ministry tasks in their local societies. Wesley's primary concern was that his preachers would remain focused on their task of preaching to "save souls" and not to get distracted by or drawn into the detailed affairs of local societies or the parishes within which they were located. After Wesley's death, and as Methodism continued to grow in the nineteenth and twentieth centuries, the movement, however, adopted more regular models of ministry.

A Settled Pattern

Beyond the orbit of Wesley's influence, Methodism settled through the course of the nineteenth century. Questions concerning the ordination of preachers and the administration of the sacraments were resolved gradually, and the young denomination adopted more familiar ecclesiastical models of ministry akin to that of other established denominations.

An important development to note concerns the designation "minister." John Lenton notes that "the term 'minister' was not used of Wesleyan preachers before 1810."[6] From this period "minister" was applied to describe the role of the itinerant preacher in Methodism, an indication of the growing status of the movement as a distinct Christian denomination. Historically, the use of the designation "minister" described those

---

4. Wesley, *Methodist Societies*, 8.
5. Baker, *John Wesley*, 78.
6. Lenton, *John Wesley's Preachers*, 35.

set apart to serve the church community. In contrast, the function of Wesley's itinerant preachers was to preach to those beyond the church community. The move to the use of the term "minister" undoubtedly indicates an increasing focus on the internal pastoral matters of a local church.

By the second half of the nineteenth century, it was evident that a document was required to collate the various constitutions, rules, and procedures of the church. In 1873 the first "Manual of Laws and Discipline" was agreed and published by the Conference of the Methodist Church in Ireland. This manual drew together material from the annual minutes of Conference and the journal of the Conference, both of which had become more sophisticated and extensive documents through the nineteenth century. Chapter 4 of the manual was entitled "Ministers and Preachers" and begins with an outline of what is understood to be the "Office and Duty of a Methodist Preacher." This first section reflects much of Wesley's "Rules for Helpers." Guidance is given on effective preaching and leading of worship and on the management of the affairs of societies. An interesting comment explores the organization and running of classes as a means of continuing to "carry on the present glorious revival of the work of God."[7] Preachers were encouraged to meet the classes monthly, and the following note is made regarding what would be understood today to be pastoral visitation of members in their homes:

> As private visits must in many cases, from our plan of continual itinerancy and village preaching, and from the number of members in the larger societies, be greatly limited, let us endeavor so to arrange in our several circuits the plans for quarterly public visitation of the classes, as to allow full time for a more minute examination into the Christian knowledge, experience, and practice of the members; and for pastoral inquiries, instructions and counsels, respecting personal and family religion.[8]

By 1900 a further edition of the Manual of Laws was published. The term "minister" is used to describe the role and function of full-time itinerant preachers. The chapter on Ministry begins with a summary reminder of the "Office and Duty of a Methodist Minister":

---

7. *Minutes of Conference*, 47.
8. *Minutes of Conference*, 47.

69 The design of God in raising up the Methodist Ministry may reasonably be believed to have been to assist in spreading Scriptural holiness over the land.

70 The office of a Christian Minister is to watch over souls, as he that must give account; and in order to do this he must feed and guide the flock.

71 The duty of a Methodist Minister, in addition to regular and faithful preaching, is to meet the Societies and Classes, to meet the Leaders, to visit the people of his charge, especially the sick, and to attend to all parts of the Methodist discipline.[9]

Further directions then given offer a deeper insight into how Methodist ministry was being practiced by this time. The themes explored include:

- regard for ministerial colleagues;
- house to house visitation for the purposes of encouraging all to embrace the Christian faith;
- personal, spiritual, and theological development in ministry;
- opening new "preaching places";
- dealing with those described as "backsliders" to the faith, i.e., those perceived to no longer be practicing Christian faith;
- the avoidance of sectarianism; and
- good relationships with other denominations.

These rules and regulations dealing with the provision of ordained ministry resembled that of other denominations as well as reflecting the origins of the Methodist preacher. Ordained ministers increasingly became involved in the routine matters of pastoral ministry and administration of circuits to sustain churches that had already been established, a far cry from Wesley's vision of extraordinary messengers. This model of pastoral ministry largely delivered by individual presbyters working alone has continued to operate to the present day as the normative approach to Methodist presbyteral ministry. This approach is facing significant challenges, however, to which we will now turn.

9. *Manual of the Laws*, 1900, 23–50.

The Contemporary Challenge

During the second half of the twentieth century, fault-lines began to appear in the landscapes of many established denominational churches, particularly in the West. Evidence of these challenges include declining membership, decreasing levels of church engagement and attendance, a drop in the number of people training for ordination, rapidly accelerating age profiles of congregations, and the rise in tensions within denominations and between denominations and the civic powers in relation to moral and ethical questions. Loren Mead describes these fault lines as "cracks in the system," which reveal the inherent weaknesses that exist in denominational structures. Closer investigation would suggest that these weaknesses have been developing for at least the last century.[10] Similarly, Stuart Murray defines this contemporary context as "post-Christendom—a culture in which central features of the Christian story are unknown and churches are alien institutions whose rhythms do not normally impinge on most members of society."[11] Like Mead, Murray argues that the church in the West is in the middle of an extended period of transition, and it remains unclear as to what forms and structures of church will emerge. While such transition and change might present institutional churches with significant challenges, it also provides the opportunity to engage in new and creative ways of relating to secular culture. Church and mission theologian Darrell Guder synopsizes the challenge in the following terms:

> As Christendom ends and the western world becomes an ever more difficult mission field, the churches are challenged to reclaim their missional calling. . . . This process means that their inherited forms of leadership are also subject to review and change.[12]

Many in the Western context are currently experiencing the symptoms of disruption as set out by Mead. Writing from a British context, Stephen Croft makes the point, "The models of mission and ministry that have nourished the church through previous centuries are no longer proving

---

10. Mead, *Once and Future Church*, 55–57.
11. Murray, *Post-Christendom*, 1.
12. Guder, *Called to Witness*, 149.

effective or sustainable for many congregations and clergy."[13] Two matters that Mead highlights will now be explored.

The Role of the Clergy

A minister in the Methodist Church is ordained to "word and sacrament." This ministry, according to the Manual of Laws of the church, is primarily focused on the "winning and watching over souls," pastoral oversight of congregational members, and the leading of worship and preaching.[14] In this regard, the Irish Methodist Church is at one with the practice of ordained ministry in other mainstream denominations operating at the end of Christendom. Mead summarizes this practice as follows:

> In Christendom, the role of the clergy was clear. It was strong, central, and unquestioned. It was a high-status role, carrying authority. Clergy were the ministry. Clergy were chaplains and guarantors of community life, with power far beyond the walls of the church.[15]

What may appear on the surface to be a relatively simple role has become increasingly complex. Guder traces this complexity back to, and even beyond, the time of the Protestant Reformation.

> In the almost five hundred years of Protestantism, there has been an enormous proliferation of concepts and structures of office in which the old patterns of Christendom and revisions of the Reformation are intertwined and adapted. For all the talk of the priesthood of all believers, there are many traces of Christendom's legacy in the ways that the ordered ministry actually functions. The clergy–laity distinction persists in spite of all Protestant affirmations that we are all part of the *laos*, the laity of God. Congregants still tend to think that their ministers are there to provide the services that meet their religious needs, based on the assumption that their ordinations, however celebrated, conferred a special status on them.[16]

In 2006 the Irish Methodist Conference received a report exploring factors affecting the health and well-being of ordained clergy.[17] The

---

13. Croft, *Ministry in Three Dimensions*, 4.
14. *Manual of the Laws*, 2011, 23.
15. Mead, *Once and Future Church*, 57.
16. Guder, *Called to Witness*, 148.
17. Methodist Church in Ireland, *Reports and Agenda*, 2006, 27–36.

report drew evidence from a survey commissioned to explore ministers' experiences. It showed that pastoral care, preaching, and teaching remained the activities that ministers found most fulfilling, along with wider community-development work, and youth and children's ministry. It also highlighted many of the issues and activities that ministers found increasingly difficult to deal with, including conflict resolution and mediation, leadership functions, time management, and change management. The conclusions of the report highlighted that the church faced significant challenges in relation to the exercise of ordained ministry. These included broad themes such as arresting the numerical decline of congregations, wider societal changes in terms of attitudes towards institutional churches, broader understanding of the nature of ministry that includes all those who are members of the church, not just those who are ordained, and the development of new forms of pioneer ministry and mission. In addition, the report highlighted the increasing difficulties of operating significant technical processes in the church, including the mechanisms for maintaining the itinerant system, the nature and scope of training for ordained ministry, and the development of leadership among both ordained and lay. Issues such as those highlighted above have continued to be discussed across the Methodist Church over the last ten years and are in line with Mead's assertions over the changing role of ordained clergy. As he states,

> Loss of role clarity lies behind much of the stress and burnout among clergy. Most clergy come to their vocations from a deep faith and commitment. Trained in institutions that were generated by the mind-set of Christendom and ordained into denominations and congregations predominantly shaped by Christendom, they discover that the rules have been changed in the middle of the game. Instead of front-line leaders and spokespersons for mission, they now feel they are being asked to take a back seat to a newly awakened laity. The role they sought out and trained themselves for no longer fits what they have to do. Many are unsure how to give leadership in the new time.[18]

Based on his research, Mead suggests that clergy are searching for roles that are clearer and less ambiguous. Some clergy see themselves as social activists or spiritual directors, "enablers" or community organizers, educators, or counsellors. Often these new role descriptions are added onto the more traditional roles of preacher, pastor, and administrator.

18. Mead, *Once and Future Church*, 59.

The multiplicity of options and opportunities, however, has resulted in less clarity, not more, as individual clergy simply decide for themselves their preferred approach to ministry.[19]

In addition, the Methodist Church in Ireland faces a decline in the numbers of ordained ministers available for service in local churches. There is a decrease in the number entering the ministry and those offering as candidates are of an older age profile and therefore unable to serve for as many years as their predecessors. The number of people leaving the ministry through resignation, retirement, or transferring to other churches overseas is also increasing. This reality increases pressure on remaining clergy who by necessity are spread over more local congregations. At the same time, the challenge of competing expectations of congregations and lay leaders further increases the pressure on the ordained. The significant reality is that the denomination, local congregations, and clergy must adapt considering changing circumstances. As Croft states,

> Changes in deployment patterns call for a different set of skills and a different mindset among the clergy. We are moving further and further away from the concept of the ordained as the person whose primary responsibility is to lead the worship of the people, to do the primary work of pastoral care, and teach the faith to the children and young people. We are moving much more rapidly towards the primary skills of the ordained being focused around leading and building communities of faith who are able to engage in God's mission to the world.[20]

The Role of the Laity

"All People Are Called to Minister" is the title of a strategic paper adopted by the Methodist Conference in June 2017.[21] It outlines a strategy for the reinvigoration of lay ministry that builds on a previous church publication from 2014 entitled "God's Mission, Our Mission," which stated,

> The concept of whole life discipleship is one where disciples engage in mission wherever they are every day—at the "frontlines" of everyday life—and the local worshiping and nurturing church fully supports and equips such discipleship shaped by and for comprehensive mission; such an understanding provides a rich

---

19. Mead, *Once and Future Church*, 58.
20. Croft, *Ministry in Three Dimensions*, 12.
21. Methodist Church in Ireland, *Reports and Agenda*, 2017, 209–12.

underpinning for how we might seek to fulfil our mission at local society and district levels in particular but also as a whole Connexion.[22]

These ideas relate to Mead's second observation, which explores the changing role of the lay members of local churches. He argues that during the last fifty years the United States has seen a shift in the understanding of how congregational members express their religious convictions in their everyday lives. In the past, involvement in local congregational work by volunteer lay members focused on the maintenance of church programs and involvement in the upkeep of church buildings. Mead shows that lay leaders are confronted by this dislocation now and face several complex and often competing demands including:

- a demand to increase the amount of time committed to and financial resources given to the function of the congregation;
- an understanding that the ministry of the laity should be expressed beyond the activities of the church in members' everyday lives, within family life, workplace, and leisure activities;
- the need to understand the nuances of often complex social and theological issues such as human sexuality, migration, and global politics and economics; and
- embracing significant changes in worship style and liturgies with little sense of ownership or consultation.

In Ireland and Britain, as in the United States, the challenge of declining church attendance and increasing age profile within the older denominational churches means that local churches cannot depend on the presence of children and young people to ensure a future. The challenge that the church faces is to engage in mission to families currently beyond the fringes of the church. As Croft states,

> Churches which do not attempt to engage in mission in this way will, in the course of time, simply have to close. The existing congregation grows older and declines as people become too infirm to attend church or as they die. The income of the church declines and so the congregation is unable to support a full-time vicar or minister. The pastoral oversight they receive from the denomination by way of part-time ministry has energy only for maintenance of the existing congregation. The decline

---

22. Methodist Church in Ireland, *Reports and Agenda*, 2014, 222–45.

continues until the circuit or diocese makes the decision to close the building and focus its energies elsewhere.[23]

The arguments made by both Croft and Mead are applicable to all mainstream churches. The conference documents cited earlier on ministry, ministers' health, and mission all provide evidence of a debate within the church regarding the perceived need for a changing understanding of the role of the laity. One example of this issue concerns the role of the ordained minister as the primary provider of pastoral care within the context of a local circuit. A recent series of comments, articles, and letters by semi-anonymous commentators published in the monthly magazine of the Methodist Church in Ireland focus on this question. The first commentator writes,

> Here is the ministerial ethic I grew up to believe to be universal: the minister of a congregation cares about every single individual within his/her remit of care. The minister, at varying suitable intervals, visits the members of the congregation. The minister knows the congregation and their cares, responsibilities, and joys—even if a small notebook of reminders is needed. Am I foolish in thinking that this is part of a minister's remit? Modern lifestyles make this more challenging, but isn't it still in the job description? There were many more Methodists in Ireland in past years, but the ministers called on their people, even if they had to cycle miles to do it. Pastoral teams of lay people are wonderful and necessary but when people are in distress, they want to see the person into whose pastoral care they have voluntarily placed themselves, someone whom they know and who knows them.[24]

In response to the comment above, a different correspondent stated, "In my opinion this is a matter of concern to many. We are all aware that membership of our Church continues to fall and I wonder if lack of pastoral care is a contributing factor."[25] The writer proceeded to infer that this was because of ordained ministers not engaging in pastoral visitation to the same degree as they did in the past. Similarly, a comment in the June 2016 edition of the same magazine suggested that ordained ministers were neglecting or rejecting their role in relation to pastoral

---

23. Croft, *Ministry in Three Dimensions*, 6-7.
24. "If Methodism," 33.
25. "Importance of Pastoral Visitation," 31.

visitation.[26] A second correspondent went further, highlighting the dislocation raised by Mead:

> As the church is reminding us to pastor each other, it appears to have forgotten that this has always been an important part of a Methodist minister's responsibility. How can a minister preach effectively to people without knowing their joys, sorrows, and difficulties? To whom do people address their questions about faith in relationship to society today? I, for one, will not discuss concerns with someone with whom I do not have an established, trusting relationship. Society may have changed but people have the same needs and more than ever require a pastor/counsellor. If the Methodist ministers of the twentieth century were able to fulfil this role, with much larger congregations, why can they not do so now?[27]

In contrast to these perspectives on pastoral care, Luscombe, writing about the practice of ordained ministry within the Methodist Church in Britain, articulates something of the tension between an understanding of pastoral care today and the original understanding of the role of a Methodist minister. As he states,

> Today, improved communications allow the ordained minister to be called in as the expert, allowing or forcing the minster into the role of professional pastoral carer, which is very far from Wesley's original concept of his helpers. This might be simply the inevitable working out of the change from new movement into settled denomination.[28]

There can be no doubt that the tension as outlined by Luscombe is a feature of the current debate within many mainstream churches. At the Irish conference of 2017, it was agreed to add a preamble to the church's criteria for selection for ordained ministry training, stating,

> "Ministry" is about the whole Church's calling to serve God in worship, in each other, and in the world. Particular ministries express this service in different ways, but the ordained minister is especially related to the total ministry of the body of Christ, as leader and enabler of others. The ordained minister acts as

---

26. "Destination Station," 31.
27. "Confused and puzzled," 34.
28. Luscombe, "Where Is the Minister?," 40.

a sign of the Church which is itself a sign of the Kingdom of God.[29]

The key words in this preamble are undoubtedly "leader" and "enabler," which emphasize that the role of the ordained is not simply to be those who "do" the ministry but, in exercising their specific ministry, the role of the ordained is to inspire, equip, train, and release the laity into the exercise of ministry. While the Methodist Conference agreed to this statement, the greatest challenge is implementation in local settings. Successful implementation requires a significant shift in culture across the denomination where there are significant numbers of members, such as those quoted above, who are of an older demographic and hold to a more traditional and settled view of the role of the ordained. In addition, among ordained ministers, many want to retain the classical Reformed model of a "pastor/teacher," which provides a degree of certainty and comfort in times where there is significant change and uncertainty in the wider culture and society. The challenges the church faces cannot be avoided, and the implications for the practice of ministry are widespread, as Croft states categorically:

> Changes in society and emerging ways of being church call for new ways of being church and therefore make new demands on the ordained ministry. A cluster of skills which, for the moment, we will call enabling or collaborating leadership skills has now become one of the primary skills of those who exercise their ordained ministry within the local church.[30]

Contemporary Presbyteral Leadership: A Ministry that Enables

We return to the account of my early pastoral ministry experience and the question of how effective pastoral ministry might be delivered in the contemporary church. Given the patterns of early Methodism, it is evident that the instinct that the key lay in enabling others to exercise ministry was a correct one. Quickly we established a team of lay members of the congregation who demonstrated pastoral care gifts, we developed a pattern of initial and ongoing formation, and we communicated with the congregation about the model of pastoral ministry we were now

---

29. Methodist Church in Ireland, *Reports and Agenda*, 2017, 223.
30. Croft, *Ministry in Three Dimensions*, 16.

deploying. I preached on the pastoral ministry of Jesus and his teaching in John's Gospel chapter 13 on the need for his followers to "love another." I also drew from the New Testament letters and the instructions given by Paul as to how disciples of Jesus should care, have due regard of, and love one another (see Rom 12; 2 Cor 13; Gal 5; Eph 4; and 1 Thess).

This pattern of developing teams to offer pastoral care and other ministries in the church is one that I have followed in subsequent appointments and in my view is a critical necessity for the future of the church in contemporary society. Though it must be said, helping some in our churches to accept pastoral ministry from lay volunteers remains a challenge. More recently, in research carried out as part of my doctoral studies, I explored the relationship between presbyteral ministry and servant leadership theory as originally formulated by Robert Greenleaf, writing in the 1970s. Greenleaf understood his theory as a collection of "intuitive insights" out of which he was able to formulate his view of leadership. His enigmatic and almost elusive approach to definition corresponds well with the often undefined nature of the practice of presbyteral ministry. We will now explore several of Greenleaf's insights and how they address the question of enabling pastoral ministry. First, however, a brief comment about the concept of leadership.

The application of leadership theory to Christian ministry, including that of servant leadership is contested.[31] Aspiring to a leadership role may be problematic for the person of faith as it runs counter to the values and character of a Christian. As Yung states, "Genuine Christian leadership can never be attained by going after it for its own sake; it has to flow out of a life of love and servanthood for our neighbor."[32] My research shows that those who have entered presbyteral ministry have not done so because they want to be leaders, but they recognize that their role and function within the life of the local church and the denomination requires them to exercise leadership.[33] It is important to affirm the principle that an element of healthy skepticism concerning the place of leadership in the church is useful, but wholesale rejection of the concept of leadership is unhelpful. The kind of leadership exercised therefore becomes the crucial matter. The ordained status of ministers should not result in a top-down hierarchy of leadership where the ordained minister is perceived to be above the congregation in some form. Rather the ordained minister

---

31. Alderdice, "Irish Methodism," 141–43.
32. Yung, *Leadership or Servanthood*, 136.
33. Alderdice, "Irish Methodism," 218–19.

should endeavor to work with lay leaders and church members in pursuing a shared vision for the local church.

Guder argues that the historical and inherited forms of pastoral leadership and ministry are themselves evolving.[34] Rather than exercising a palliative ministry, the ordained of today are called to lead and minister with and to their congregations, helping them to grapple with emerging models of ministry and mission. Such leadership and ministry necessitate a framework of leadership analogous to servant leadership involving working collaboratively with people, listening deeply, and understanding people's perspectives, as well as helping communities to discern vision. The ultimate intention of the ministry and leadership activity of the ordained must be to develop other people as servant leaders. In the setting of the church, the tools at the disposal of the ordained minister are ironically the ones they have already been trained for—that of word and sacrament—but deployed in a way that enables and equips congregations to live out their faith in a changed world.

The ordained minister is to set an example in their personal lives and spirituality and to serve those around them. This is the form of countercultural servant leadership that is required in the church:

> Leadership is the result of practicing genuine servanthood wherever we are and whatever position we are called to by Christ. By living and ministering as servants, our loving and humble service will impact those around us as great leadership.[35]

At the core of this form of leadership is a deep-seated concern for people and a desire on the part of the leader to see human beings flourish. We will now explore this in more depth under four headings.

(1) Sense of Call

A significant historical characteristic of Methodist ministry is a deep-seated sense of call. Wesley's own motivation was shown in his indefatigable passion which stemmed from a deep spirituality and underlying motivation to serve God. Wesley regarded such a call as essential for his colleague preachers if they were to flourish.

My own research shows that a spirited sense of call to serve remains a vital feature of the experience of ministers of all those called to pastoral

34. Guder, *Called to Witness*, 149–50.
35. Yung, *Leadership or Servanthood*, 14.

ministry. Furthermore, the minsters who participated in the research recognize that the process of nurturing their personal spirituality is essential in sustaining their sense of call to ministry and leadership.[36] The person of Jesus is therefore both inspiration and role model to those engaged in ordained ministry. The fundamental motivation to serve others arises from the minister's obedience to God's call and the example of the sacrifice and service of Jesus. This corresponds with Robert Greenland's foundational argument that the servant-leader is first a servant.[37]

Responding to the call of God to serve is by no means a straightforward endeavor especially given the significant challenges facing the contemporary church, as discussed above. These challenges include secularization, increasing age demographics, and declining numerical strength. The ministers interviewed in my research recognize that they face a church culture that can be predominantly focused on the maintenance and internal well-being of congregations rather than on the wider mission to the world as envisaged by Wesley.[38] Such challenges have the potential to be overwhelming and necessitate a spiritual vigor and commitment to maintain effectiveness.

Applying Wesley's call to service to today's context is perhaps best understood as not simply relevant to individual church ministers and leaders but to all members of local church congregations. In this context, the Methodist minister exercises spiritual service and leadership, enabling members of congregations to grow in terms of their personal spiritually and to foster servant leadership within the church community. Central to this task is equipping and releasing congregations to move out of their church buildings, and to engage with, and minister to, their wider communities with humility and sacrifice. Though it may not always be understood or received in this way, this is servant leadership in operation.

(2) Virtuous Love

A second essential aspect of servant leadership relates to what might be described as virtuous love. In fact, Kathleen Patterson considers such love to be an antecedent of servant leadership:

---

36. Alderdice, *Irish Methodism*, 194.
37. Greenleaf, *Servant Leadership*, 27.
38. Croft, *Ministry in Three Dimensions*, 25–26.

Servant-leaders lead with love, are motivated by love, and serve their followers with love. This love is a force, a force so intense that it changes lives—the lives of the followers, the life of the organization, and even the life of the leader.[39]

Undoubtedly loving people and leading them at the same time is extremely demanding for those in ministry. The people with whom ministers engage are initially those who are already members of their congregations. These members have their own worries, concerns, and pastoral expectations of their ministers that are not always fully aligned with the wider mission of the church.

My experience of building collaborative pastoral care teams has taught me of the need not to take the team for granted, and indeed, that it is a mistake to expect them to keep on serving effectively without being loved or cared for themselves. This requires discipline and intentionality in terms of regular team meetings and ongoing one-to-one support and encouragement.

(3) People over Programs

Taking the concept of virtuous love a step further, Greenleaf argued the key difference between his framework for servant leadership and other leadership theories centered on "the care taken by the servant to first make sure that other people's highest priority needs are being served."[40] To a person, the participants who took part in my research argued that leadership is predominantly concerned with working for and with people.[41] Furthermore, the participants noted that the leadership skills required for effective ministry focused on the wisdom to listen well, empathize, understand people and contexts, build trust, and to work collaboratively. These leadership skills mirror those required to exercise effective pastoral ministry. In other words, there is a deep resonance between the pastoral ministry role and the outworking of servant leadership. Such an approach builds relational trust and, as Nigel Wright argues, this is essential for effective Christian ministry:

> Showing oneself to be a caring pastor with clear and honorable motives who is a transparent disciple of Christ and has a

---

39. Patterson, "Servant Leadership and Love," 72.
40. Greenleaf, *Servant Leadership*, 27.
41. Alderdice, "Irish Methodism," 221.

self-sacrificing love for the church, it is possible to create the conditions in which constructive change can come about.[42]

The participants in my research declared their commitment to building relationships within the life of local congregations. Love for people, as well as love for God, was seen as crucial in the exercise of ministry. There is no escaping the reality, however, of the interviewees' experience of significant pressure and expectation particularly in relation to delivery of pastoral care and relationship building. Increasing age demographics and numerical decline are among the factors that feed pastoral expectations. Significant effort is required to provide a form of pastoral care that encourages people to grow and develop rather than the offering of a passive model of personal support and counsel.[43]

A further skill required on the part of a presbyter is to involve a wider variety of people in the mission and ministry of the church. It may be a temptation for leaders to look to those already deeply involved to pursue yet other initiatives. It is essential however, to listen to and engage people not normally included or deeply involved in the life and witness of the church. Such an approach is inherently Methodist, building on the example of John Wesley who viewed participation in ministry and mission as a vital feature of Christian discipleship and service.

(4) Withdrawal and Awareness

The practice of ordained ministry implies a commitment to personal spiritual growth. The contemporary challenges facing those in church leadership only serves to underline the importance of this issue. Nurturing others to serve in ministry teams not only requires the development of leadership skills on the part of the ordained minister, but also their character formation so that they have the necessary spiritual and emotional depth for the role. Wesley placed a significant emphasis on the importance of his preachers paying attention to their personal holiness. This emphasis on spirituality resonates with Greenleaf's argument concerning perception and self-awareness. Christian leaders must maintain the discipline of periodic withdrawal from the intensity of activity to reflect, to recharge, and to recall the broader meaning of their calling and circumstances. Without such discipline, the servant leader runs the risk

---

42. Wright, *Church Minister*, 120.
43. Alderdice, "Irish Methodism," 222.

of losing perspective, suffering burnout, and ultimately becoming unable to lead effectively.

Conclusion

Drawing from my ministry experience and own research, this chapter has sought to explore the theme of collaborative pastoral ministry. Methodism as a movement and denomination possesses a heritage and model that offers the contemporary church a template for how it might function effectively considering the challenges it faces today. Furthermore, the chapter has explored how those who exercise presbyteral ministry today need to be committed to enabling and developing the ministry and mission of those within their church communities. Servant leadership theory as outlined by Robert Greenleaf provides a template for how those exercising presbyteral ministry can lead in such a way as to enable people to flourish and the wider ministry and mission of the church to grow.

13

Ministering Cross-Culturally and to Those on the Margins

Laurence Graham

Setting the Scene

For several centuries Ireland's greatest export was its people, with emigrants leaving the island in search of work and a new life in Britain, the United States, Australia, or Canada. But in the late 1990s that began to change as Ireland's economy started to grow rapidly, and, quite suddenly, Ireland became a destination for migration. For all kinds of reasons people began to arrive from almost every country in the world. As a result, during the last two decades, many churches in Ireland, as is the case elsewhere, have benefited from an influx of enthusiastic Christians arriving in their midst. Dublin Central Mission, where I am currently based, is a good example of this trend.

Established in 1893 by the Methodist Church, Dublin Central Mission served the needs of people in the inner city for over one hundred years. But by the late 1990s the Sunday morning worshiping congregation greatly declined and was mostly populated by people who travelled into the city center from the suburbs. They began to wonder if they should cease to meet as a worshiping congregation while continuing with the social outreach work of the mission. However, after a process of discernment, the leaders felt God's call to stay in the city. A short time after this decision was made new people started to arrive so that the congregation doubled in a few short years. This led to the church resourcing a new project called "Welcoming the Stranger," and the congregation grew further.[1] As a result, when I arrived in 2015, I found a vibrant congregation comprised of people from many different nations but wonderfully united in worship and witness. For me, this followed similar experiences in my previous posting in County Kerry. Hence the reflections in this chapter on pastoral care in a multicultural context are based on approximately twenty years of ministry among people who have recently come from somewhere else to live in Ireland. The chapter itself will be divided into two main sections: an outline of the underlying principles of this form of ministry followed by some reflections on practice.

Underlying Principles

The Fundamental Unity of the Body of Christ

The Christian church has been multicultural and multiethnic since its foundation at Pentecost. As Peter declared in the home of Cornelius, "I now realize how true it is that God does not show favoritism but accepts from every nation the one who fears him and does what is right."[2] Based on his detailed study of the account of the commissioning of Saul and Barnabas at Antioch, which is recorded in Acts 13:1–4, Werner Kahl of the Goethe Institute argues that it seems likely that two of the three pairs of hands that were laid on Barnabas and Saul were from Africa and therefore black.[3] A similar argument is made by David G. Peterson in his Pillar Commentary on the Acts of the Apostles.[4] Some years later that same Saul, now called Paul wrote,

> For he himself is our peace, who has made the two groups one
> and has destroyed the barrier, the dividing wall of hostility, by

---

1. Stephens, "Developing a Multi-Ethnic Congregation," 30–40.
2. Acts 10:34–35. Unless otherwise indicated, all Scripture is taken from the NIV.
3. Kahl, "Migration and Transcultural."
4. Peterson, *Acts of the Apostles*, 374–75. "What is most obvious is the ethnic diversity of the leadership of this church. *Barnabas* was from Cyprus, *Simeon called Niger* may have been from Africa (*Niger* is a Latinism, meaning 'black'), and *Lucius of Cyrene* certainly came from North Africa (cf. 11:20 note). *Manaen* is described as having been *brought up with Herod the tetrarch*, the ruler of Galilee when Jesus was born (Lk. 3:1), and *Saul* was from Tarsus. The remarkable diversity of the backgrounds and origins of these leaders was 'appropriate to the cosmopolitan context of Antioch."

> setting aside in his flesh the law with its commands and regulations. His purpose was to create in himself one new humanity out of the two, thus making peace, and in one body to reconcile both of them to God through the cross, by which he put to death their hostility. He came and preached peace to you who were far away and peace to those who were near. For through him we both have access to the Father by one Spirit. Consequently, you are no longer foreigners and strangers, but fellow citizens with God's people and also members of his household, built on the foundation of the apostles and prophets, with Christ Jesus himself as the chief cornerstone. (Eph 2:14–20)

This passage spells out that those who have been reconciled to God by the cross are consequently reconciled to another. Both Jew and gentile are granted equal access to the Father, through the Son, by the Spirit (v. 18). So, within God's family the Father makes no distinction between those children who are Jewish by birth and those who are gentile but adopted. To us today the abolition of the barriers separating Jews and gentiles may not be so revolutionary as it was then, but there are other divisions within the human family that are equally irrelevant in the sight of God and ought to be irrelevant in his children's sight. In the body of Christ, the church, there is no place for divisions or distinctions based on race or ethnicity.

At the outset of this chapter, then, let us note that a multicultural church is not a recent phenomenon. In fact, for as long as there has been a church it has been multicultural and the New Testament makes it clear that, from the beginning, Christian leaders taught that all people are fundamentally equal in God's sight. Indeed, as Kahl notes,

> The current processes of global migration have the potential of making us aware of the fundamental significance of gospel in early Christianity. . . . They pose two challenges for European churches, similar to the challenges Jewish early Christians faced: to overcome prejudice and superiority complexes, [and] to create spaces of cross-cultural encounter and the formation of transcultural, sharing and caring faith-communities, for all involved to grow together.[5]

---

5. Kahl, "Migration and Transcultural Faith."

The Need to Acknowledge the Reality of Racism

At this point I want to suggest that you, the reader, have probably agreed with every word in the previous section. Most people are not proactively racist. However, we must never forget that we all make distinctions in our mind when we notice people of a different race. Imagine you are driving along a road and suddenly a car pulls out in front of you so that you must brake to avoid them. You will be upset and probably angry. But I am also certain that you will notice the ethnicity of the driver and I am guessing that your reaction may well be slightly different depending on the racial background of the driver of the other car.

Racism can be subtle, or it can be blatant. I remember a taxi driver in Dublin who had come from Nigeria telling me that he regularly saw people passing him over in the taxi rank lane and going to the taxi behind him which had a white driver. My response to him was one of regret and apology, but I was also glad that he told me. For very few of the many people from other countries with whom I have had pastoral contact have told me about incidents of racism in their lives in Ireland. Furthermore, on one occasion we organized a focused storytelling circle at the church with a professional facilitator. The meeting was advertised as being a mix of Irish and those of other ethnic origins and was organized in the hope that it would lead to some healing. Sadly, it transpired that very few were interested in coming.

A further point to note when discussing racism, is that I have discovered that it is not necessarily confined to how white Irish people view those who have come from other parts of the world. Racism can also be manifest among those who have come. These prejudices can be localized or much more broadly based. For example, most African countries contain many different tribal groups because their borders were drawn by colonial powers with little regard for the ethnic makeup of the various regions. This can then be accentuated among people who have come to seek asylum because there is conflict in their homeland. It is quite conceivable that people representing both sides of that conflict could be worshiping in the same congregation in Ireland. Another example is the fact that some of the countries of the world still have a more pronounced class structure than we now have in Western Europe. For instance, the caste system in India, which is a mystery to Europeans, can still cause prejudice in churches in the West.

The Fact of Common Pastoral Needs

Another important principle to note at the outset is that basic pastoral needs are the same in a multiethnic congregation as they would be in any other group of people. While the focus of this chapter is to highlight some of the specifics relating to pastoring in a multiethnic context, all the themes of this book apply just as much in that context as they would in any other. The normal spread of pastoral issues arise in a multiethnic congregation. Birth, marriage, death, issues of faith, and so on are no respecter of race or ethnicity.

> Look again and you will see
> familiar people . . .
> mothers and fathers,
> sisters and brothers,
> grandparents.
> Listen and you will hear
> familiar sounds . . .
> talking, crying, laughing.
> Understand and you will know
> the stuff of which your dreams are made . . .
> love and laughter, safety and security,
> peace and prosperity . . .
> Are their dreams too.[6]

The Requirement for All to be Willing to Change

A further fundamental principle to note is that when someone new joins a group, the whole group should change, not just the newcomer. Helen Richmond helpfully points out that hospitality in the church context can lead a congregation to think that it is the host while newcomers are the guests. This attitude is based on an understanding that it is our church. However, if we remember that it is God's church, not ours, then those who come move from being guests to new members and therefore changes need to be made so as to accommodate these new members.[7]

---

6. From the poem "Call No One Stranger" by Sr. Patricia Mulhall. Used with permission. This poem was published the Catholic Agency for Overseas Development (CAFOD), and reproduced in Rebekah Chevalier, *On Frequent Journeys*, 119.

7. Richmond, quoted in Stephens, "Developing a Multi-Ethnic Congregation," 157–58.

This principle is especially important to remember in congregations that are located in countries from which hundreds of missionaries travelled to Africa, Asia, and Latin America during the great colonial missionary expansion of the eighteenth and nineteenth centuries. During that period, it was generally assumed that European culture was superior to the culture of the countries they travelled to, and, furthermore, it was assumed that true Christianity could only be expressed fully through European culture. As Murray summarizes, "The church wrongly assumed that people could be a true Christian only if they accepted European values and European ways of worship."[8] I would contend that this notion remains deeply embedded in the general mindset of many congregations in the Western world. Furthermore, when those same congregations receive people from countries which were once called "the mission field," this assumption could cause us to try to change the culture of those whom we receive. So, when those whom God sends to us are different to us, we have a decision to make: either we can try to mold them to be just like us or we can accept God's gift and allow it to change us. In my experience, when congregations pray for new people to come, they are usually subconsciously praying for more people just like themselves. But often, God answers that prayer by sending people who are different and so there is a decision to make.

This can also happen the other way round. People can arrive from around the world whose Christian faith and practice have been shaped by European culture. But it is the European culture of perhaps a century ago. The culture here has now changed and so they can be very surprised when they find that the culture of the church to which they have come seems different. In fact, offense and uncertainty can be caused when practices that they grew up understanding were fundamental to Christianity are not practiced in the church here because in fact those practices were more to do with nineteenth-century European cultural norms.

There is a West African proverb that states, "The person who has not visited another village will think only his mother's cooking is sweet."[9] Most of us tend to assume that our culture is normal and natural while many of us assume that our culture is superior. But, in truth, all cultures can learn from each other. Time after time, I still sometimes get frustrated on the phone when I call someone with just a quick message, but we

---

8. Murray, *Being Black in Britain*, 17.
9. See Schachtel et al., *Changing Lanes, Crossing Cultures*, 71.

spend much of the time inquiring about each other's well-being, how our families are, and so on. But I am wrong. One of the best-known cultural frustrations is with regard to attitude to time, yet who are we to say that it is not more important to stop and give time to the person that we meet on the way than it is to arrive on time for the meeting.[10] As Schachtel, Lim, and Wilson note,

> We need to be learning continuously. We don't have all the answers, or the only, or best, approaches to worship, prayer, Bible study or hospitality. This book's authors have learnt, and continue to learn, so much from the "strangers" with whom God has brought them into contact, including lessons about patience, respect for the elderly, perseverance, strong families and much more.[11]

The Importance of Commitment to the Process

Pastoral work in a multiethnic context takes effort. Indeed, multiethnic church itself takes effort. Even basic communication can be difficult and that is not just because of language. There is a huge variety of accents among English language speakers around the world. But do not dismiss someone simply because you are unwilling to listen carefully in order to understand what they say. Someone can appear to be shy and hesitant, yet when they are among people of their own culture and language it becomes clear that they are enthusiastic and gifted followers of Jesus with leadership qualities.[12] I have known people whose giftings I would have completely missed had I not subsequently seen them among others from their own country.

When ministering among people for whom English is not their first language, a simple step we can take is to try to learn a word or two of their language. This can open doors and build a little bridge of trust in that it "can send a strong message that you value your friend's culture and language and are willing to be vulnerable as you botch up the pronunciation."[13]

---

10. Schachtel et al., *Changing Lanes, Crossing Cultures*, 93.
11. Schachtel et al., *Changing Lanes, Crossing Cultures*, 99.
12. Schachtel et al., *Changing Lanes, Crossing Cultures*, 99.
13. Schachtel et al., *Changing Lanes, Crossing Cultures*, 99.

But if we ever feel that this all sounds like too much effort, then let us remember two things. First, the adjustment or effort will always be much greater for those who have come than it is for those of us who welcome people from other countries to our church. Secondly, the effort is always worthwhile. It is one of my greatest joys to have had the opportunity to serve in multicultural congregations for most of my ordained ministry. How wonderful to be among people from every continent united in Christ, worshiping together, and learning from each other as we seek to follow our common Lord. Every Sunday I rejoice to see the prophecy of Rev 7:9–10 being fulfilled.[14] As a leader in one Anglican congregation in Dublin that has recently received international newcomers put it,

> There has been the active engagement in worship by our overseas parishioners bringing enthusiasm, colorfulness, spontaneity and a different world view. Their enthusiasm, dedication and commitment to Sunday worship and their very joyful and positive attitude is so refreshing.[15]

Practical Guidelines

Remember, my reflections on pastoral care in a multi-cultural context are based on ministry among people who have recently come from somewhere else to live in Ireland. When such people arrive, they are both strong and weak. Let me explain. First, they are strong because they have taken the initiative to come here. Whatever the reason for the decision, it takes great strength to leave your home place and travel somewhere else with a view to settling there. People who have arrived have demonstrated enough strength to take the initiative to travel to a completely new place. The very fact that they have travelled demonstrates motivation and industriousness. Another strength that is clear to behold in those who have come to churches where I have served is depth of faith. The fact that they have gone looking for a church when they have arrived in a new place usually indicates that Christian faith and church connection is an important part of their lives. This applies even if there is some delay between

---

14. "After this I looked, and there before me was a great multitude that no one could count, from every nation, tribe, people and language, standing before the throne and before the Lamb. They were wearing white robes and were holding palm branches in their hands. And they cried out in a loud voice: 'Salvation belongs to our God, who sits on the throne, and to the Lamb.'"

15. Lodge, "But the Lord," 1:17.

their arrival in Ireland and their coming to church. In fact, in my experience, if there is a delay it can make them even more strongly determined in their church commitment at the point they do connect. I can think of several families and individuals who came to Ireland for work having had a strong church connection in their home country but did not link up with a church when they came here. Yet, some years later they realized that they really wanted to reconnect, and so when they came it made their subsequent connection all the stronger.

Secondly, however, those who have recently arrived from another country are also weak. They are weak because they have arrived in a place where they do not know the culture or perhaps even the language. They do not know how to work the system or even to do many of the basics of daily living. Many will also be in a position of financial weakness. Even if they have found work immediately, relocation and settling in a new country is an expensive business. Their weakness is further compounded because they are now away from their previous support networks of family, friends, and other familiar props of life. After two weeks spent alone in Paurmiana, a rural village in Pakistan but which was not far from the large city of Rawalpindi, Martin Forward movingly writes,

> In Paurmiana, I discovered how remote one can feel from the known and the taken-for-granted. A few miles away in Rawalpindi, there were people who shared my language, class identity, reliance on phone and electricity. In Paurmiana, I often felt vulnerable, at the mercy of others' acts of kindness, not so much out of control as unable to control my life.[16]

This gave him a much deeper understanding of what life felt like for the multiethnic community around his church in inner city Leicester, including one Antiguan woman who told him that the sense he had "of living on a knife-edge and the constant feeling of queasiness in [his] stomach were exactly her experience of daily living."[17] We now proceed to enumerate some of the lessons I have learned through my experience of new members entering the church from elsewhere.

---

16. Forward, "Culture," 251.
17. Forward, "Culture," 251.

They Understand the Church as Family

The cities of the Roman Empire were populated by people who had often travelled from somewhere else. In addition to this, society was very stratified. In this context, the establishment of professional associations (*hetaeria*) became a common feature among craftsmen, artisans, merchants, and shopkeepers. By this means such people derived a shared sense of belonging and provided each other with community and even friendship. Something similar happened in the fledgling Christian church where the common link was devotion to Jesus Christ, which could overcome all other potentially divisive classifications.[18]

I have seen something rather similar happen in congregations where people have gathered who have recently migrated from other parts of the world. The church can end up being their "Irish family," sharing in and supporting one another through the normal joys and sorrows of life while far away from their blood relatives. Something similar is apparent in this quotation from a recent survey of Church of Ireland parishes in Dublin and Glendalough, which have recently received people from other countries: "I think the whole church, and everybody is very warm and well supporting. There's a moral support and they help, it's like an extended family to be honest. Yes, like extended family."[19]

Perhaps the time when this is most apparent is when someone in the congregation suffers bereavement due to the death of a parent or other close relative far away in their country of origin. Quite often I have led a short service of readings and prayers in the home or even at the church on the same day and at the same time as the funeral is taking place in a distant land. Having said that, this is more unusual since the COVID-19 pandemic, because it has become quite common for funeral services to be live streamed and so the people in Ireland usually want to be alone to watch proceedings on the internet. An important annual service in our church is the Sunday morning in November where we read a list of names of loved ones of people in our congregation who have passed away during the previous twelve months. This is often quite meaningful for many in our congregation and also for their surviving family members across the world.

Over the years of pastoring in multiethnic contexts I have been asked to conduct some rites and rituals that are quite unfamiliar to me

18. Graham, *Hope from the Margins*, 35.
19. Lodge, "But the Lord," 2:14.

but are common practice in the home country of the person who has asked me. These include the blessing of a new home or a first car. Quite often I have been asked to invite parents and their newborn baby to the front of the church on the baby's first visit for thanksgiving prayers. This in no way precludes a more formal baptism or dedication service later. It is also not unusual to be asked to lead prayers at parties celebrating a significant birthday or, just recently, I was asked to meet in the church for a service of Holy Communion with someone on the afternoon of their sixty-fifth birthday. My response to these requests is almost always "Why not?" It seems to me that when requested, it is always appropriate to pray on any occasion, be it prayers for blessing or rededication. Having said that, there have been a few occasions where I have been anxious to stress that my prayers are not any more important than those of anyone else, and that the occasion, while important and sincere, is not of major theological significance.

A further consequence of seeing the church congregation as your family means that you may understand going to church on Sunday as much more than just for the service itself. Particularly for an African Christian, arriving for worship at the church can be understood as something similar to arriving at a relative's home to spend the day.[20] In this mindset, coming to church is not a rushed, functional thing but is a gathering for worship, conversation, and sharing food together. In contrast, as my predecessor at Dublin Central Mission points out,

> An Irish Christian will see attendance at worship as something they may want to do or feel obliged to do for a fixed period of time. For many Irish people it is a private act done in the company of others. Such a gulf in perception creates potential dissatisfaction for either group if their expectations are not met.[21]

Speaking of sharing food together, this is a very important component of ministry in a multicultural context. As well as the importance of table fellowship and the opportunity to build relationships, which eating together provides, the sharing of food in a multicultural context has a further benefit in that it enables people to share something of their homeland. I have often had the pleasure of being at bring-and-share lunches in the church or at picnics that are a festival of food from around the world. But it is not only the food itself that is enjoyed on these occasions.

20. Martin, *Ephesian Moment*, 4.
21. Stephens, "Developing a Multi-Ethnic Congregation," 149.

It is also beautiful to see the pride and joy on the faces of people who are sharing the culinary delicacies of their homeland and enjoying watching others partaking in what they have brought. These occasions are a wonderful way to bridge across different cultures and can really help to build bonds of acceptance and understanding within the congregation.

They See the Church as Important

Over the last few centuries churches in Ireland have sent thousands of missionaries across the world (e.g., Africa, Latin America and large parts of Asia) in order to spread the faith. For most of that time our churches were strong and the missionaries' role was to teach the Gospel and establish churches in areas where they had not been before. During this period stories from what was known as the "mission field" were told back at home to encourage Irish Christians to pray for the "missions" and also to fund future missionary endeavors. But now in recent decades, we in Ireland have begun to discover that churches which we had a part in planting are stronger and more vigorous than here in Ireland. David Smith recounts the incongruity of being at a service in Northern Nigeria in 2002 where there were over a thousand people engaged in Spirit-filled worship but at one point a Victorian hymn was sung which made reference to the "heathen faraway." At first it seemed ridiculous and laughable but then he continues "and yet, perhaps sung in modern Africa it does make sense because, from the perspective of those Churches, the heathen are now far away—in London, Birmingham and Glasgow."[22]

A consequence of this is that many, if not most, of the people who come from countries in the global south to churches in Ireland which I have pastored were very often mature and committed Christians. The very fact that they actively looked for a church when they migrated to a new place implies that Christian faith and Church membership are important to them. This is different to other, local, newcomers who might be coming to church because they are seeking faith or beginning to wonder about Christianity. So, when pastoring in a multi-ethnic context it is important to be careful not to underestimate the Christian commitment of a newcomer because it may well be that they have come from a country where the church is strong and that they bring with them committed faith and active discipleship.

22. Smith, *Against the Stream*, 108.

A related fact is that many who come from countries where the church is strong and growing will come with a high view of the power of the pastor. It is important for a pastor in a multi-ethnic context to be very aware of the fact that it is very likely that some of the congregation will have her or him on some sort of a "pedestal." This can manifest itself in many different ways. One consequence is that sometimes people are not inclined to share their trials and difficulties with me but are much more likely to divulge these to our lay pastoral assistant. This makes it even more important for the pastor in a multi-cultural setting to make every effort to come alongside people, to be available and to get to know people in the hope that they will lower their view of the pastor. Having said that, another reason why some people, particularly women, may share more with our lay pastor than with me is because she is female and in many cultures around the world, women will talk and share more openly with other women.

Another consequence is that people who have recently come to Ireland from countries where the church is central in society will often have an overly inflated view of the importance and influence of the pastor, not just in the church but in the wider community. There was a time in Ireland when a church leader could make effective representation with government agencies on behalf of people, but those days are gone. Nevertheless, in a multi-ethnic context there continue to be people in the congregation who will believe that my influence on the immigration process or the housing list or the hospital waiting times counts for something. Hooker and Lamb summarize this from a context of Asian people living in England.

> As a white religious leader he is presumed to have influence. He may be asked to help in trying to get a relation admitted to this country, or to track down a daughter who has run away from home. His equivalent in the societies of the Indian subcontinent would normally have such influence and be expected to use it, but the English clergyman finds such expectations embarrassing, for he knows he cannot fulfill them.[23]

Having said that, it is my experience that when people realize that the minister is not an omnipotent problem-solver it can actually help more than hinder a pastoral relationship. It is much easier to get alongside

---

23. Hooker and Lamb, *Love the Stranger*, 23–24.

people pastorally if they do not have the view that you are much more powerful and influential than they are.

They Experience Home Life as Challenging.

Many of the people among whom I pastor have experienced substantial changes in their home life and family dynamics as a result of moving to Ireland. For example, many nurses and other healthcare workers have come to Ireland in recent decades because they can get visas for working here. Often, they come alone for a year or two, leaving their spouse and children behind until they get settled. So, this creates a period of family separation that is never easy. Then if the family do come, further issues arise. Sometimes spouses are not given work permits and so they can move from being the main provider of the household to being a stay-at-home parent. Even if they are granted a work permit, the qualifications of the spouse may not be recognized in Ireland with the result that someone who was working as an engineer, research scientist, or university lecturer at home can end up working in Ireland as a shop assistant or a hospital porter. Needless to say, this is a huge adjustment and can create tensions of which the pastor must be aware. Another scenario I have seen is when the spouse may travel to another nearby country to find work in his/her profession and so the parents are again separated, which can be difficult.

Another dynamic of home life that can change radically arises from the fact that some families who have come to Ireland have come from countries where it is still common for domestic staff to be employed to help with the household chores. Of course, there is no chance of this in Ireland and then this adjustment is further compounded by the fact that, in general, the family who has moved to Ireland will be away from their extended family group who may have been living close by in the home country. A pastor in this context must be watchful for such stresses and strains in home life.

Issues can also arise in the family due to different models of parenting. For example, there are very different understandings of what is appropriate for disciplining children in Ireland compared to some of the countries from which people have relocated. Also, at school children can notice a difference in the way teachers and other authority figures are treated here compared with the deference and respect that would still be shown in many African and Asian countries. Tensions can then begin to arise in the family as these children gradually begin to see authority figures differently, including their parents.

Some of these dynamics increase with the passage of time as children of migrant families who were born in Ireland or who came to Ireland when they were very young grow up to be teenagers and young adults. They can begin to rebel against cultural expectations which their parents still hold but which are no longer their culture. I have particularly noticed this when the teenage children no longer want to attend a culture- and language-specific Christian fellowship within the church. They have become used to Westernized forms of worship through the medium of English language, and they prefer to wear Western clothes. I have watched teenagers literally roll their eyes when mention is made of attending the language-specific fellowship group that their parents still love to attend. Martin Forward summarizes this when he speaks of the children of the Antiguan lady mentioned above: "They were Britons, but often made [to] feel as if they weren't. Yet they had nothing else to be. Antigua was as remote to them as the moon, not the focus of nostalgic childhood reminiscences."[24]

Another big strain on home life, especially in the early years after arriving in the West, can be finance. People who have moved country for whatever reason and are settling in the new place can often experience significant financial vulnerability. The pastor will want to help in this regard. There may be funds in the church that can be confidentially offered in cases of need, and also the pastor can have a role in pointing people towards relevant charitable organizations that may be able to assist. It is of course good if the pastor can help in this way, but I would also offer a few words of warning. The key job of a pastor is to offer pastoral support. We may be able to help but we must exercise discretion if we are not to become seen simply as problem solvers. There have been times when I have become uneasy when I have begun to sense that a member of the congregation seems to see me as the first port of call for any financial challenge. This has not happened very often, but I simply offer it as a word of caution that the pastor in a multicultural setting must be wise in separating financial help from pastoral support. Hooker and Lamb write perceptively on this danger of the pastor being seen primarily as a problem solver who can access financial and other supports:

---

24. Forward, "Culture," 251.

If he is insecure and uncertain of what he is about he can very easily let this role take him over.... He will simply be colluding with the expectations of others, making no demands of them, provoking no questions from them—or for himself. He will simply be encouraging people to be dependent on him for this area of need. In other words, while problem-solving can and should be an element in his ministry he needs to keep it under control and in proportion.[25]

A further danger for the pastor who becomes primarily perceived as a helper or a problem solver is that it can increase the power gap between the pastor and those whom she or he is trying to get alongside. On his return to England after living in the small village in Pakistan where he had been completely powerless and had felt so insecure, Martin Forward asks, "How, then, do churches and persons give to people of different cultures, religions and racial groups a sense of power within society?"[26] His conclusion was that in fact churches could easily end up doing the opposite by helping people in a condescending way, which increases dependence rather than reducing it.

The Pastor's Responsibilities

If pastoring means getting alongside people, then pastoring in a multicultural context means that the pastor should seek to develop a basic understanding of the geography of our world. For me, this means not listening to local news only but also listening to world news daily. I have found both BBC World Service and Al Jazeera English language version invaluable in keeping me up-to-date with elections, tragedies, natural disasters, and other significant events in countries around the world. Of course, we cannot know everything, but it can be very helpful in a pastoral relationship if the pastor is in a position to make sensible comments or ask informed questions about the situation in the home country of the person they are talking to. It is also a good discipline, after meeting someone about whose home country you know very little, to do some research and learn a little about that country before the next time you meet. Asking questions can also build bridges. If you have very little familiarity

---

25. Hooker and Lamb, *Love the Stranger*, 49.
26. Forward, "Culture," 251.

with the home country of someone you have just met, then it is acceptable to say that and to ask them to tell you a little about their homeland.

However, one word of warning about questions. For the first few years after people began arriving from countries around the world into churches that I led, my opening question on meeting someone was usually "Where are you from?" This is the wrong question. They may have lived in Ireland for years, or they may have come from another European country or they may be wary of announcing where they are from until they know who I am and where I stand on certain issues.[27] So now when I meet someone who has come to the church for the first time my opening questions will be something like "Are you visiting in Dublin or do you live here?" "Have you lived in Ireland for long?" "Where did you live before you came to this country?"

It is also important not to generalize. Africa is not a country any more than Europe is a country. So, do not assume you know more than you actually do about someone's country of origin. The key is to be honest and transparent. And remember, it is okay to make mistakes if you make them graciously. In fact, getting it wrong can even help to develop the relationship because it can create "a moment when someone perceived to have power, status or ability was suddenly and unexpectedly brought down to the normal level of humanity"[28] In a multicultural setting everyone will make mistakes, but they need not create barriers, in fact they can lower them. As Schachtel, Lim, and Wilson comment, "When your friends begin to tell you about a *faux pas* you have made, it could well be a good sign—they like and trust you enough to tell you."[29]

Another important point in navigating geography is to not assume that all the people of one nation or region in your church will necessarily get along. As already mentioned above, there may be ethnic, political, or other tensions within that country, with people from both "sides" represented in one congregation. Having said that, it is more likely that people of one country or language group will gather together in groups. This is of course natural. We tend to drift towards those who are like us, with whom we are most comfortable, and with whom we can chat easily and freely. Furthermore, it is a good thing when the church can provide a comfortable space for people to relax together. "In this setting the church

---

27. One infamous example of this led to the resignation of the lady-in-waiting of the late Queen Elizabeth II in England. See Coughlan, "Lady Susan Hussey Quits."

28. Hooker and Lamb, *Love the Stranger*, 52.

29. Schachtel et al., *Changing Lanes, Crossing Cultures*, 100.

can become a place of refuge from racism and a community center to help the group in their attempt to settle in a new land."[30]

But the pastor in a multicultural setting must also ensure that the church does not end up as a collection of monocultural groups. "Left to themselves friendships and fellowships across cultures do not just happen."[31] So we need to do some intentional mixing:

> Becoming multiracial is generally the result of hard work by the leaders and laity of integrated congregations. In those few instances where a church is fortunate enough to develop a racially integrated congregation with little work, effort is still needed for that church to maintain its racial mix.[32]

While the pastor can do some of this work, by thinking carefully about the cultural mix of any small groups or other gatherings that are being set up, members of the congregation can also play a part. So, for example, if after church someone observes a group that seems to be of just one culture it can be helpful to intentionally drift into that group and become part of the conversation.[33]

This intentional mixing is also important at an organizational level. The church leader must work hard to ensure diverse representation on the church leadership committees, in the worship group, among the lay preachers, and the team of Sunday school teachers and others playing a leadership role. The church where I am currently based in Dublin is a wonderful multicultural mix of people at every level of its organization with no nationality or ethnicity dominating. But this did not happen automatically—it was carefully built by my predecessors and I do all I can to maintain it. The result is that the church can offer a model to the nation that multicultural communities can work and are a blessing to everyone.

A Closing Thought

Having begun this chapter with a reminder of the fundamental equality of all people, let me finish with a reminder that all human beings are not the same:

---

30. Stephens, "Developing a Multi-Ethnic Congregation," 152.
31. Schachtel et al., *Changing Lanes, Crossing Cultures*, 117.
32. Yancey, *One Body, One Spirit*, 117.
33. Schachtel et al., *Changing Lanes, Crossing Cultures*, 118.

> The basis of our rhetoric against exclusion of particular groups of human beings is a proclaimed belief in human equality. In fact, however, we do not believe that human beings in general are equal: not in height, weight, age, strength, speed, health, beauty, moral virtue, intelligence, wealth, power or in any other respect. In proclaiming the equality of human beings, neither do we believe that human beings should be treated equally: instead we think that those who are thirsty should be given water, rather than those who have just drunk, that those who are sick should receive medical care, rather those who are healthy, that those who are unable to feed themselves should be fed by others, rather than those who are capable of feeding themselves independently, and so on. What we mean by the claim that all human beings are equal, then, is not that they are all equal or that they should all be treated equally, but that we should not base unequal treatment on irrelevant characteristics of persons. Thus, for example, the electorate in a democracy should be defined according to those capable of voting, rather than those of a particular gender, judges should reach decisions based on the merits of a case, rather than on the relative privilege of the contesting parties, and academic examiners should decide grades according to the quality of work assessed, rather than on the basis of their personal relationship with students.[34]

Pastoral care in a multicultural setting is not about working to create uniformity in the church but rather about honoring, nurturing and celebrating diversity within the united body of Christ as expressed in a local congregation. As Christians, we must never forget that it is God who created the diversity among us—it seems to be God's plan that we are diverse and different. As a prayer published by the Methodist Church in Britain puts it,

> Creator God, in the beginning, when all was chaos and color had yet to be born, you painted across the blank canvas with your brush strokes of love. From your palette, grace, color, diversity and passion blended together and a universe of contrast, beauty and drama was created.[35]

In the famous story of the tower of Babel, we read that in ancient history people gathered and said to themselves, "Come, let us build ourselves a city, with a tower that reaches to the heavens, so that we may make

---

34. Clough, "Problem of Human Equality," 83.
35. Youngson and Gnanapragasam, *Radical Hope, Transforming Grace*.

a name for ourselves" (Gen 11:4). The end result of this tower-building was diversity and movement. We are told that "the Lord scattered them from there over all the earth" (Gen 11:8) And not only were people physically scattered, but they were separated by language as well. Then, in the New Testament, we see that on the day of Pentecost many people from around the world received the blessing of God. Again, we see a picture of a very diverse group of people who travelled to Jerusalem from all over the known world speaking many different types of languages. Yet God, by his Spirit through the apostles, touched each one of them.

Sometimes sermons are preached in which Pentecost is described as a reversal of the tower of Babel. The sermon goes that at Babel people were divided and separated because of their language but now at Pentecost all of that is undone. But is Pentecost the reversal of Babel? It was an American Methodist minister in Denmark who helped me think of it differently. If we look carefully at what happened in Pentecost, what we see is that redemption came to the diversity. We see people experiencing and receiving the redemptive grace of God in Christ where they were and whoever they were. At Pentecost all the people were not made the same and were not all made to speak the same language or to have the same culture. Rather, what happened at Pentecost was that people speaking different languages and from different cultures and different ethnicities all received the same touch of God by his Spirit.[36]

So, at the birth of the church at Pentecost it seems that it was not God's intention to remove diversity from the world or to make everybody the same but rather to meet people where they were and to offer his grace, love, and forgiveness in the context of every language and every nation. I, for one, rejoice in this. To finish, let me share the prayer of David Anderson, the African American pastor of a multicultural congregation in the United States:

> My prayer is that the church, whether Anglo, African, or Afghan, would refuse to be colorblind. Why would we ever want to dull a sense that we've been given by our creator? We don't need colorblind stages, staffs, and structures. We need churches who know how to see beauty and celebrate diversity. Who among us would ever desire to walk through a garden to behold only one color and one kind of flower?[37]

---

36. The idea comes from an unpublished sermon delivered by Mark Lewis at the European Methodist Council meeting in Haslev, Denmark on Sept. 8, 2018.

37. Anderson, *Multicultural Ministry*, 119.

14

The Role of Mentoring in Pastoral Development

Christina Baxter

This chapter aims to make clear the value of mentoring through different stages of the Christian life, and to explore how it may be done well, by developing some strategies to avoid any dangers as we build such a working relationship. Finally, it focuses on the work of the Holy Spirit in both the mentor and mentee as they serve the Lord maturely and well in their different roles.

What is Mentoring?

The term "mentoring" is used in a number of ways, so an initial definition is important. According to Parsloe and Leedham, "At their heart coaching and mentoring are simply conversations. But not just any conversations; they are conversations in which skillful use of human interaction supports and catalyzes change, growth, and development."[1] Such conversations may be occasional and informal, or part of a deliberate professional relationship with regular meetings between mentor and mentee. They are usually one-on-one conversations. Most people will be able to identify such conversations in their lives, and I am among them.

---

1. Parsloe and Leedham, *Coaching and Mentoring*, 2.

Receiving Mentoring

I am indebted to a number of mentors, who without exception intervened without asking my explicit permission (though it was always tacitly given). These figures did not suggest a contract to offer mentoring, but they were on the scene when I needed it. It began with a Sunday school supervisor who trained me to capture the attention of the children. "Wear bright colors," she urged us, "Children love bright colors!"—there beginning my lifelong love of pink jackets. She emphasized the importance of praying for our charges, giving rise to a habit of intercession. My history teacher in secondary school was also a hugely significant role model. She emphasized "having the courage of your convictions," manifesting that herself and demonstrating its importance to personal integrity. It reinforced a lesson from the Bible verses that formed my vocational call:

> Only be strong and very courageous, being careful to act in accordance with all the law that my servant Moses commanded you.... This book of the law shall not depart out of your mouth; you shall meditate on it day and night; so that you may be careful to act in accordance with all that is written in it.... Do not be frightened or dismayed, for the Lord your God is with you wherever you go. (Josh 1:7-9)[2]

Her example sealed into my heart a conviction that I needed to speak plainly, being ready to give account of my faith or offer challenging or unwelcome words (albeit graciously) where necessary.

Later, the curate of my parish church gave me a lot of time as I grappled with the complexity of Scripture both at advanced level and university. Once he travelled to Durham to advise how to approach Philosophy of Religion lest my faith be overturned. His influential example endures to this day.

Eventually, while I was teaching in a sixth form college, the local vicar encouraged me to become a reader,[3] challenging me continually to spread "the boundaries of my tent" (Isa 54:2), by preaching across the diocese, while also contributing to deanery and diocesan ventures. He saw potential I did not recognize in myself. That same skill of opening a world of possibilities to me was a key feature of the professional supervision I subsequently had from the Principal of St. John's College

---

2. Unless otherwise indicated, all Scripture is taken from the NRSV.

3. An Anglican lay ministry involving preaching and the leading of liturgical worship.

Nottingham—who sent me to Malaysia to teach one summer vacation. Later, he guided and supported me into General Synod, the Archbishops' Council and the Anglican Consultative Council. With him, mentoring was hugely interrogative—there were many questions and challenges, and it sometimes involved robust debate. It was also at points seriously hilarious. Through this relationship I gained more perspective, widened my circle of contacts, and was afforded time to reflect in dialogue.

Mentoring became intentional when I asked someone to mentor me in areas where I was inexperienced as a new principal of a theological college. Even in retirement I am glad to seek advice. Towards the end of life, I know I will need the example and support of those who have gone before me into old age and who are approaching their own death, though most of that may come from my memories of those who have aged and died well.

I have demonstrated from my own case that mentoring involves modelling life habits that make for a reliable and effective ministry as a preacher, teacher, youth worker, or any other Christian ministry. But, of course, there are also things to learn intellectually, skills to hone, and attitudes to espouse that together contribute to inhabiting well the roles, voluntary or professional, to which we aspire.

Many others taught me the wondrous gift mentoring can be, sharing the kind of wisdom that is not readily gained from books, as they demonstrated silently how to live out their values. Like medieval apprenticeships, mentoring can teach, not only technical understanding but also practical skills and appropriate attitudes. Conversations between mentor and mentee enable growth in all three areas. The mentee can explore what it means to be an adult who is becoming a "something"—whether that be a teacher, banker, manager, caterer, or minister. The mentee learns the reasons for routine skills, or how to respond to the trickier situations of life in a way that enables flourishing, not only for the young mentee but for all those who surround her in family life, in the workplace, or in a voluntary organization.

Mentoring—Part of a Family of Assistance

It is important to acknowledge that there are a number of ways in which a person may be supported to maturity and flourishing in their Christian life and ministry. These different ways are not necessarily mutually exclusive. We might think of it as a series of overlapping circles. Some practice or write about "discipling" recent converts,[4] others offer soul friendship,[5] or spiritual direction,[6] all of which aim to help disciples live their pilgrimage wholly open to God. Others refer to pastoring that enables the welfare of others—so can include practical as well as moral support.[7] Mentoring is usually focused on role or vocation, aiming to enable the client to be proficient.[8] Very similar, "coaching is unlocking people's potential to maximize their own performance."[9] Counselling is chiefly therapeutic.[10] All of these can help a person become "mature in Christ" (Col 1: 28–29). While there are some skills and gifts that are specific to each of these practices, it does not seem possible or perhaps even desirable to draw hard and fast distinctions between them, especially as differing traditions use terms in varying ways. There are overlapping bodies of literature, with some unique ways of proceeding. For some methods, such as counselling, there is a formal accreditation system to ensure that practitioners are qualified and accountable to others through supervision.[11] This ensures vulnerable people receive proper professional advice. It is within what we might think of as a Venn diagram of circles of competencies relating to these different ways of encouraging others that we may place mentoring. Clutterbuck argues wisely that there is need for multiple mentors in a lifetime, both formal and informal.[12]

Mentoring in the Workplace

Much literature is aimed at people who are engaged in mentoring in the workplace.[13] There is extensive discussion as to whether the line manager of someone can also be their mentor, or whether it is better to arrange for people to have mentors to whom they do not directly report. The

4. See Robinson, *Mentor for Life*.
5. Leech, *Soul Friend*.
6. Guenther, *Holy Listening*.
7. Campbell, "Pastoral Care," 188–90.
8. Clutterbuck, *Everyone Needs a Mentor*.
9. Whitmore, *Coaching for Performance*, 13.
10. See Jacobs, *Counselling*, 54–56.
11. For example, the British Association for Counselling and Psychotherapy (BCAP) or the American Psychotherapy Association.
12. Clutterbuck, *Everyone Needs a Mentor*, 6.
13. For example, see Parsloe and Leedham, *Coaching and Mentoring*.

latter seems to be favored, though it is clear that there can be conflicts when line manager and mentor offer contrary advice. In order to present standard features, I rely on the work of Linda Phillips-Jones, the results of whose research is published online.[14] Her work focuses chiefly on long term workplace mentoring relationships and includes suggested tools for mentoring. She identifies "Mentee-Specific Skills" as learning quickly, showing initiative, being capable of following through, and managing the relationship with the mentor. Some "Shared Core Skills" to be found in mentor and mentee alike are listening actively, building trust, encouraging, and finally, identifying goals and current reality. "Mentor-Specific Skills" were found to be instructing/developing capabilities, inspiring, providing corrective feedback, managing risks, and opening doors. She elaborates on each of these.[15]

Because this is a highly developed secular field, with good research published to help mentors in a range of professions, I confine myself in this chapter to a discussion of mentoring that may take place in Christian and chiefly church contexts. We have much to learn from other workplaces. But in the church, much mentoring does not involve employer/employee relationships, since so much is voluntary. There are, of course, some exceptions.

Mentoring in a Christian Context

It is important to realize that the *purpose* of mentoring controls its nature. In all three types of mentoring, which I identify below, we may find a dialectic between syllabus-based learning (usually in a group) and person-directed learning where individual one-to-one accompaniment is the most effective learning method.

I want to suggest there are three kinds of Christian mentoring, differentiated by their purpose. First, *mentoring for maturity*, which is the way people who become disciples by conversion from pagan, other faith, or non-Christian backgrounds, come to understand what discipleship ultimately involves. Such learning is only partly intellectual. It may be accomplished through group learning, often based on a syllabus, but it inevitably involves person-centered learning that is harder to achieve through group work in syllabus-dominated settings and requires either

---

14. Phillips-Jones, *Mentee's Guide*.
15. Phillips-Jones, *Mentees Guide*, 28.

a very small group or one-on-one attention. In these more person-centered contexts, mentoring will come to the fore. For many, coming to faith will involve a major shift in worldview, which may be best learned in a residential Christian community or in "temporary communities" such as those created at Christian conferences; or, for a few, it may be by being welcomed into the home life of a Christian family who make room for an "adoption," or a lodger, or a student. Being Christian cannot be easily learned in formal or informal Sunday worship only. We should probably think of learning to be a Christian as being mentored by a whole church community.

Context is everything. One of the dawning realizations for the contemporary church is that the methods employed in previous generations are no longer effective since many people are several generations away from any kind of Christian faith, though not, Grace Davie argues, from an interest in spirituality.[16] The church can no longer expect people to be lifelong Christians because their parents have brought them up in the faith. And when the gospel is offered to them through process evangelism programs such as Alpha, the church cannot assume that people who decide to follow Jesus know how to do this. It is a serious mistake to "leave to chance" their deepening discipleship. For this reason, many schemes are available to help them to understand what this will mean for them. One such program, "Holy Habits" produced by the Bible Reading Fellowship, suggests that the whole church could benefit from in-depth teaching, which is not purely intellectual, about the basic themes of discipleship.[17]

We should be cautious in assuming that all mentoring can be done in groups. At points this may be necessary because there are not enough people to mentor converts one-on-one. However, this approach lacks an emphasis on self-directed learning that characterizes most mentoring, omits the personal tailoring of learning that takes account of previous lifestyles, and may preclude recognition of potential "door opening," which is also part of the purpose of mentoring.

Secondly, there will be *mentoring for leadership*—most of this will be leading small groups or other churchly or Christian initiatives, but there will be important lessons to learn in the small scale for larger leadership responsibilities later. While there is certainly a syllabus of learning about

---

16. Davie, *Religion in Britain*, 198. "Religious life . . . is not so much disappearing as mutating, for the sacred undoubtedly persists . . . but in forms that may be very different from those which have gone before."

17. See Holy Habits, "Story"; cf. Robinson, *Mentor for Life*.

leadership, there will be much that needs to take account of a person's context and transferable skills that is best achieved through one-on-one mentoring. Characteristic of this stage is that people engaging in this kind of leadership are working within a collaborative leadership group under formal or informal supervision. This is important for them as they begin this journey as a mature Christian. It assures them that they have others to whom they may refer when they encounter, as they surely will, difficult situations where their prior learning, experience, and skills offer few pointers to the way ahead. But it is also important to those to whom they offer leadership. The "led" need to know that they may refer to senior people if the new leader is struggling, misguided, or abusive. When it is going smoothly, it assures them that even when approaches in the group seem unusual, they can be sure that this has been considered by more than their one inexperienced group leader. Mentoring in this area, even more than mentoring for maturity, needs to give significant attention to the context in which the person is leading. We could helpfully adopt the model that Peterson offers in *Working the Angles: The Shape of Pastoral Integrity*.

He suggests that we need to pay attention to a triangle: (a) the context of the ministry—the community of faith; (b) the person who is learning the task, i.e., the mentee—their background, training, and experience; and (c) the mentor—their background, training, and experience, most especially whether they are prayerful, reading the Bible and offering spiritual counsel to individuals.

Finally, I want to suggest that there can also be *mentoring for strategic oversight leadership*, which is offered to those who are wholly responsible for a local church. Such responsibility may encompass more than one congregation, alongside some other groups such as Scouts who also have allegiances outside the church. Often it encompasses some other charitable activities, as well as relationships with those outside the Christian community. It may also be mentoring for those whose oversight extends far wider, such as a bishop or Methodist circuit superintendent minister, or district chair, or Baptist regional team leaders. Occasionally, it may be mentoring a leader of a parachurch group, which may be operating as a charity. Here, the burden of learning may be best done in a mentoring relationship, although some seminar-type learning as well as book, video, or online learning can make a significant contribution if well directed.

As a Christian passes through these three stages—maturity, leadership, strategic oversight—the emphasis falls increasingly on to the mentee's shoulders to identify areas where they realize they need to learn more. Mentoring must always keep the purpose of the mentee's role in view, so it is crucial to affirm here that part of the role of strategic leadership is to mentor others. Only so can the whole Christian community/ church operate well, collegially, and collaboratively. Strategic leadership must be shared with those who are learning these skills, so that there is some opportunity for others to be ready for succession in due course. Strategic leadership should include opportunities to hone an understanding of mentoring, to develop skills to enable mentoring, and to learn attitudes that make their generous gifts of wisdom and time warmly welcomed by those they mentor. As always in the Christian faith, grace is key.

Fairness in the Sphere of Mentoring

One of the matters discussed in the secular literature is the question of egalitarianism with which Christians must be concerned because of their belief that God created all human persons and, in his providence, loves them all equally. From this flows Jesus' injunction to love all our neighbors. In a secular company it is understandable that some employees may think it is unjust if mentoring is offered to some people who may therefore subsequently have an advantage in preferment while others are excluded from mentoring on the basis that a line manager or the human resources department do not regard them as having sufficient potential. Such judgments are hard to defend if the "usual suspects" are sidelined and predominantly white males are chosen.[18]

Fairer selection procedures are beginning to influence the Church of England, which is creating "pathways" for groups not normally found in ordained ministry to access opportunities to offer themselves as candidates. It also now has a system that prepares some ordained ministers for larger responsibilities. Criticized by some, there is much to be said for ensuring that serious preparations are made for and by individuals who are to assume public and widely responsible positions. But there are hazards if the learning is not holistic, encompassing the head, hands, and heart of which we wrote above.

As far as what I have called "mentoring for maturity" is concerned, there is no reason not to make this universally available, indeed rather the opposite. A key feature of some churches still operating in "Christendom

---

18. See Clutterbuck, *Everyone Needs a Mentor.*

mode," has been that not only do they not have regular opportunities for people to explore the Christian faith so that they may decide whether they want to follow Jesus, but many of these churches do not offer any kind of follow up to allow adults or young people who have been baptized and come to faith to learn how to be Christians. Process evangelism provides material that enables people to have engagement that leads to faith, and sometimes continues beyond it, but unless the church takes the second stage of faith development seriously, it is falling down on its duty to fulfil Jesus' command to "make disciples" (Matt 28:19–20) whom we now recognize need to be more than just converts. While it is properly the concern of the church to ensure that such opportunities are appropriate to the age and capabilities of the participants, mentoring for maturity *for everyone* is essential. And since growing in grace (2 Pet 3:18) is a lifetime activity, it is important that all Christians are given regular chance to develop "holy habits."

Most persons who receive a stipend for the work they do will have oversight. In Christian contexts, it may be less important than in secular ones whether a person is in receipt of payment for the role they do, since whether one is ministering in an episcopal or congregational church, line management will be very unlike that found in regular secular employment, which is regulated by national laws. In an episcopal church, the bishop is not the employer of the clergy, though there are mutual responsibilities. And in the congregational model, while the congregation or its representative deacons meeting may in some ways act like an employer, both the faith context and the plural nature of the supervisory group make it more complex.

Universal access has to be balanced against the theology of gifting when it comes to mentoring for leadership or strategic oversight. The New Testament makes much of this while also making clear that different giftings are not to be considered as privileges or distinctions but under the *one* banner of serving.[19] My capacity to make marmalade or cakes for a church event is not to be seen as in competition with another person's capacity to bring people to faith. And since there is usually no question of financial reward or preferment, there can be no question that in selecting some to be trained to be youth leaders, charity workers, and/or small group leaders, the church is favoring anyone. Rather the church is helping each person to fulfil their God-given natural potential as well

---

19. See 1 Cor 12:1–11.

as to fulfil their supernatural gifting as they receive the Holy Spirit. For this reason, I do not think we can say that it is anti-egalitarian to provide some (but not all) mentoring for leadership or for strategic oversight. But since the church can easily fall into the trap of acting or speaking as if some roles are more important than others, we need to ensure that both teaching and practice honor all equally as members of Christ's body, the church. This is an ongoing challenge.

Transitioning from Mentee to Mentor

At some point in my career, I realized that the mentoring role was now expected of me. Gradually I moved from feeling, as a very young teacher, that I was on the wrong side of the teacher's desk and should be sitting alongside the sixth-formers whose education was now entrusted to me! From this "imposter syndrome," years of experience brought me to a recognition that I was in the right place. Decades later, others recognized in me what I did not know of myself: that I now had learning, skills, and attitudes—that they called maturity or wisdom—that I could share with others who were coming after me. So, my chief role was no longer to preach, conduct worship, chair meetings, or strategize but to create opportunities for others while I stood alongside or behind them preparing, encouraging, and giving feedback so they could grow their readiness for all that lay ahead in a lifetime of mission and ministry. My task was to spot potential, to see where others had skills and gifts beyond my own, and name that to them. Coaching, correcting, giving chances to fail were all significant gifts to those who sought me out as mentor even when we did not use that term to describe it.

Mentoring requires that we have a holistic appreciation of the nature of any work or profession, but especially in the church context. It is not only about learning what to do, or practicing skills, but allowing that to shape one's internal life. Perhaps it is impossible to prevent it changing one's ways of looking at things. After a few months teaching in a sixth form college, I was no longer *acting* as a teacher, but I had *become* a teacher—and others recognized the change. Of course, in the case of church life, we want people's ministry to *flow out of who they are*, as disjunction between being and doing leads to hypocrisy, against which Jesus himself warns us (Luke 11:42–44). Mentoring is perhaps most valuable as we negotiate the delicate transitions that we need to make as we move into new areas of mission and ministry. Often that is personally costly.

So an important task for me has been to help others carry the internal costs of external ministry and management by guiding them: (a) to biblical passages on which to reflect; (b) to the lives of the saints who have gone before and developed many differing styles of response to challenges; and (c) by being willing to share personal stories of how the Lord has taught me to manage similar challenges where appropriate—such examples not always being "success stories." Beyond that it has been possible to direct mentees to: (d) relevant secular literature; and (e) to solid theological discourses to give a wider perspective on how to approach matters with a Christian perspective.

Generous gifts of time need to be matched with generous sharing of experience. I came to realize that with those I mentor, I do not have the right to undue privacy. It is tough to "unlearn" lessons about boundaries and humility that guide us not to share too much, but it seems that with mentees it is important to be willing to share the deep costs of discipleship and ministry in a way that allows them to see how the grace of God is sufficient to sustain in the bleakest times.[20] It has also been important to acknowledge where I cannot help them, as it is beyond my competence or outside my experience. Fortunately, it has sometimes been possible to direct them to others who are competent to talk issues through with them constructively. Opening doors to a network of other people able to advise is a significant mentoring gift.

Mentoring Volunteers

There is one other point to keep in mind: in Christian contexts many will be volunteers, some may even be found in the third group—the strategic oversight leaders. Mentoring volunteers will vary greatly according to the formality or informality of their relationship to the organization. For instance, in the college where I was principal, when people volunteered to assist with our charitable work, there was a written agreement of how this was to be done, some indication of their expected involvement with the college (purpose of work and likely weekly time offered), and the institution's expectations and responsibilities as well as clarity concerning whom they should report and to whom they were answerable. But church

---

20. See 2 Cor 12:9.

membership rarely knows of such arrangements, which is why bullying and inappropriate use of power can occur so easily—"fogginess" as to the exact arrangements is an open invitation to ignorant, irregular, or even abusive behavior. Indeed, the Church of England is currently considering some kind of code of conduct for lay people that would match that already provided for clergy, so that everyone can be clear about what may be expected.

Volunteers are exactly that; they usually cannot be penalized for irregular attendance; they cannot be held to account easily, except where they break national laws, are office holders governed by ecclesiastical (canon) law, or regulated by codes of conduct. They cannot be forced to train for their roles, though safeguarding policies have changed the culture in that regard, as has the expectation that only those who have been trained as readers or lay preachers can be licensed to preach. This does not usually present a significant problem, as most Christians want to do the very best they can in Christian service and welcome help to achieve that. But it is naive to assume that this is the case for everyone.

What Might We Expect in Meeting With Our Mentor/Mentee?

Whether this is a professional development meeting or a voluntary session, there are guidelines that it would be helpful to follow.

First, the arrangement needs to begin well. This will mean that we are clear about what expectations each person has, and that this is to be mentoring. A suitable time and place to meet should be agreed, as well as the frequency and length of each meeting. It is important that the mentor makes clear to the mentee how they themselves are working/volunteering with appropriate supervision or accountability. This needs to be explained so that the mentee understands that their case may be discussed but name and circumstances will be kept confidential. Mentees need to know that there will be a regular review in which a frank discussion can occur as to whether mentoring meetings are constructive. Perhaps the best way to initiate that is to write a brief note annually (or at another agreed interval) to the mentee to indicate that it is good to review arrangements from time to time and to ask them to consider before their next meeting how helpful the past number of meetings have been, and how they could have been better. The mentor will also prepare some reflections. This forms the first part of the next encounter, and new plans can be laid as necessary. As with spiritual direction, it is important that it is entirely clear that this arrangement can be brought to a courteous conclusion by either side if it seems to be counterproductive in any way.

Secondly, it will be helpful initially to come to understand one another—thus the mentor may want to share something of their background and relevant experience so the mentee knows to whom they are talking. Similarly, the mentee may share something of their context, their life journey, or training, so that the mentor can assess at what level to conduct discussions. Then they may wish to discuss how long there is to be mentee-led agendas, so the mentee comes having prepared what they wish to raise with sketched-out background information. Person-centered or self-directed learning occurs when the mentee identifies challenges or areas of ignorance and seeks help. This requires of the mentor capacity to respond unprepared; often the way forward is to regard the mentee's agenda as an opportunity to work through the problem together. The mentor does not provide answers but guides the mentee as they create some ways forward.

As the meetings progress, the mentor may discern that there are areas that are "known unknowns"—that is, the mentor recognizes that the mentee does not seem aware of some knowledge, skills, or attitudes that could help them in their progress. Perhaps they have not yet had sufficient experience to assess hidden risks that need to be identified. So, from time to time, there may be an agenda to be explored that is offered by the mentor who can show how this may enlighten the challenges or perplexities that the mentee is experiencing.

Always there will be very attentive mutual listening and deep and reflective questioning to ensure that the full picture has been disclosed and understood by both parties. Then there will be the kind of discussion that respects the unique responsibilities that the mentee has (they will be doing the job, leading the group, talking to an individual, planning a conference) so the mentor assists by clarifying, advising possible ways forward, exploring what may be feasible for the mentee to achieve, and encouraging them to make their own decisions in the light of all that they now recognize.

At their next meeting, some feedback may be helpful, and the mentor will be uniquely placed to offer some informal assessment—helping those who are self-deprecating to recognize their good achievements and moderating the over-confidence of those prone to boasting or self-congratulation. Their wide experience should enable them to offer balanced praise or gently to point out weaknesses.

Some mentees may wish to make notes during a session or soon afterwards, and this should be encouraged in those who find it helpful. Mentors should make clear whether they will take notes while they talk or afterwards and how they ensure that they are kept confidential and retained according to best practice in relation to data protection. Some find they can better analyze with paper and pen or remind themselves what was talked about perhaps a month or two ago if they take notes.

When Things Go Wrong

Recently there have been a number of high-profile cases where those in positions of responsibility have been subject to serious allegations of inappropriate behavior in relation to those they have been mentoring.[21] We must address this thorny problem and suggest some solutions. First, those who offer mentoring should be self-aware. We must recognize that every person, however long or distinguished their life of discipleship, has weaknesses, such as a need to be affirmed or valued or attractions to certain groups of people. Knowing these tendencies in themselves is essential for any mature minister, so they can be alert to that danger in their relationship with others who look to them for guidance. In moments of tiredness, illness, depression, or temptation, such weaknesses may be the catalyst for wholesome boundaries to be crossed. Anyone who offers to mentor another has to live with this knowledge and monitor themselves as they weigh up how to respond to any situation where their vulnerability may be tested.

Secondly, mentoring is clearly a power relationship, even if there is no "line-manager" relationship. Someone who looks to another for mentoring clearly regards them as a person who has more experience, contacts, or wisdom than they do. They will therefore be likely to accept what is suggested to them even if they feel uncomfortable about it. The greater the power or age disparity, the more likely this is to happen.

Thirdly, we need to acknowledge that each of us must pray for integrity in all our dealings as our first and continuous help is to rely on the Lord. But there is more to be done.

---

21. For example, Scolding and Fullbrook, *Independent Review*.

Fourthly, it is imperative that we keep up-to-date with best practice in safeguarding and appreciate gender boundaries, so the mentor can adhere to current norms. This may be done by reading, face-to-face courses, or online provision. Anyone in later adult life must be adapting their earlier professional practice to a more cautious and publicly accountable framework since there has been so much change in recent decades. Since this book may reach different parts of the world, it is important that readers realize that this is a specialist area. Mentors and mentees must follow national or local legal and institutional guidelines when people disclose matters that relate to safeguarding issues, consulting with professionals to ensure that they are dealt with promptly and appropriately.

This takes me to a fifth way in which we may guard against abuse. Everyone who offers mentoring, informally or professionally, occasionally or regularly, needs to set up relationships in a mutually agreed manner. Thus, every mentee will understand the terms by which this relationship will be conducted. It is important that they also know to whom they may go if they have any concerns about its conduct. It needs to be absolutely clear that they can withdraw from this arrangement at any time with no threat of penalty—actual or imagined.

In secular settings, the relationship may be organized by the company in which it is happening, and there may be training that can address these issues. Often there is also supervision by an experienced practitioner or mutual supervision and learning among those offering mentoring. All of these arrangements can protect mentor and mentee from developing unhealthy relationships of any kind. In church settings, these oversight arrangements may be harder to find but are equally important. Mentors need to be accountable, either to their own line manager or to a supervisor or peers who meet to offer mutual supervision and accountability. In churches this is not always easy to arrange. However, especially where ordained or licenced ministers have access to ministerial review, it should be part of that review to consider whether there is anything, such as mentoring, which should be included in their job description. Those reviewing ministers have a responsibility to ensure that they themselves have had some training in how this may best be delivered. As well as personal responsibility for deviant practices developing, there may be institutional negligence in considering these matters.

Mentoring for growth from conversion to maturity may well be done in groups initially and perhaps entirely, and any lay person leading such groups should be clear to whom they are answerable. When there is a vacancy in the parish or church in which they operate, they deserve to know to whom they are answerable so that proper supervision can be provided. Other lay persons such as churchwardens or deacons may be able to offer such support. Mentoring for leadership of groups or congregations will broadly follow similar lines. Perhaps most vulnerable are the ministers who have sole charge of one or more congregation, since mentoring may become part of their ministry only after the initial phases of their post have been completed. There can be a loneliness about ministry that leads to mentoring being potentially abused as the admiration of a younger person may become a pathway into codependency, for which the older and more experienced person must take entire responsibility. To ensure that this does not happen, it may be necessary either to change practice or to bring the relationship to a good end without disclosing the personal reasons for its conclusion, perhaps signposting them to another person or opportunity that will support them.

With these warnings in place, we can now turn to a much more positive discussion of Christian mentoring.

What Role does the Holy Spirit Play in Mentoring?

Much secular wisdom and guidance may be transferable into the Christian context, but the church believes that the Holy Spirit is present in all interpersonal relationships, indeed he has been called the "Go-Between God."[22] His role in mentoring needs to be elaborated.

The Holy Spirit is the Spirit of Love (2 Timothy 1:7 and Romans 5:5)

This means that mentor and mentee need to listen to each other with all the attention and respect that they can achieve so that they really understand one another. This will certainly include being capable of interrogating each other and speaking plainly but with courtesy when they think that either is speaking in a biased or prejudicial way. It will also include praying for one another, probably in the meeting before they begin to discuss business and certainly between meetings.

I have learned that it is important to take the other person's concerns seriously; they may not be my concerns, but they will be the Lord's concerns even if they need to be reframed so we can have a constructive

---

22. Taylor, *Go-Between God*.

conversation around them. Even in casual conversations it is important to make sure that I have understood as deeply as possible what the other is sharing—so there may be questions about other circumstances, history, feelings, understandings, and future possibilities. Generally, it is important to make the conversation iterative—"Is it like this, or that?" or "What does it seem like to you?"

The Holy Spirit is the Spirit of Conviction (John 16:8–11)

Only the Holy Spirit can bring a person to repentance that leads to faith in Jesus, baptism, and discipleship (Acts 11:15–17). Equally, it is the work of the Holy Spirit that opens a Christian to exploration of and volunteering for local leadership. Similarly, literature about vocation makes clear that it is the internal work of the Holy Spirit (as well as the guidance of the Holy Spirit in the community) that brings people to readiness to accept strategic leadership responsibilities. That same Holy Spirit is at work in the mentors who make themselves available to disciples, local leaders, or strategic overseers. They will be experienced enough to know that it is only as they rely on the guidance of the Holy Spirit that they are able to fulfil this mentoring role at all. And this will all occur within the community of faith that is directed and held together by the same Spirit.

The Holy Spirit is the Spirit of Truth (John 14:17; 16:13; 17:17).

Initially, Philips-Jones suggests that acquiring a mentor is an essential skill for those who are to enter into this kind of arrangement.[23] Recognizing your needs for support is as essential as being open to all that you may learn, so knowing yourself well enough to be able to make good use of a mentor. But disclosure is not only something for the mentee. In the conversations that follow, both mentor and mentee will need the disclosure of the Spirit of truth who enlightens their minds about the reality of the situation in which the mentee finds themselves. Such an acknowledgment of the reality of this specific context is essential if a realistic strategy for how to approach it is to be found. Here, the Spirit of Truth is crucial—making clear what the issues really are. And the mentor will need the disclosure of the Spirit as she or he accepts that the Lord

---

23. Phillips-Jones, *Skills for Successful Mentoring*, 6.

has given them the skills to help this person, and the wisdom to listen perceptively as a way forward is discerned.

The use of pictures or images in these conversations can often bring enlightenment. Sometimes I need to suggest possible starting points in their thinking, although it is also good to ask them where they want to begin. Like a tailor making a garment, sometimes mentors know better than the mentees: we may need to start with the fit on the shoulders of a jacket because everything hangs from there and other adjustments need to follow on. But on other occasions, the length of a troublesome cuff may need to be adjusted because the wearer cannot "hear" what the source of the other problems is until that annoying uneven cuff has been remedied.

The Holy Spirit is the Spirit of Power (Acts 1:8; Eph 3:16; Rom 8:26)

After the conversation has happened, for the mentee there will be significant follow-through. Because situations may change, they may need to vary the approach which they had originally crafted in a mentoring session. The mentee learns not only how to deal with foreseeable upcoming circumstances, but how to make judgments in new or evolving times. Phillip-Jones suggests that assessing risk is a responsibility for the mentor, who helps mentees take appropriate risks while guarding them from unnecessary mistakes.[24] In this, the mentee can learn how to assess their own risks and make judgments when there is no time for lengthy reflection. It is important to help them to prepare well but trust their own decisions and actions. Most circumstances discussed will involve risk, and recognition of that will be part of the Spirit's gift of disclosure, but capacity to face up to risk, assess and embrace it, while taking appropriate mitigating actions, will trigger reliance on the Spirit's empowering.

The Holy Spirit is the Spirit of Insight (John 14:25)

By far, the majority of the time the mentee will live, work, and serve on their own, without the benefit of being able to consult a mentor about how to respond in each novel situation. For this reason, it will be important that the lessons previously learned can be brought to mind much later—sometimes months or years later. This, too, is the work of the Holy Spirit, our remembrancer, of whom Jesus says that he will bring to mind

---

24. Phillips-Jones, *Skills for Successful Mentoring*, 6.

for the disciples all that they have learned from him. Much of this is about learning wisdom and calling to mind what has been learned when it is needed. The ability to recognize true parallels and false ones is important. Sometimes a superficial reading of the situation suggests that a previous good strategy will be successful, but closer examination may suggest significant differences that may mean that the mentee needs to develop new approaches. Cool-headed assessment of problems needs to be married with creative solutions and a readiness to improvise and innovate. There are many examples in the New Testament of how early church leaders had to remember not to replicate slavishly but to have the courage to reimagine the gospel in a new cultural setting.

Of course, what is true for the mentee is also true for the mentor, who will sometimes need an imaginative leap into the past or future to empathize with the mentee and recall what viable options may be explored with them at this stage in their development.

The Holy Spirit is the Spirit of Knowledge (John 14:26)

In a healthy mentor–mentee relationship, both people will be learning, and both will be relying on the work of the Holy Spirit, their teacher, to enable that to happen. In one-on-one exchanges, the mentor will serve the mentee best by judicious questions that enable them to think through for themselves the context in which they are submerged. Being alert to the Spirit's prompting as to what to ask and in what order, what to press and what to leave to one side, is perhaps the most important skill. Encouraging responding questions is essential and requires of the mentor a high degree of maturity, which can live with the uncertainty of what may arise in the conversation. There are some occasions where the mentor in an informal way has to use the more usual didactic teacher role, either by referring mentees to the places or people where they can learn, such as relevant literature, an internet video, a conference, or by narrating parallel events, helping the mentee draw out lessons from them.

Perhaps most important is the skill of enabling the mentee to travel round the figure 8, as identified by Laurie Green. According to this, the top circle comprises identifying an experience, exploring it, reflecting on the exploration, and formulating a response. To this circle is added another below (making the figure of 8) in which reflection is elaborated to include a biblical or theological "intuition," leading to an "exploration" of this, and finally a "new witness" that is carried back into the upper circle's consideration of a response.[25] So a mentee presenting a situation where a group member is frequently behaving disruptively so as to upset the group dynamics might just be considered in psychological or social terms (the upper circle), but Christian mentoring must also consider the theological issues that this raises (the lower circle), such as forgiveness, reconciliation, and perhaps some deeper issues that indicate that there is need for healing of memories that may give rise to this tricky behavior. Essential in Christian mentoring is the integration of Christian theology with everyday life. This will enable the mentor to understand better, to offer better practice, or the mentee to experience attitudinal change that make them able to respond in a more mature Christian way.

The Holy Spirit is the Spirit of Freedom (Romans 8:2)

Frequently there is a need for clarity about boundaries. As mentor I may offer ideas, possibilities, parallels, or perspectives, but as mentor I do not hold any responsibilities—in law, the mentee is the office holder. I cannot intervene or make decisions as to lines of actions. I may only be consulted once, so there are things for me to ponder:

a) Can I be "hands off" and objectively interested?
b) Can I let the matter rest in my mind and between us, determining not to try to initiate any follow up?
c) Can I pray as long as the memory remains, content to let go or to discern for how long to intercede as I am led?

The aim of this kind of relationship is so that the mentee may be able to serve, think, or work competently as well as or better than the mentor. Here the Holy Spirit is the liberator, for lengthy dependency is never the purpose of mentoring. At the end, the mentor has to learn when to step back and renegotiate the relationship into peer collegiality. The Holy Spirit liberates the mentee from their fears so that they can use their unique gifts, learned skills, and mature wisdom to negotiate their own way through their life and career (2 Tim 1:7).

---

25. Green, *Let's Do Theology*, 95.

Conclusion

I have already indicated how significant mentoring has been in my own development and practice. It has also been a privilege to learn from the narratives of others because mentoring does not only change the mentee, it will also gloriously enlarge the perspective and practice of the mentor. As with so many things, God's providential provision means that there is a rich harvest beyond what might be anticipated. Gospel economy means that nothing is one dimensional; the Holy Spirit bears fruit in many places simultaneously. It repays the mentor far more than anything given; it is a deeply enriching ministry.

Conclusion

Patrick McGlinchey

"Pastoral care" is a value rooted in the Christian vision of a nurturing and merciful society. Its ongoing potency is evidenced by its successful migration from the purely religious domain to the secular. "Pastoral care" of employees and the sick is even today a major priority within the post-Christian West. One explanation for why this distinctively Christian emphasis has maintained itself so thoroughly was put forward by Tom Holland in his ground-breaking publication *Dominion*. There, the author makes the claim that although belief in Christian doctrine has declined significantly in recent centuries, the church's teaching on human equality and the value of the individual has remained central for contemporary society. As Holland comments wryly, "In a West that is often doubtful of religion's claims, so many of its instincts remain—for good or ill—thoroughly Christian."[1] Whether he is correct or not in his interpretation of history—the editors suspect he is—many of us (Christian and non-Christian alike) know little about the origins and scope of pastoral ministry within the church or what it potentially offers a society that retains a high view of the human person. Five major themes emerge over the course of the book that are valuable, not only for those attempting to understand the practicalities of pastoral ministry (i.e., those individuals inside the church) but also those others who find themselves intrigued or challenged by the Christian view of the person.

---

1. Holland, *Dominion*, xxix.

Human Beings as the Image of God

Perhaps the most consistent claim made throughout the book is that human beings are made in the image of God. This single conviction fuels all pastoral ministry and accounts for the immense value placed on every single individual. Joseph Ratzinger (later Pope Benedict XVI), writing on the theme of "Creation and Fall" in Genesis, articulates the classic Christian perspective on humanity as the image of God. His words echo the perspective of the whole book, but he is also at pains to alert us to the harm that may come to society if a high view of humanity is lost. We can detect resonances with Columba Toman's emphasis on human dignity in the healthcare setting from Ratzinger's note of warning.

> Each human being is known by God and loved by him. Each is willed by God, and each is God's image. . . . Human life stands under God's special protection, because each human being, however wretched or exalted he or she may be, however sick or suffering, however good-for-nothing or important, whether born or unborn, whether incurably ill or radiant with health—each one bears God's breath in himself or herself, each one is God's image. This is the deepest reason for the inviolability of human dignity, and upon it is founded ultimately every civilization. *When the human person is no longer seen as standing under God's protection and bearing God's breath, then the human being begins to be viewed in utilitarian fashion. It is then that the barbarity appears that tramples upon human dignity.*[2]

Interestingly, pastoral ministry is not only a response to the fact that we are all in our original constitution image-bearers, but to the additional reality that this "image" has a profound bearing on the "goal" of the church's pastoral activity. McGlinchey and Mitchel in their chapters highlight St. Paul's overarching pastoral vision, which was of human beings (Paul's converts) restored to the divine image. Mitchel utilizes Scot McKnight's fascinating term "Christoformity" to underscore the Christological nature of this transformation. Christ was the perfect image of God, and therefore it is the image of Christ that pastoral ministry aims to help restore. This core understanding of the *telos* of pastoral ministry flags up something essential that is often missed. Pastoral care is not primarily *reactive* and aimed towards the alleviation of immediate difficulties. It should always have a goal in mind, and this goal is moral and

---

2. Ratzinger, *"In the Beginning"*, 45; emphasis added.

spiritual transformation. It is therefore *proactive* and aimed at facilitating an interior spirituality and relational interdependence that will allow the character of Christ to become evident in frail and wounded people. This is a vision encompassing the whole church.

The Centrality of the Pastor-Teacher Role

Although, in many ways the publication reflects an Anglican perspective on pastoral ministry, it is balanced by insights from other theological traditions. Indeed, even the "distinctively Anglican" parts of this book often contain generic wisdom applicable far beyond the boundaries of Anglicanism. One of these generic pieces of wisdom concerns the crucial need for the ministry of the pastor-teacher.[3] This combined role is referenced in St. Paul's list of ministries given to the church by the ascended Christ (Eph. 4:11–13). It accompanies the ministry of apostles, prophets, and evangelists and is likely more relevant to the internal pastoral life of the church than these other ministries, which are focused, respectively, on the founding of churches, prophetic utterance, and evangelism. Harold Miller's detailed study of the early Anglican Ordinal sets out the qualities expected of those undertaking the pastor-teacher role. The dominant image is that of "shepherd," and much of what this evokes is summed up in the charge given to priests: "Have always therefore printed in your remembrance, how great a treasure is committed to your charge. For they are the sheep of Christ, which he bought with his own death, and for whom he shed his blood."[4] Pastoral engagement without real cognizance of the immense worth placed on the recipients of such ministry dramatically misses the mark and scuppers pastoral effectiveness. Conversely, sensitive pastoral reflection taking individuals and their stories seriously (as illustrated in Robin Stockitt's chapter on pastoral visiting) can bring very different outcomes and the possibility of substantial healing through the grace-inspired empathy of the pastor.

Miller also emphasizes the inseparability of these two ministerial gifts (pastor and teacher), suggesting that they should be viewed as two sides of the same coin. The image of a superb expository preacher with a cold pastoral manner juxtaposed with the image of a warm and effusive pastor with banal preaching content highlights the need for ministers

---

3. See the evidence for this claim in Stott, *God's New Society*, 163-64.
4. *BCP* 2004, 532.

to embody both these gifts, at least to some degree. William Olhausen showcases the pastoral theology of Archbishop Michael Ramsay to underscore this core principle. These words from Ramsay's *Durham Essays* encapsulate beautifully this pastoral commitment to both truth and love. Interestingly, they also echo the view already expressed by Miller. "The tasks of the pastor and the teacher are like two facets of the one reality: they interpret one another. . . . The lover of human lives who for their sake studies the mysteries of God: the student of truth whose books are marked with the love of human lives—that is the great tradition which our Ordinal sets before us."[5] Good and focused pastoral care has these key proactive elements with pastor-teachers, giving of themselves emotionally and intellectually for the benefit of their flock. However, even this kind of ministry has limits when it is confronted with loss, moral confusion, and overwhelming tragedy. Here the ministry of presence comes into its own. This idea is explored in the chapters written by the two hospital chaplains (Nuzum and Toman) who both view pastoral ministry as embodying regard, acceptance, and radical availability. Sometimes this kind of being present *for the other*—which is ultimately an interior disposition reflective of the minister's own closeness to God—does more than what might be achieved by more conventional pastoral ministrations.

The Need of Self-Care for Effective Pastoral Ministry

While pastoral ministry is others-centered, its effectiveness is derived from the minister's own relationship with God. What is offered pastorally does not emanate from an inexhaustible spring within the individual themselves; rather it is the product of prayer, worship, and what Eugene Peterson once described as "a long obedience in the same direction."[6] At its root, true pastoral ministry flows out of a human personality touched by the grace of God, submitted to the purposes of God, and available as a conduit of grace to others roundabout. Without this divine aspect, pastoral care cannot be more than a human endeavor, limited in the ways that all such endeavors are limited.

Three chapters from our book touch on this vital theme, highlighting the ways that ministers themselves are nurtured and renewed as channels of divine grace. In summary, self-care for this fundamental

---

5. Ramsey, *Durham Essays*, 121.
6. Peterson, *Long Obedience*, 11.

aspect of ministry will ideally have three distinct components: *genuine self-knowledge, rigorous commitment to the avoidance of hurry,* and *the wisdom and support of others who have shared the same journey.* In relation to the first of these elements, Elliott advises those in ministry to keep a dutiful watch over their own souls in the ways that the Ordinal advises clergy to oversee the souls of their congregation. Without attention to this matter, the pathway towards resilience recommended by Elliott will be missed or ignored. What, then, should this self-scrutiny involve? At the very least, this will entail self-honesty of the sort envisaged by John Wesley in his rigorous list of questions formulated for band meetings and other gatherings.[7] The psalmist's prayer that he would be taught truth "in the inward parts" (Ps 51:6) is also a fitting stimulus for this journey towards self-knowledge. A useful daily exercise might be the practice of the examen, which allows the person involved to explore their actions and motivations in ways that nurture self-awareness. Practices such as this (and there are numerous examples to draw upon from the wider Christian tradition) can be instrumental in helping individuals gain genuine self-knowledge. A fitting complement to these interior exercises might be a wise spiritual director or accountability partner who would, among other things, play a role in helping the "directee" avoid self-deception.

One of the great challenges of ministry is busyness, much of which is unavoidable, and Bishop Storey, in her chapter, draws on that perennial piece of Christian wisdom that the busier we are, the more time we should spend in prayer. Self-care involves spending enough time in prayerful engagement with God to allow him to care for us amid our own stresses and busyness. The establishment of one or two non-negotiable points in the day when appropriate time can be given to prayer or spiritual disciplines will be the anchor point needed to not only survive but to thrive in ministry. Storey gives prominence to John Mark Cromer's publication *The Ruthless Elimination of Hurry* as a guide for those seeking to order their lives towards God.

---

7. See New Hope, "John Wesley's Small Group." The below sampling of small group questions devised by John Wesley highlights the degree of self-honesty he was requiring of his converts.
   1. Am I consciously or unconsciously creating the impression that I am better than I am? In other words, am I a hypocrite?
   2. Am I honest in all my acts and words, or do I exaggerate?
   3. Do I confidentially pass onto another what was told me in confidence? Can I be trusted?
   4. Am I a slave to dress, friends, work, or habits?
   5. Am I self-conscious, self-pitying, or self-justifying?

The chapter on mentoring by Dr. Christina Baxter highlights one of the most crucial elements in anyone's spiritual growth. This is the presence of a mentor figure who has already walked a similar ministerial path and who accompanies the mentee at crucial points on their journey. As a theological student, I sensed a profound need for a mentor and prayed that God would lead such a person into my life. I saw clearly how mentors function as sources of encouragement and example on the Christian way. Their input could be transformational and might even account for some of the significant ways that God would care for and guide us. Speaking personally, it was Dr. Christina Baxter's mentoring role in my own life over some decades that helped me discern a vocation, step out in new forms of ministry, and ultimately embrace the challenge of being a theological educator. This type of figure may not always be available, but it is advisable to be open to this form of relationship (especially early on in ministry) and indeed to be willing to become a mentor should the opportunity arise. Such openness either way is vital to the nurturing of effective pastoral service.

Pastoral Ministry as a Source of Insight and Inspiration for the Wider Culture

Cynthia Bennett Brown, in her review of pastoral care in the Christian tradition, noted how breakthrough insights in modern psychology around the human personality and its emotional shape were already being modelled out in the pastoral writings of figures such as Gregory the Great.[8] I cite this example to underscore the church's historic capacity to meet pastoral needs intelligently and out of a profound grasp of the human personality. I would expand this point further to suggest that the increasingly materialistic and atomistic culture of today has indirectly diminished access to the profound pastoral wisdom embodied in the church. This is a wisdom not only of theory but of practice. The church, when spiritually healthy, has lived out its values in persuasive and life-affirming ways and certainly been able to comprehend what will lead to human flourishing.

This was evidenced, particularly, in our chapters on marriage and cross-cultural ministry where a positive image of both was held up in a culture struggling to maintain healthy romantic relationships and come

---

8. Pope Gregory ministered in the late sixth century.

to terms with deep cultural differences. Gibson, in a sympathetic and pastorally informed account, demonstrates that the essentially contractual view of marriage present in today's culture can be transformed by a covenantal view in which the rich treasures of marriage are unlocked. This sense of the church really having something to offer culture in relation to marriage resonated with some of my own pastoral experience. I was part of a parochial team that offered extensive marriage preparation to largely non-churched couples with little exposure to either Christian teaching about marriage or practical wisdom relating to themes like debt and conflict. The sessions were enhanced by the winsomeness of my clergy colleague and his wife who both exuded pastoral warmth and accessibility. This "gift" to those approaching marriage (i.e. a relevant and engaging course of marriage preparation) may be augmented within the community life of the church by the encouragement of married couples in their vocation and the offer of additional supports such as parenting classes. While these scenarios are only realizable in thriving pastoral contexts, they do exemplify what the church can potentially offer in the domain of marriage. Pastoral ministry benefits not only insiders but can be life-enhancing for those who are on the peripheries.

The chapter on cross-cultural ministry written by Laurence Graham shows the church trailblazing a vision for ministry in this area. His Methodist congregation in central Dublin is radically diverse and thus reminiscent of the early New Testament church. Indeed, its bringing together of disparate ethnic groupings also reflects the highest secular ideals for a functioning, multiracial society. But even these statements do not do full justice to what the church can potentially offer in this context. Like the Lord's Supper as it was celebrated in the early decades of the church, this style of church functions as a melting pot of ethnicities and social classes who might not come together in any other circumstances. In this regard, it perhaps exceeds the culture's best hopes and successfully models out welcome and harmony. Moreover, as demonstrated by Graham, valuable lessons are also learned about how best to integrate diverse communities and promote genuine understanding. Most significant of all perhaps is Christianity's powerful vision of each church member being made equally in the image of God. Taken to heart, this metaphysical reality provides the necessary foundation for a real eclipsing of the racist past and disabling of present prejudices. The church's unique potential in this area shows what it can offer to a secular society that may not otherwise be readily available.

The Collaborative Nature of Ministry

This final section pivots around a theological question more than a directly pastoral one. John Alderdice, in his chapter, describes a partial retrieval of John Wesley's own collaborative approach to ministry within Methodism. Essentially, the founder of Methodism had discovered that, in a thriving missional context, the absence of ordained clergy demanded the creation of lay leadership. While being a worthy pragmatic option, this broader vision of pastoral ministry accords quite strongly with New Testament precedent and the heritage of the post-Reformation church. The discussion of Paul's pastoral ministry early in the book highlighted that the model of holiness he envisaged was not realizable outside of a context where congregants are actively involved in each other's lives and schooled in the ways of discipleship. Indeed, the pastor-teacher model promoted by Miller and Olhausen is derived from a passage of Scripture in which each of Christ's ministerial gifts (apostle, prophet, pastor-teacher, evangelist) are given to facilitate the ministry of the whole body. Conventional ordained ministry must be seen as an enabling ministry for the fuller and arguably more significant ministry of the church in the world.

Having thus argued for the significance of lay ministry, I would hasten to add that this must not be construed as my attempt to diminish the importance of ordained ministry. There is a theological and pastoral necessity for an educated clergy who can lead effectively because of their roots in Scripture and the tradition. Cynthia Bennett cites pastoral theologian Thomas Oden to the effect that good pastoral care will entail "the constant interweaving of scriptural wisdom, historical awareness, constructive theological reasoning, situational discernment, and pastoral empathy."[9] This kind of capacity is not easily achieved without substantial training and reflection. Rather than dumbing down the demands of ministerial formation within the training context because of a diminution of the role, there is perhaps the need to educate the laity in a way that keeps speed with other forms of adult education. By this means they may gain the requisite depth of theological and pastoral understanding for the exercise of lay pastoral ministry.

---

9. Oden, *Care of Souls*, 12.

Final Thoughts

This exploration of pastoral ministry has highlighted both its diversity and its challenge. In God's economy, though, it is surely the highest calling. Those who undertake this role are a channel of God's mercy to the world, and there is no greater purpose to pursue than that. It is an activity that not only enables profound needs to be met but which ironically perfects and purifies the "giver." We live in a post-Christian West where the values that formed our culture are eroding, albeit at a slower rate than we might have thought. Culture tends to be increasingly about immediate gratification and there is little appetite for selfless engagement with the "other." Viewed through a missional lens, authentic pastoral ministry points to a hope beyond what Charles Taylor labelled in *A Secular Age* "the buffered self," a condition in which human beings are cut off from the transcendent. This kind of care can embody a love and reality that ministers hope into even this spiritual void. Moreover, it remains God's means of transforming those in the church into the image of Christ. What greater vocation can there be than to be a bearer of such radical consolation—the sign of hope where there is no hope and the agent of a healing and transforming God?

Bibliography

Ainsworth, Mary. *Patterns of Attachment: A Psychological Study of the Strange Situation*. Hove: Psychology, 1979.
Alderdice, John. "Irish Methodism and Servant Leadership—A Vision of Ministry for the Twenty-first Century." PhD diss., Dublin City University, 2023.
Anderson, David. *Multicultural Ministry*. Grand Rapids: Zondervan, 2004.
Anglican Communion. "Intentional Discipleship." https://www.anglicancommunion.org/mission/intentional-discipleship.aspx.
———. "Marks of Mission." https://www.anglicancommunion.org/mission/marks-of-mission.aspx.
Anglican-Methodist International Commission for Unity in Mission (AMICUM). *Into all the World: Being and Becoming Apostolic Churches*. London: Anglican Consultative Council, 2014. https://www.anglicancommunion.org/media/102827/Into-All-The-World-AMICUM-Report-2014.pdf.
Aquinas, Thomas. *Summa Theologica*. Translated by Fathers of the English Dominican Province. New York: Benziger Bros., 1947. https://dhspriory.org/kenny/CDtexts/summa/index.html.
Arieli, Y. "On the Necessary and Sufficient Conditions for the Emergence of the Dignity of Man and His Rights." In *The Concept of Human Dignity in Human Rights Discourse*, edited by D. Kretzmer and E. Klein, 1–18. The Hague: Kluwer, 2002.
Ash, Christopher. *Marriage: Sex in the Service of God*. Leicester: InterVarsity, 2003.
———. *Zeal Without Burnout: Seven Keys to a Lifelong Ministry of Sustainable Sacrifice*. London: The Good Book Company, 2016.
Ashcroft, Richard. "Making Sense of Dignity." *Journal of Medical Ethics* 31 (2005) 679.
Atherstone, A. *The Anglican Ordinal: Gospel Priorities for the Church of England Ministry*. Oxford: The Latimer Trust, 2020.
Atkinson, David J. and David F. Field, eds. *New Dictionary of Christian Ethics and Pastoral Theology*. Nottingham: InterVarsity, 2020.
Atkinson, Nigel. *Richard Hooker and the Authority of Scripture, Tradition and Reason*. Vancouver: Regent College, 2005.
Baab, Lynne M. *Nurturing Hope: Christian Pastoral Care in the Twenty-First Century*. Minneapolis: Fortress, 2018.
BACP. *Managing Confidentiality Within the Counselling Professions*. Sept. 2024. https://www.bacp.co.uk/media/21757/bacp-managing-confidentiality-lr-gpia014-sept-24.pdf.
Bailey, Kenneth. *Jacob and the Prodigal: How Jesus Retold Israel's Story*. Downers Grove, IL: InterVarsity, 2011.

———. *Poet and Peasant and Through Peasant Eyes: A Literary-Cultural Approach to the Parables in Luke*. Grand Rapids: Eerdmans, 1983.

Baker, Frank. *John Wesley and the Church of England*. London: Epworth, 2000.

Barclay, John. *Paul and the Gift*. Grand Rapids: Eerdmans, 2015.

Barnett, Paul. "Paul as Pastor in 2 Corinthians." In *Paul as Pastor*, edited by Brian S. Rosner et al., 55–69. London: T&T Clark, 2018.

Barr, Beth Alison. *The Pastoral Care of Women in Late Medieval England*. Cambridge: Boydell and Brewer, 2008.

Barrett, C. K. *The First Epistle to the Corinthians*. London: A & C Black, 1987.

Barth, Karl. *The Doctrine of Creation*. Vol. 3.1 of *Church Dogmatics*. Translated by G. W. Bromily et al. London: T&T Clark, 2009.

———. "The Strange New World Within the Bible." In *The Word of God and the Word of Man*, edited and translated by Douglas Horton, 28–50. Pilgrim, 1928.

Bates, Ursula, et al. "Implementation and Evaluation of a National Bereavement Support Line in Response to the COVID-19 Pandemic in Ireland." *Journal of Public Health* 45 (2023) e296–e302. https://doi.org/10.1093/pubmed/fdac119.

Baxter, Richard. *The Reformed Pastor*. Wheaton: Crossway, 2021. Ebook.

Beaumont, Susan. *How to Lead When You Don't Know Where You're Going: Leading in a Liminal Season*. London: Rowman & Littlefield, 2019.

Beeson, G. W. "Counseling the Newly Married." *Currents in Theology and Mission* 5 (1978) 105–9.

Bell, Simon. "SMART Goals." Mindtools. https://www.mindtools.com/a4wo118/smart-goals.

Bender, Kimlyn J. *1 Corinthians*. Brazos Theological Commentary on the Bible. Grand Rapids: Baker Academic, 2023.

Benner, David G. *Care of Souls: Revisioning Christian Nurture and Counsel*. Grand Rapids: Baker, 1998.

Bennett, David W. *Metaphors of Ministry: Biblical Images for Leaders and Followers*. Grand Rapids: Paternoster, 1993.

Bennett, Gaymon. *Technicians of Human Dignity*. New York: Fordham University Press, 2016.

Bicknell, E. J. *The Thirty-Nine Articles*. 3rd ed. Edited by H. J. Carpenter. London: Longmans, Green, 1919.

Bill, George. *True North: Discover Your Authentic Leadership*. San Francisco: Jossey-Bass, 2007.

Birkett, Kirsten. *Resilience: A Spiritual Project*. Oxford: Latimer House, 2015.

Body, Andrew. *An Introduction to Marriage Preparation*. Cambridge: Grove, 2014.

Bolsinger, Tod E. *It Takes a Church to Raise a Christian: How the Community of God Transforms Lives*. Grand Rapids: Brazos, 2004.

Bonhoeffer, Dietrich. "The Bible Alone: A Letter to Dr. Rüdiger Schleicher." In *Meditating on the Word*. Cambridge, MA: Cowley, 1986.

———. *The Cost of Discipleship*. London: SCM, 2006.

The Book of Common Prayer. Dublin: Columba, 2004.

Bornkamm, Günther. *Paul*. London: Hodder & Stoughton, 1985.

Bowlby, John. *Attachment*. London: Pimlico, 1997.

———. "Attachment and Loss: Retrospect and Prospect." *American Journal of Orthopsychiatry* 52 (1982) 66–78. http://www.ncbi.nlm.nih.gov/pubmed/7148988.

———. "Attachment Theory and Its Therapeutic Implications." *Adolesc Psychiatry* 6 (1978) 5–33. http://www.ncbi.nlm.nih.gov/pubmed/742687.

———. "The Making and Breaking of Affectional Bonds. I. Aetiology and Psychopathology in the Light of Attachment Theory. An Expanded Version of the Fiftieth Maudsley Lecture, Delivered Before the Royal College of Psychiatrists, 19 November 1976." *British Journal of Psychiatry* 130 (1977) 201–10. http://www.ncbi.nlm.nih.gov/pubmed/843768.

Bradshaw, Paul. *The Anglican Ordinal: Its History and Development from the Reformation to the Present Day*. London: SPCK, 1971.

Brain, Peter. *Going the Distance: How to Stay Fit for a Lifetime of Ministry*. Kingsford: Matthias, 2004.

Brown, Raymond E. *The Sensus Plenior of Sacred Scripture*. Wipf and Stock, 2008. Originally published in 1955 by St. Mary's University.

Bruce, F. F. *Paul: Apostle of the Free Spirit*. London: Paternoster, 1977.

Buber, Martin. *I Thou*. New York: Simon & Schuster, 2008.

Bucer, Martin. *Concerning the True Care of Souls*. Translated by Peter Beale. Edinburgh: The Banner of Truth, 2009.

Buechner, Frederick. *Now and Then: A Memoir of Vocation*. New York: Harper & Row, 1983.

Burnett, Gary W. *Paul's Gospel of Love*. Cambridge: Grove, 2023.

Byrne, Michael J., and Daniel R. Nuzum. "Pastoral Closeness in Physical Distancing: The Use of Technology in Pastoral Ministry during COVID-19." *Health and Social Care Chaplaincy* 8 (2020) 206–17. https://doi.org/10.1558/hscc.41625.

Cajthaml, Martin. *Europe and the Care of the Soul*. Nordhausen: Traugott Bautz, 2014.

Caldwell, Taylor. *The Man Who Listens*. London: Collins, 1961.

Calhoun, D. H. "Human Exceptionalism and Imago Dei: The Tradition of Human Dignity." In *Human Dignity in Bioethics: From Worldviews to the Public Square*, edited by Stephen Dilley and Nathan J. Palpant, 19–46. New York: Routledge, 2012.

Campbell, Alistair V. "Pastoral Care." In *A Dictionary of Pastoral Care*, edited by Alistair V. Campbell, 188–90. London, SPCK, 1987.

———. *Rediscovering Pastoral Care*. 2nd ed. London: Darton, Longman, and Todd, 1986.

Campbell, Douglas A. *Pauline Dogmatics: The Triumph of God's Love*. Grand Rapids: Eerdmans, 2020.

Carroll, B. *Survey of Childhood Bereavement Services in Ireland*. Dublin: Irish Hospice Foundation, 2010.

Carson, Don. *For the Love of God*. Vol. 1. Downers Grove, IL: IVP, 1998.

Carson, Marion. "For Now We Live: A Study of Paul's Pastoral Leadership in 1 Thessalonians." *Themelios* 30 (2005) 23–41.

Carter, John D. "Personality and Christian Maturity: A Process Congruity Model." *Journal of Psychology and Theology* 2 (1974) 190–201.

Cathie, Sean. *The Clergy's Experience of Pastoral Care*. Cambridge: Grove, 2024.

Center for Pastor Theologians. "Vision & Mission." https://www.pastortheologians.com/vision-mission.

Challis, William. "The Word of Life: Using the Bible in Pastoral Care." Handbooks of Pastoral Care. London: Harper Collins, 1997.

Chapell, Brian, and Kathy Chapell. *Each for the Other: Marriage as It's Meant to Be*. Grand Rapids: Baker, 2006.

Chapman, Gary. *The Five Love Languages*. Chicago: Moody, 2015.

Chapman, Mark D., et al., eds. *The Oxford Handbook of Anglican Studies*. Oxford: Oxford University Press, 2018.

Cheng, Joanna Oi-Yue, et al. "A Pilot Study on the Effectiveness of Anticipatory Grief Therapy for Elderly Facing the End of Life." *Journal of Palliative Care* 26 (2010) 261–69. http://www.ncbi.nlm.nih.gov/pubmed/21268518.

Chevalier, Rebekah. *On Frequent Journeys*. Toronto: United Church, 1997.

"Chicago-Lambeth Quadrilateral." Anglican Communion. https://www.anglicancommunion.org/media/109011/Chicago-Lambeth-Quadrilateral.pdf.

Chochinov, Harvey Max. "Dignity and the Essence of Medicine: The A, B, C, & D of Dignity-Conserving Care." *British Medical Journal* 335 (2007) 184–87.

———. *Dignity Therapy: Final Words for Final Days*. Oxford: Oxford University Press, 2012.

Chochinov, Harvey Max, et al. "Dignity in the Terminally Ill: A Cross-Sectional, Cohort Study." *Lancet* 360 (2002) 2026–30.

Clebsch, William A., and Charles R. Jaekle. *Pastoral Care in Historical Perspective*. New York: Jason Aronson, 1983.

Clough, David. "The Problem of Human Equality: Towards a Non-Exclusive Account of the Moral Value of Creatures in the Company of Martha Nussbaum." In *Transforming Exclusion: Engaging Faith Perspectives*, edited by Hannah Bacon et al., 83–100. London: T&T Clark, 2011.

Clutterbuck, David. *Everyone Needs a Mentor*. London, Institute of Personnel and Development, 1998.

Comer, John Mark. *The Ruthless Elimination of Hurry*. London: Hodder & Stoughton, 2019.

Common Worship Ordination Services: Study Edition. London: Church House, 2007.

"Confused and Puzzled." *Methodist Newsletter* 44 (2016) 34.

Congregation for the Doctrine of the Faith. "Dignitas personae." Holy See. 2008. https://www.vatican.va/roman_curia/congregations/cfaith/documents/rc_con_cfaith_doc_20081208_dignitas-personae_en.html.

———. "Samaritanus bonus." Holy See. 2020. https://www.vatican.va/roman_curia/congregations/cfaith/documents/rc_con_cfaith_doc_20200714_samaritanus-bonus_en.html.

Costa, Ken. *Know Your Why: Finding and Fulfilling Your Calling in Life*. Nashville: W, 2016.

Cottrell, Stephen. *Priesthood: Servants, Shepherds, Messengers, Sentinels and Stewards*. London: Hodder & Stoughton, 2020.

Coughlan, Sean. "Lady Susan Hussey Quits over Remarks to Charity Boss Ngozi Fulani." BBC, Dec. 1, 2022. https://www.bbc.com/news/uk-63810468.

Croft, Steven. *Ministry in Three Dimensions*. London: Darton, Longman, and Todd, 1999.

———. *Bishops*. London: APCK, 2015.

Cross, F. L., ed. *The Oxford Dictionary of the Christian Church*. Oxford: Oxford University Press, 1957.

———. *The Selfhood of the Human Person*. Washington, DC: The Catholic University of America Press, 1996.

———. "The Two-Fold Source of the Dignity of Persons." *Faith and Philosophy* 18 (2001) 293–306.

———. "Why Persons Have Dignity." In *Life and Learning IX: Proceedings of the Ninth University Faculty for Life Conference June 1999 at Trinity International University, Deerfield, IL*, edited by J. W. Koterski, 79–92. Washington, DC: University Faculty for Life, 2000.

Cummings, Thomas G., and Christopher G. Worley. *Organization Development and Change*. 10th ed. Stamford: Cengage, 2015.

Dagg, John L. *A Treatise on Church Order*. Vol. 2 of *Manual of Theology*. Charleston, SC: Southern Baptist Publication Society, 1858.

Dalton-Smith, Saundra. *Sacred Rest*. New York: Hachette, 2017.

———. "What Sort of Rest Do You Lack?" Church Times, Apr. 1, 2022. https://www.churchtimes.co.uk/articles/2022/1-april/features/features/what-sort-of-rest-do-you-lack.

Davie, Grace. *Religion in Britain Since 1945*. Oxford, Blackwell, 1999.

Davie, Martin. *Bishops: Past, Present and Future*. Great Britain: Gilead, 2022.

Davies, Madeleine. "Clergy Are in the Dark About How Well They're Doing, New Study Finds." Church Times, Jan. 6, 2022. https://www.churchtimes.co.uk/articles/2022/7-january/news/uk/clergy-are-unsure-about-performance-living-ministry-study-finds.

"Destination Station." *Methodist Newsletter* 44 (2016) 31.

Demacopoulos, George E. *Five Models of Spiritual Direction in the Early Church*. Notre Dame: University of Notre Dame Press, 2007.

———. *Gregory the Great: Ascetic, Pastor, and First Man of Rome*. Notre Dame: University of Notre Dame Press, 2015.

Department of Health, Social Services and Public Safety. *Living Matters, Dying Matters: A Palliative and End of Life Care Strategy for Adults in Northern Ireland*. Mar. 2010. https://www.health-ni.gov.uk/sites/default/files/publications/dhssps/living-matters-dying-matters-strategy-2010.pdf.

DeVries, Reijer J. "Models of Mutual Pastoral Care in the Footsteps of Martin Luther." *Journal for Theology and the Study of Religion* 72 (2018) 41–56.

Dicastery for the Doctrine of the Faith (DDF). "Dignitas infinitas." Holy See. Apr. 8, 2024. https://www.vatican.va/roman_curia/congregations/cfaith/documents/rc_ddf_doc_20240402_dignitas-infinita_en.html#_ftn2.

Dilley, Stephen, and Nathan J. Palpant. "Human Dignity in the Throes? An Introduction to the Volume." In *Human Dignity in Bioethics: From Worldviews to the Public Square*, edited by Stephen Dilley and Nathan J. Palpant, 3–18. New York: Routledge, 2012.

Dix, Gregory. *The Image and Likeness of God*. Westminster: Dacre, 1953.

———. *The Question of Anglican Orders*. Westminster: Dacre, 1944.

Doehring, Carrie. *The Practice of Pastoral Care: A Postmodern Approach*. Louisville: Westminster John Knox, 2015.

Doka, Kenneth J. "Disenfranchised Grief." *Bereavement Care* 18 (1999) 37–39.

Dowling, R. H., and D. R. Holeton, eds. *Equipping the Saints: Ordination in Anglicanism Today: Papers from the Sixth International Anglican Liturgical Consultation*. Dublin: Columba, 2006.

Downs, David J. "Collection for the Saints." In *The Dictionary of Paul and His Letters: A Compendium of Contemporary Biblical Scholarship*, edited by Scot McKnight et al., 136–39. London: InterVarsity Academic, 2023.

Dunn, James D. G. *The Theology of Paul the Apostle*. Grand Rapids: Eerdmans, 2006.

Egan, Kevin. "Pastoral Care Today: Widening the Horizons." In *The Bloomsbury Guide to Pastoral Care*, edited by Bernadette Flanagan and Sharon Thornton, 5–19. London: Bloomsbury Continuum, 2014.

Elliott, Maurice and Patrick McGlinchey, eds. *Perspectives on Prayer and Spirituality*. Eugene, OR: Wipf and Stock, 2021.

———. *Perspectives on Preaching: A Witness of the Irish Church*. Dublin: Church of Ireland, 2017.

Erhueh, Anthony. *Vatican II: Image of God in Man: An Inquiry into the Theological Foundations and Significance of Human Dignity in the Pastoral Constitution on the Church in the Modern World, "Gaudium et Spes."* Rome: Urbaniana University Press, 1987.

Etymonline. "Bereavement." https://www.etymonline.com/word/bereavement.

Fee, Gordon, *The First Epistle to the Corinthians*. Grand Rapids: Eerdmans, 1987.

———. *The Spirit and the People of God*. London: Hodder and Stoughton, 1997.

Fernandes, Ashley. "The Loss of Dignity at the End of Life." *The National Catholic Bioethics Quarterly* Autumn (2010) 529–46.

Flanagan, Bernadette, and Sharon Thornton, eds. *The Bloomsbury Guide to Pastoral Care*. London: Bloomsbury Continuum, 2014.

Forward, Martin. "Culture, Religious Faiths and Race." In *The Blackwell Reader in Pastoral and Practical Theology*, edited by James Woodward and Stephen Pattison, 248–56. Malden: Blackwell, 2000.

Francis. *Evangelii gaudium*. Apostolic exhortation. Holy See. Nov. 24, 2013. https://www.vatican.va/content/francesco/en/apost_exhortations/documents/papa-francesco_esortazione-ap_20131124_evangelii-gaudium.html.

———. "Homily of Pope Francis." Holy See. Mar. 28, 2013. https://www.vatican.va/content/francesco/en/homilies/2013/documents/papa-francesco_20130328_messa-crismale.html.

Francis, Leslie. "Healthy Leadership: The Science of Clergy Work-Related Psychological Health." In *The Future of Lived Religious Leadership*, edited by R. Brouwer, 116–34. Amsterdam: VU University Press, 2018.

Furnish, Victor. *The Love Command of the New Testament*. London: SCM, 1973.

———. *Theology and Ethics in Paul*. Nashville: Abingdon, 1968.

Gallagher, Ann, et al. "The RCN Survey and Implications for Leaders." *Nursing Management UK* 16 (2009) 12–16.

Garand, Linda, et al. "Anticipatory Grief in New Family Caregivers of Persons with Mild Cognitive Impairment and Dementia." *Alzheimer Disease Associaiton Disorder* 26 (2012) 159–65. https://doi.org/10.1097/WAD.0b013e31822f9051.

Gatiss, Lee, ed. *Feed My Sheep: The Anglican Ministry of Word and Sacrament*. London: Church, 2016.

———. *Reach, Build, Send: A Pattern for Anglican Ministry*. London: Church Society, 2019.

Gay, Doug. *God Be in My Mouth: 40 Ways to Grow as a Preacher*. Edinburgh: Saint Andrew, 2018.

George, Bill. *True North: Discover Your Authentic Leadership*. San Francisco: Jossey-Bass, 2007.
Gerkin, Charles. *An Introduction to Pastoral Care*. Nashville: Abingdon, 1997.
Goodreads. "Hélder Câmara." https://www.goodreads.com/quotes/1485304-when-i-feed-the-poor-they-call-me-a-saint.
Gorman, Michael J. *Becoming the Gospel: Paul. Participation and Mission*. Grand Rapids: Eerdmans, 2015.
Gottmann, John, and Nan Silver. *The Seven Principles for Making Marriage Work* Rev. ed. New York: Harmony, 2015.
Graham, Laurence. *Hope from the Margins*. Dublin: Praxis, 2022.
Graham-Wisener, Lisa, et al. *Fostering Compassionate Communities: A Call to Transform Caregiving, Dying, Death and Grieving on the Island of Ireland*. 2025. https://aiihpc.org/wp-content/uploads/2025/01/Compassionate-Communities-Position-Paper-2025.pdf.
Graveling, Liz. *How Clergy Thrive: Insights from Living Ministry*. London: Church House, 2020.
Green, Laurie. *Let's Do Theology*. London, Continuum, 2008.
———. *Let's Do Theology: Resources for Contextual Theology*. London: Mowbray, 2009.
Greenleaf, Robert. *Servant Leadership*. Mahwah, NJ: Paulist, 1977.
Gregory of Nazianzus. "In Defence of His Flight to Pontus, and His Return, After His Ordination to the Priesthood, with an Exposition of the Character of the Priestly Office." Catholic Library Project. https://catholiclibrary.org/library/view?docId=Synchronized-OR/npnf.000358.gr.html;query=;brand=default.
Gregory the Great. *Pastoral Rule*. https://www.newadvent.org/fathers/3601.htm.
Griffin-Heslin, Venessa Lynne. "An Analysis of the Concept Dignity." *Accident and Emergency Nursing* 13 (2005) 251–57.
Guder, Darrell. *Called to Witness*. Grand Rapids: Eerdmans, 2015.
Guenther, Margaret. *Holy Listening: The Art of Spiritual Direction*. London: Darton, Longman, and Todd, 1992.
Hansen, David. *The Art of Pastoring: Ministry Without All the Answers*. Downers Grove, IL: InterVarsity, 1994.
Hanson, Richard. *Christian Priesthood Examined*. London: Lutterworth, 1979.
Hays, Richard. B. *The Conversion of the Imagination: Paul as Interpreter of Israel's Scripture*. Grand Rapids: Eerdmans, 2005.
Hempton, David. *Methodism: Empire of the Spirit*. New Haven: Yale University Press, 2005.
Hendron, Jill. *When It Hurts to Care: Clergy Working with Crisis*. Champaign: Common Ground, 2022.
Heywood, David. *Reimagining Ministerial Formation*. London: SCM, 2021.
Hiestand, Gerlad, and Todd Wilson. *The Pastor Theologian: Resurrecting an Ancient Vision*. Grand Rapids: Zondervan, 2015.
———, ed. *Becoming a Pastor Theologian: New Possibilities for Church Leadership*. Center for Pastor Theologians. Downers Grove, IL: IVP Academic, 2016.
Holland, Tom. *Dominion: The Making of the Western Mind*. London: Abacus, 2019.
Holley, C. K., and B. T. Mast. "The Impact of Anticipatory Grief on Caregiver-Burden in Dementia Caregivers." *The Gerontologist* 49 (2009) 388–96. https://doi.org/10.1093/geront/gnp061.
Holmes, Anne C. *Creative Repair: Pastoral Care and Creativity*. London: SCM, 2023.

Holy Habits. "The Story Behind Andrew Roberts." https://www.holyhabits.org.uk/andrew-roberts.
Hooker, Roger, and Christopher Lamb. *Love the Stranger*. London: SPCK, 1986.
Howe, Reuel. *Partners in Preaching*. New York: Seabury, 1967.
Hunter, James Davison. *The Death of Character: Moral Education in an Age Without Good or Evil*. New York: Basic, 2000.
Hurding, R. F. "Pastoral Care, Counselling and Psychotherapy." In *New Dictionary of Christian Ethics and Pastoral Theology*, edited by David J. Atkinson and David F. Fields, 86–93. Nottingham: InterVarsity, 2020.
Hurtado, Larry, W. *Destroyer of the Gods*. Waco: Baylor University Press, 2016.
"If Methodism Were Not in My DNA." *Methodist Newsletter* 44 (2016) 33.
"The Importance of Pastoral Visitation." *Methodist Newsletter* 44 (2016) 31.
Irish Hospice Foundation. "Adult Bereavement Care Pyramid." https://hospicefoundation.ie/our-supports-services/bereavement-loss-hub/i-work-in-bereavement/adult-bereavement-care-pyramid/.
Jacobs, Barbara. "Respect for Human Dignity: A Central Phenomenon to Philosophically Unite Nursing Theory and Practice Through Consilience of Knowledge." *Journal of Advances in Nursing Science* 24 (2001) 17–35.
Jacobs, Michael. "Counselling." In *A Dictionary of Pastoral Care*, edited by Alistair V. Campbell, 54–56. London, SPCK, 1987.
Jacobson, Nora. *Dignity and Health*. Nashville: Vanderbilt University Press, 2012.
Jeffries, Henry A. "Parish and Pastoral Care in the Early Tudor Era." In *The Parish in Medieval and Early Modern Ireland: Community, Territory and Building*, edited by Elizabeth FitzPatrick and Raymond Gillespie, 211–27. Dublin: Four Courts, 2006.
Jenkins, Daniel. *Christian Maturity and the Theology of Success*. London: SCM, 1976.
John XXIII. *Pacem in terris*. Encyclical letter. Holy See. Apr. 11, 1963. https://w2.vatican.va/content/john-xxiii/en/encyclicals/documents/hf_j-xxiii_enc_11041963_pacem.html.
John Paul II. *Dolentium hominum*. Apostolic letter. Holy See. Feb. 11, 1985. https://www.vatican.va/content/john-paul-ii/en/motu_proprio/documents/hf_jp-ii_motu-proprio_11021985_dolentium-hominum.html.
———. *Evangelium vitae*. Encyclical letter. Holy See. Mar. 25, 1995. https://www.vatican.va/content/john-paul-ii/en/encyclicals/documents/hf_jp-ii_enc_25031995_evangelium-vitae.html.
———. "Patients as Persons." In *John Paul II's Contribution to Catholic Bioethics*, edited by Christopher Tollefsen, 151–68. Dordrecht: Springer, 2004.
———. "Pope John Paul II's Address to the World Congress." *The Linacre Quarterly* 50 (1983) 31–38.
———. "To Representatives of the Italian Catholic Physicians." *Insegnamenti* 12 (1989).
———. "The Two-Fold Source of the Dignity of Persons." *Faith and Philosophy* 18 (2001) 293–306.
———. "Why Persons Have Dignity." In *Life and Learning IX: Proceedings of the Ninth University Faculty for Life Conference, June 1999 at Trinity International University Deerfield, IL*, edited by J. W. Koterski, 79–92. Washington, DC: University Faculty for Life, 2000.
Jones, David Albert. "Human Dignity in Healthcare: A Virtue Ethics Approach." *The New Bioethics* 21 (2015) 87–97.

Johnston, Bridget Margaret, and Harvey Max Chochinov. "The Therapeutic Implications of Dignity in Palliative Care." In *Palliative Care: Core Skills and Clinical Competencies*, edited by Linda Emanuel and S. Laurence Librach, 696–705. St. Louis: Saunders, 2011.

Judge, Mike. *The Biblical Basis of Marriage: God's Gift for the Whole of Society*. The Christian Institute. 2012. https://www.christian.org.uk/wp-content/uploads/biblical-basis-of-marriage.pdf.

Kahl, Werner. "Migration and Transcultural Faith Communities in Early Christianity and in Contemporary Times." Unpublished lecture delivered to the European Commission on Mission, Frankfurt, Sept. 22, 2023.

Kalib, Kathleen A. "Lessons from Pope John Paul II: 'Theology of the Body' Underpins Healthcare." Catholic Health Association of the United States. Mar.–Apr 2012. https://www.chausa.org/news-and-publications/publications/health-progress/archives/march-april-2012/lessons-from-pope-john-paul-ii-'theology-of-the-body'-underpins-health-care.

Keller, Timothy, and Kathy Keller. *The Meaning of Marriage*. London: Hodder and Stoughton, 2013.

Kelly, Ewan R. *Marking Short Lives: Constructing and Sharing Rituals Following Pregnancy Loss*. Bern: Peter Lang, 2007.

King, Martin Luther, Jr. *Strength To Love*. Philadelphia: Fortress, 1983.

Klass, Dennis. "Continuing Bonds in the Existential, Phenomenological, and Cultural Study of Grief: Prolegomena." *Omega—Journal of Death and Dying* (2023). https://doi.org/10.1177/00302228231205766.

Köstenberger, Andreas J., and David W. Jones. *God, Marriage and Family*. Wheaton, IL: Crossway, 2010.

Kouzes, James M., and Barry Z. Posner. *Credibility: How Leaders Gain and Lose It, Why People Demand it*. San Francisco: Jossey-Bass, 2003.

Lake, Frank. *Clinical Theology: A Theological and Psychological Basis to Clinical Pastoral Care*. London: Darton, Longman, and Todd, 1986.

Lawrence, James. *Growing Leaders: Reflections on Leadership, Life and Jesus*. Oxford: Bible Reading Fellowship, 2004.

Lebech, Mette. "What Is Human Dignity?" *Maynooth Philosophical Papers* 2 (2004) 59–69.

Lee, Nicky, and Sila Lee. *The Marriage Book*. London: Alpha, 2020.

Leech, Kenneth. *Soul Friend: Spiritual Direction in the Modern World*. Harrisburg, Morehouse, 2001.

Leithart, Peter J. *The End of Protestantism: Pursuing Unity in a Fragmented Church*. Grand Rapids: Brazos, 2016.

Lencioni, Patrick. *The Five Dysfunctions of a Team*. San Francisco: Jossey-Bass, 2002.

Lenton, John. *John Wesley's Preachers: Social and Statistical Analysis of British and Irish Preachers*. Milton Keynes: Paternoster, 2009.

Lewis-Anthony, Justin. *You Are the Messiah and I Should Know*. London: Bloomsbury, 2013.

Lewis, C. S. *The Four Loves*. Glasgow: William Collins Sons, 1987.

———. *Mere Christianity*. Glasgow: Fount, 1983.

Lichtenthal, Wendy G., et al. "Investing in Bereavement Care as a Public Health Priority." *The Lancet* 9 (2024) e270–e274. https://doi.org/10.1016/S2468-2667(24)00030-6.

Lightfoot, J. B. *Commentary on Philippians*. London: MacMillan, 1879.

Lobb, Elizabeth A., et al. "Predictors of Complicated Grief: A Systematic Review of Empirical Studies." *Death Studies* 34 (2010) 673–98. https://doi.org/10.1080/07481187.2010.496686.

Lodge, Anne. *But the Lord Looks on the Heart. Part 2. International Voices from the Church of Ireland Parishes of Dublin and Glendalough*. Oct. 2022. https://dublin.anglican.org/cmsfiles/files/But-the-Lord-Looks-on-the-Heart-Part-2-Oct-2022-1.pdf.

———. *But the Lord Looks on the Heart. Report of a 2020 Study of Cultural and Ethnic Diversity in the Parishes of the United Dioceses of Dublin and Glendalough*. Oct. 2020. https://dublin.anglican.org/cmsfiles/files/Cultural--Ethnic-Diversity-Report.pdf.

Lord Tennyson, Alfred. *Maud and Other Poems*. London: Edward Moxon, 1859.

Luscombe, Philip. "Where Is the Minister?" In *What Is a Minister?*, edited by Philip Luscombe and Esther Shreeve, 33-47. Peterborough: Epworth, 2002.

Mabry, Gregory. *The Priest and His Interior Life*. Racine: DeKoven, 1963.

MacDonald, Gordon. *A Resilient Life*. Nashville: Thomas Nelson, 2004.

Macquarrie, John. *The Faith of the People of God: A Lay Theology*. London: SCM, 1972.

Malone, Andrew S. *God's Mediators: A Biblical Theology of Priesthood*. London: Apollos, 2017.

Manual of the Laws and Discipline of the Methodist Church Ireland. 3rd rev. ed. Dublin: Robert T. White, 1900.

Manual of the Laws and Discipline of the Methodist Church in Ireland. Belfast: The Methodist Church of Ireland, 2011.

Manetsch, Scott M. *Calvin's Company of Pastors: Pastoral Care and the Emerging Reformed Church, 1536-1609*. Oxford: Oxford University Press, 2013.

Marcu, Marinel Laurențiu. "The Orthodox Christian Church Fathers Pastoral Counseling and Specific Patristic Pastoral Approaches." *Journal for the Study of Religions and Ideologies* 21 (2022) 81–95.

Marek, Franziska, and Nathalie Oexle. "Supportive and Non-Supportive Social Experiences Following Suicide Loss: A Qualitative Study." *British Medical Council Public Health* 24 (2024) 1190. https://doi.org/10.1186/s12889-024-18545-3.

Marshall, Catherine. *A Man Called Peter*. Wheaton: Evergreen, 1951.

Martin, Francis. *Sacred Scripture: The Disclosure of the Word*. Naples, Florida: Sapientia, 2006.

Martin, Alan. "The Ephesian Moment." MPhil diss., Irish School of Ecumenics, 2003.

Massey, Denise. *Caring: Six Steps for Effective Pastoral Conversations*. Nashville: Abingdon, 2019.

McClure, Barbara. "Pastoral Care." In *The Wiley-Blackwell Companion to Practical Theology*, edited by Bonnie J. Miller-McLemore, 269–78. Oxford: Blackwell, 2012.

McFerran, Louise, and Liz Graveling. *Clergy Wellbeing in a Time of Covid: Autonomy, Accountability and Support*. London: Church of England, 2022.

McGrath, Alister E. "Theology of the Cross." In *Dictionary of Paul and His Letters*, edited by Gerald F. Hawthorne et al., 192–97. Leicester: InterVarsity, 1993.

McKnight, Scot. *Pastor Paul: Nurturing a Culture of Christoformity in the Church*. Grand Rapids: Brazos, 2019.

McMichael, Ralph. "What Does Canterbury Have to Do with Jerusalem: The Vocation of Anglican Theology." In *The Vocation of Anglican Theology*, edited by Ralph McMichael, 1–34. London: SCM, 2014.

McNeill, John T. *A History of the Cure of Souls*. London: SCM, 1952.
McSherry, Wilfred, and Joanna Smith. "Spiritual Care." In *Care in Nursing*, edited by Wilfred McSherry et al., 117–31. Oxford: Oxford University Press, 2012.
Mead, Loren. *The Once and Future Church Collection*. Herdon, VA: The Alban Institute, 2001.
Meadows, Mary. "How to Set SMARTER Goals for the New Year." BA Online, Jan. 7, 2019. https://baonline.org/smart-goals/.
The Methodist Church in Ireland. *Reports and Agenda of the Methodist Conference*. 2006.
The Methodist Church in Ireland. *Reports and Agenda of the Methodist Conference*. 2014.
The Methodist Church in Ireland. *Reports and Agenda of the Methodist Conference*. 2017.
Miller, Harold. *The Desire of Our Soul*. Dublin: Columba, 2004.
Miller, Rachel Green. *Beyond Authority and Submission: Women and Men in Marriage, Church, and Society*. Phillipsburg, NJ: P&R, 2019.
Minutes of Conference of the Methodist Church in Ireland, 1873.
Mitchel, Patrick. "Eschatology." In *The Dictionary of Paul and His Letters: A Compendium of Contemporary Biblical Scholarship*, edited by Scot McKnight et al., 265–79. 2nd ed. London: InterVarsity Academic, 2023.
———. "Love." In *The Dictionary of Paul and His Letters: A Compendium of Contemporary Biblical Scholarship*, edited by Scot McKnight et al., 663–70. 2nd ed. London: InterVarsity Academic, 2023.
———. *The Message of Love: The Only Thing That Counts*. London: InterVarsity, 2019.
———. "The New Perspective and the Christian Life: *Solus Spiritus*." In *The Apostle Paul and the Christian Life: Ethical and Missional Implications of the New Perspective*, edited by Scot McKnight and Joe Modica, 71–102. Grand Rapids: Baker Academic, 2016.
Moberly, Robert C. *Ministerial Priesthood: Chapters on the Rationale of Ministry and the Meaning of Christian Priesthood*. London: John Murray, 1910.
Moltmann, Jürgen. *Theology of Hope*. London: SCM, 2021.
Montgomery, James. "Pour Out Thy Spirit from On High." Hymnary.org. 1833. https://hymnary.org/text/pour_out_thy_spirit_from_on_high.
Moore, Alison. *The Puzzle of Pastoral Care: A Practical Approach*. Buxhall, Stowmarket: Kevin Mayhew, 2019.
Moore, Peter, ed. *Bishops, But What Kind?* London: SPCK, 2015.
Moorhead, John. *Gregory the Great*. London: Routledge, 2005.
Morgan, Patricia. *The Marriage Files*. London: Wilberforce, 2014.
Morris, Leon. *Testaments of Love: A Study of Love in the Bible*. Grand Rapids: Eerdmans, 1981.
Morrison, Richard. "A Year Before and a Year After: Patterns of Support for Couples Being Married in the Route Presbytery." Undergraduate diss., Queen's University Belfast, 2018.
Murray, Judith, and Geoffrey Mitchell. "A Framework for Considering Life-Limiting Illness Across the Life Cycle." In *Palliative Care: A Patient-Centred Approach*, edited by Geoffrey Mitchell, 80–90. Oxford: Radcliffe, 2008.
Murray, Leon. *Being Black in Britain*. London: Chester House, 1995.
Murray, Stuart. *Post-Christendom: Church and Mission in a Strange New World*. Milton Keynes: Paternoster, 2005.

Neimeyer, Robert A., et al. "The Measurement of Grief: Psychometric Considerations in the Assessment of Reactions to Bereavement." In *Handbook of Bereavement Research and Practice: Advances in Theory and Intervention*, edited by Margaret S. Stroebe et al., 133–61. Washington, DC: American Psychological Association, 2008.

New Hope. "John Wesley's Small Group Questions." https://www.newhopefree.org/art-and-poetry/2015/9/28/john-wesleys-small-group-questions.

Newitt, Mark. "Chaplaincy Support to Bereaved Parents—Part 1: Liturgy, Ritual and Pastoral Presence." *Heath and Social Care Centre Health and Social Care Chaplaincy* 2 (2015) 179–94.

Niebuhr, Reinhold. *The Irony of American History*. Chicago: University of Chicago Press, 1952.

Noorani, Salim. "Pastoral Care in a Modern Workplace." LinkedIn. https://www.linkedin.com/pulse/pastoral-care-modern-workplace-salim-noorani.

Northern Ireland Department of Health, Social Services and Public Safety. *Living Matters, Dying Matters: A Palliative and End of Life Care Strategy for Adults in Northern Ireland*. 2010. www.dhsspsni.gov.uk/8555_palliative_final.pdf.

Null, Ashley. *Eastertide: Meditations on the Easter Collects of Thomas Cranmer*. Newport Beach: Anglican House, 2024.

Nuzum, Daniel. "Pastoral care." In *Irish Anglicanism, 1969–2019: Essays to Mark the 150th Anniversary of the Disestablishment of the Church of Ireland*, edited by Ken Milne and Paul Harron. Dublin: Four Courts, 2019.

Nuzum Daniel, et al. "The Impact of Stillbirth on Bereaved Parents: A Qualitative Study." *PLoS One* 13 (2018) e0191635. https://doi.org/10.1371/journal.pone.0191635.

———. "Pregnancy Loss: A Disturbing Silence and Theological Wilderness." In *Modern Believing* 60 (2019) 133–45. https://doi.org/10.3828/mb.2019.12.

O'Connor, Mary-Frances. "Grief: A Brief History of Research on How Body, Mind, and Brain Adapt." In *Biopsychosocial Science and Medicine* 81 (2019) 731–38. https://journals.lww.com/bsam/fulltext/2019/10000/grief__a_brief_history_of_research_on_how_body,.8.aspx.

Oden, Thomas C. *Care of Souls in the Classic Tradition*. Philadelphia: Fortress, 1984.

Oord, Thomas Jay. *Pluriform Love: An Open and Relational Theology of Well Being*. Grasmere: SacraSage, 2022.

Origen. *Homilies on Leviticus: 1–16*. Translated by Gary Wayne Barkley. The Fathers of the Church 83. Washington, DC: The Catholic University of America Press, 1990.

Osmer, Richard R. *Practical Theology: An Introduction*. Grand Rapids: Eerdmans, 2008.

Packer, James I. *Your Father Loves You*. Carol Stream, IL: Harold Shaw, 1987.

Park, Nick. *Ministry to Migrants and Asylum Seekers*. Dublin: Evangelical Alliance, 2015.

Parrott, Les, and Leslie Parrott. *The Complete Guide to Marriage Mentoring: Connecting Couples to Build Better Marriages*. Grand Rapids: Zondervan, 2005.

Parsloe, Eric, and Melville Leedham. *Coaching and Mentoring: Practical Techniques for Developing Learning and Performance*. Edited by Diane Newell. 4th ed. New York, Kogan Page, 2022.

Patterson, Kathleen. "Servant Leadership and love." In *Servant Leadership: Developments in Theory and Research*, edited by Dirk van Dierendonck and Kathleen Patterson, 67–76. Basingstoke: Palgrave Macmillan, 2010.

Patterson, Neil. "Clergy Discipline Is Not About Taking Sides." Church Times, Mar. 5, 2021. https://www.churchtimes.co.uk/articles/2021/5-march/comment/opinion/clergy-discipline-is-not-about-taking-sides.
Pembroke, Neil. *Foundations of Pastoral Counselling*. London: SCM, 2018.
Percy, Martin, ed. *The Study of Ministry: A Comprehensive Survey of Theory and Best Practice*. London: SPCK, 2019.
Petersen, David. G. *Acts of the Apostles*. Nottingham: Apollos, 2009.
Peterson, Eugene H. *The Contemplative Pastor: Returning to the Art of Spiritual Direction*. Grand Rapids: Eerdmans, 1989.
———. *Five Smooth Stones for Pastoral Work*. Grand Rapids: Eerdmans, 1980.
———. *A Long Obedience in the Same Direction*. Downers Grove, IL: InterVarsity, 2021.
———. *The Pastor: A Memoir*. New York: HarperOne, 2011.
———. *Working the Angles: The Shape of Pastoral Integrity*. Grand Rapids: Eerdmans, 1989.
Phillips-Jones, Linda. *Skills for Successful Mentoring: Competencies of Outstanding Mentors and Mentees*. 2003. https://my.lerner.udel.edu/wp-content/uploads/Skills_for_Sucessful_Mentoring.pdf.
Pickard, Stephen. *Theological Foundations for Collaborative Ministry*. Farnham: Ashgate, 2009.
Piper, John. *Desiring God*. Leicester: InterVarsity, 1996.
Pope, Alexander. "An Essay on Criticism." Poetry Foundation. https://www.poetryfoundation.org/articles/69379/an-essay-on-criticism.
Post, Stephen G. *More Lasting Unions: Christianity, the Family and Society*. Grand Rapids: Eerdmans, 2000.
Prime, Derek, J., and Alistair Begg. *On Being a Pastor*. Chicago: Moody, 2004.
Proeschold-Bell, Rae Jean and Jason Byassee. *Faithful and Fractured: Responding to the Clergy Health Crisis*. Grand Rapids: Baker Academic, 2018.
Puchalski, Christina. M., et al. "Improving the Spiritual Dimension of Whole Person Care: Reaching National and International Consensus." *Journal of Palliative Medicine* 17 (2014) 642–56. https://doi.org/10.1089/jpm.2014.9427.
Purves, Andrew. *Pastoral Theology in the Classical Tradition*. Louisville: Westminster John Knox, 2001.
Quinlan, John. *Pastoral Relatedness: The Essence of Pastoral Care*. Lanham, MD: University Press of America, 2002.
Ramsey, Michael. *The Christian Priest Today*. London: SPCK, 1972.
———. *Durham Essays and Addresses*. London: SPCK, 1956.
Rando, Therese A. *Clinical Dimensions of Anticipatory Mourning: Theory and Practice in Working with the Dying, Their Loved Ones, and Their Caregivers*. Champaign, IL: Research, 2000.
Ratzinger, Joseph. *"In the Beginning . . ." A Catholic Understanding of the Story of the Creation and the Fall*. Translated by Boniface Ramsay, O. P. Grand Rapids: Eerdmans, 1995.
Reddrop, Mary, and Bruce Reddrop. *For Better, for Worse: A Guide to Contemporary Marriage Counselling*. London: Harper Collins, 1995.
Rittgers, Ronald K. *The Reformation of Suffering: Pastoral Theology and Lay Piety in Late Medieval and Early Modern Germany*. Oxford Studies in Historical Theology. Oxford: Oxford University Press, 2012.

Roberto, Mark D. "Pastor, Paul As." In *Dictionary of Paul and His Letters: A Compendium of Contemporary Biblical Scholarship*, edited by Scot McKnight et al., 749–55. 2nd ed. London: InterVarsity, 2023.

Rosner, Brian S., et al., eds. "The Household Setting of Paul's Pastoral Practice and its Biblical and Jewish Roots." In *Paul as Pastor*, edited by Brian S. Rosner et al., 1–16. London: T&T Clark, 2018.

———. *Paul as Pastor*. London: T&T Clark, 2018.

Saint Benedict. "The Rule of St. Benedict." Translated by Boniface Verheyen. Christian Classics Ethereal Library. https://ccel.org/ccel/benedict/rule/rule.i.html.

Sallnow, Libby, et al. "Report of the Lancet Commission on the Value of Death: Bringing Death Back into Life." *Lancet* 399 (2022) 837–84. https://doi.org/10.1016/S0140-6736(21)02314-X.

Saunders, Cicely M. *Cicely Saunders: Selected Writings 1958–2004*. Oxford: Oxford University Press, 2012.

Schachtel, Andrew, et al. *Changing Lanes, Crossing Culture*. Sydney: Great Western, 2016.

Scharfenberg, Joachim. "The Babylonic Captivity of Pastoral Theology." *The Journal of Pastoral Care* 8 (1954) 125–34.

Schmemman, Alexander. *The Journals of Father Alexander Schmemman, 1973–1983*. Translated by Julianna Schmemman. Crestwood, NY: St. Vladimir's Seminary Press, 1998.

Schulz, R., et al. "Caregiving and Bereavement." In *Handbook of Bereavement Research and Practice: Advances in Theory Intervention*, edited by M. S. Stroebe et al. Washington, DC: American Psychological Association, 2011.

Scolding KC, Fiona, and Ben Fullbrook. *Independent Review into Soul Survivor*. Sept. 26, 2024. https://static1.squarespace.com/static/547c7dfde4b028a1612a4736/t/66f5374e329e35524f9c0f7c/1727346512153/Soul+Survivor+Review+-+Final+Report+260924.pdf.

Second Vatican Council. *Gaudium et spes*. Pastoral Constitution on the Church in the Modern World. Holy See, 1965. https://www.vatican.va/archive/hist_councils/ii_vatican_council/documents/vat-ii_const_19651207_gaudium-et-spes_en.html.

Senkbeil, Harold L. *The Care of Souls: Cultivating a Pastor's Heart*. Bellingham, WA: Lexham, 2019.

Sistrunk Robinson, Natasha. *Mentor for Life*. Grand Rapids, Zondervan, 2016.

Skoglund, Elizabeth. *Burning Out for God: How to be Used by God Without Being Used Up*. Leicester: InterVarsity, 1988.

Smith, David. *Against the Stream*. London: InterVarsity, 2003.

Smith, Gordon T., *Called to Be Saints: An Invitation to Christian Maturity*. Downers Grove, IL: InterVarsity Academic, 2014.

Standing, Roger, and Paul Goodliff, eds. *Episkope: The Theory and Practice of Translocal Oversight*. London: SCM, 2020.

Stansbury, Ronald. *A Companion to Pastoral Care in the Late Middle Ages (1200–1500)*. Brill's Companions to the Christian Tradition, 22. Leiden: Brill, 2010.

Stedman, Ray C. "Supreme Priority." Ray Stedman Authentic Christianity, Jan. 14, 1979. https://www.raystedman.org/new-testament/1-corinthians/supreme-priority.

Stephens, John. "Developing a Multi-Ethnic Congregation and New Ministries in Dublin's Changing City Center Context." DMin diss., Fuller Theological Seminary, 2004.

Stern, Karl. *The Pillar of Fire: A Modern Psychiatrist's Personal Story of His Life and His Spiritual Voyage to Catholicism*. Garden City, NY: Image, 1959.
Stevens, Margaret. *Preparing Couples for Marriage*. Grove Pastoral Series 28. Bramcote: Grove, 1991.
Stewart, James S. *A Man in Christ*. New York: Harper, 1955.
Stjerna, Kirsi. *Women and the Reformation*. Oxford: Blackwell, 2009.
Stott, John. *God's New Society: The Message of Ephesians*. Leicester: InterVarsity, 1979.
Stroebe, Margaret, and Henk Schut. "The Dual Process Model of Coping with Bereavement: Rationale and Description." *Death Studies* 23 (1999) 197–224.
Sulmasy, Daniel P. "Dignity and the Human as a Natural Kind." In *Health and Human Flourishing: Religion, Medicine and Moral Anthropology*, edited by Carol Taylor and Roberto Dell'Ora, 71–87. Washington DC: Georgetown University Press, 2006.
Taylor and Francis. "Pastoral Care in Education." https://www.tandfonline.com/journals/rped20.
Taylor, John V. *The Go-Between God*. London, SCM, 1975.
"The Teaching of the Twelve Apostles, Commonly Called the Didache." In *Early Christian Fathers*, edited by Cyril C. Richardson, 148–56. Grand Rapids: Christian Classics Ethereal Library. https://www.ccel.org/ccel/r/richardson/fathers/cache/fathers.pdf.
Temple, William. *About Christ*. London: SCM, 1963.
———. *Readings in St. John's Gospel*. London: Macmillan, 1950.
Thatcher, Adrian. *Marriage After Modernity: Christian Marriage in Postmodern Times*. Sheffield: Sheffield Academic, 1999.
Thomas, Columba, OP. "Christ the Physician: A Theological Framework for Healing in Catholic Health Care." *The Linacre Quarterly* 91 (2024) 243–53.
Thomas, Gary. *Sacred Marriage*. Grand Rapids: Zondervan, 2000.
Thompson, James W. *Moral Formation According to Paul: The Context and Coherence of Pauline Ethics*. Grand Rapids: Baker Academic, 2011.
———. *Pastoral Ministry According to Paul: A Biblical Vision*. Grand Rapids: Baker Academic, 2006.
Tilby, Angela. "Angela Tilby: Pastors, Not Persuaders, Are Needed." *Church Times*, June 25, 2021. https://www.churchtimes.co.uk/articles/2021/25-june/comment/columnists/angela-tilby-pastors-not-persuaders-are-needed.
Toman, Gary C. M. "A Critical Examination of the Understanding and Application of the Term 'Dignity' in End-of-Life Care." PhD diss., The Queen's University of Belfast, 2019.
Tomlin, Graham. *The Widening Circle: Priesthood as God's Way of Blessing the World*. London: SPCK, 2014.
Treasure, Julian. "5 Ways to Listen Better." TED Talk, July 29, 2011. 7:50. https://www.youtube.com/watch?v=cSohjlYQI2A&list=PLS5XOICJQYn3cfw2-KqoV5wOfM5zbpK9Y.
United States Catholic Conference. *Health and Healthcare: A Pastoral Letter of the American Bishops*. Washington, DC: United States Catholic Conference, 1981.
Van der Maas, P. J., et al. "Euthanasia and Other Medical Decisions Concerning the End of Life." *Lancet* 338 (1991) 669–74.

Van der Watt, Stéphan. "Wholehearted Commitment to Sound Pastoral Theology and Care: What Martin Bucer and John Calvin Can Teach Today's Pastors." *Calvin Theological Journal* 56 (2021) 231–63.

Vanhoozer, Kevin J., and Owen Strachan. *The Pastor as Public Theologian: Reclaiming a Lost Vision.* Grand Rapids: Baker Academic, 2018.

Village, Andrew, and Leslie Francis. *Coronavirus, Church and You.* York: St. John University, 2020.

———. "Exploring Affect Balance: Psychological Well-Being of Church of England Clergy and Laity During the Covid-19 Pandemic." *Journal of Religion and Health* 60 (2021) 1556–75.

———. "Introducing The Index of Balanced Affect Change (TIBACh): A Study Among Church of England Clergy and Laity." *Mental Health, Religion & Culture* 24 (2021) 770–79.

———. "Wellbeing and Perceptions of Receiving Support Among Church of England Clergy During the 2020 Covid-19 Pandemic." *Mental Health, Religion & Culture* 24 (2021) 463–77.

Wainwright, Geoffrey. *Doxology: The Praise of God in Worship, Doctrine, and Life.* New York: Oxford University Press, 1984.

Walcott, Mackenzie E. C. "An Introduction to the Ordinal." In *The Annotated Book of Common Prayer Being an Historical, Ritual, and Theological Commentary on the Devotional System of The Church of England*, edited by John Henry Blunt, 655–672. London: Longmans, Green, and Co., 1892.

Wells, Samuel. *Improvisation: The Drama of Christian Ethics.* London: SPCK, 2004.

Wesley, John. *The Methodist Societies: History, Nature, and Design.* Vol. 9 of *The Works of John Wesley.* Edited by Rupert E. Davies. Nashville: Abingdon, 1989.

Westcott, Brooke Foss. *Some Thoughts on the Ordinal.* London: Macmillan, 1884.

White, B. G. "Second Letter to the Corinthians." In *The Dictionary of Paul and His Letters: A Compendium of Contemporary Biblical Scholarship*, edited by Scot McKnight et al., 181–194. 2nd ed. London: InterVarsity Academic, 2023.

Whitmore, John. *Coaching for Performance.* London: Nicholas Brearley, 2017.

Wilson, Todd, and Gerlad Hiestand, eds. *Becoming a Pastor Theologian: New Possibilities for Church Leadership.* Center for Pastor Theologians Series. Westmont, IL: InterVarsity Academic, 2016.

Wojtyła, Karol. *Person and Community: Selected Essays.* Translated by Theresa Sandok. Catholic Thought from Lublin, 4. New York: Peter Lang, 1993.

Worden, J. W. *Grief Counselling and Grief Therapy.* 4th ed. New York: Springer, 2009.

Wright, Nigel G. *How to Be a Church Minister.* Abingdon: Bible Reading Fellowship, 2018.

Wright, N. T. *The New Testament and the People of God.* London: SPCK, 1992.

———. *Paul and the Faithfulness of God.* 2 vols. Minneapolis: Fortress, 2013.

Yancey, George. *One Body, One Spirit: Principles of Successful Multiracial Churches.* Downers Grove, IL: InterVarsity, 2003.

Youngson, Michaela A., and Bala Gnanapragasam. *Radical Grace, Transforming Hope: Joining in with God's Longing for a World Transformed by Love.* London: Methodist, 2018.

Yung, Hwa. *Leadership or Servanthood.* Carlisle: Langham, 2021.

Zell, Katarina Schütz. *Church Mother: The Writings of a Protestant Reformer in Sixteenth-Century Germany.* Edited and translated by Elsie McKee. Chicago: University of Chicago Press, 2006.

Name Index

Ainsworth, Mary, 157
Ambrose of Milan, 20
Anderson, David, 251
Ash, Christopher, 117, 122, 131, 132
Ashcroft, Richard, 193n22
Atherstone, Andrew, 102–3
Atkinson, Nigel, 80
Augustine of Hippo, 20

Bailey, Kenneth, 157
Baker, Frank, 214
Barnes, M. Craig, 29
Barr, Beth Alison, 23
Barth, Karl, 57–58, 85, 86, 87
Basil the Great, 30
Baxter, Christina, 278
Baxter, Richard, 27–28, 131
Beaumont, Susan, 146
Begg, Alastair, 4
Bender, Kimlyn J., 62n33
Benedict of Nursia, 20
Benner, David, G., 17
Bernard of Clairvaux, 22
Bicknell, E.J., 83
Birkett, Kirsten, 119, 127, 133
Boisen, Anton, 190–91, 196
Bonhoeffer, Dietrich, 82, 87, 91
Bowlby, John, 157, 203
Brain, Peter, 122
Brock, Darrell, 101–2
Brown, Raymond E., 57n 16
Bruce, F.F., 44
Buber, Martin, 165
Bucer, Martin, 24, 25
Buechner, Frederick, 161

Burnett, Gary, 46
Byassee, Jason, 115, 116, 122, 124

Caldwell, Taylor, 196–97
Calvin, John, 26, 27
Câmara, Hélder, 66
Campbell, Alastair, 1
Campbell, Douglas, 35
Carson, Don, 94 fn5
Carson, Marion, 34, 40, 49
Carter, John, 54
Cathie, Sean, 2
Challis, William, 79–80, 85
Chochinov, Harvey, Max
Chrysostom, John, 18, 20
Clebsch, William A., 17
Climacus, John, 30
Clough, David, 250n34
Costa, Ken, 144
Cranmer, Thomas, 92, 126
Croft, Steven, 136, 146, 218, 221, 222, 223, 225
Crosby, John, 190

Davie, Grace, 257
Davie, Martin, 136
Dentière, Marie, 26
Dix, Gregory, 78, 86
Dunn, James D.G., 34, 41

Fee, Gordon, 56–57
Ford, David, 130
Forward, Martin, 240
Francis of Assisi, 22
Francis, Leslie, 116, 123, 128

300 NAME INDEX

Francis, Pope, 105

Gay, Doug, 4
George, Bill, 142
Gerkin, Charles, 186
Gerson, Jean, 23
Gorman, Michael J., 48n56
Graham, Billy, 65
Graveling, Liz, 117, 125
Green, Laurie, 271
Greenleaf, Robert, 226, 228
Gregory the Great, 19, 137, 278
Gregory of Nazianzus, 30–31
Grumbach, Argula von, 26
Guder, Darrell, 218, 227
Guzman, Dominic (St Dominic), 22

Hauerwas, Stanley, 130
Hays, Richard, 37
Hempton, David, 214
Heywood, David, 127
Hildegard of Bingen, 22
Holland, Tom, 273
Holmes, Anne, 122–23
Hooker, Richard, 80, 83
Hooker, Roger, 244
Howe, Reuel, 181n19
Hunter, James Davison, 57
Hurding, Roger, 16n3
Hurtado, Larry, 41, 48n55

Jaekle, Charles R., 17
Jeffries, Henry A., 22
John of Ravenna, 20
Jones, David, 207

Kahl, Werner, 233, 234
King, Martin Luther, 59–60, 61
Kouzes, James, 124

Lake, Frank, 197
Lamb, Christopher, 244
Lawrence, James, 3n5
Leedham, Melville, 252
Leithart, Peter, 64–65
Lencioni, Patrick, 143
Lenton, John, 215
Leo XIII, Pope, 112

Lewis-Anthony, Justin, 121–22
Lewis, C.S., 6, 52, 54, 88
Lightfoot, J.B., 93n4
Lodge, Anne, 239n15
Luscombe, Philip, 224
Luther, Martin, 3
Luther, Katherine, 26

Mabry, Gregory, 123
MacDonald, Gordon, 147
Marcu, Marinel, 30
Marshall, Catherine, 121
Marshall, Peter, 121
Massey, Denise, 184
McCheyne, Robert Murray, 119
McGrath, Alister, 89
McKnight, Scot, 33, 40
McMichael, Ralph, 76
McNeill, John T., 15n2, 24
Mead, Loren, 218, 219, 220, 224
Moltmann, Jürgen, 178n15
Montgomery, James, 108
Moore, Alison, 182
Murray, Leon, 237
Murray, Stuart, 218

Niebuhr, Reinhold, 132
Null, Ashley, 11

Oden, Thomas, 17
Origen, 189

Packer, J.I., 63
Parsloe, Eric, 252
Patterson, Kathleen, 228–29
Peterson, David, 233–34
Peterson, Eugene, 49, 50, 73, 84, 85, 258
Phillips-Jones, Linda, 256, 268
Pickard, Stephen, 125, 129
Piper, John, 131
Pope, Alexander, 179n16
Posner, Barry, 124
Prime, Derek, 4
Proeschold, Rae Jean, 115, 116, 122, 124

Quinlan, John, 206

Ramsey, Michael, 6, 73, 76, 77, 78, 79, 81, 124, 131
Ratzinger, Joseph, 274
Richmond, Helen, 236
Rittgers, Ronald K., 23
Rosner, Brian, 33

Saunders, Cicely, 199
Schachtel, Andrew, 238, 248
Schmemman, Alexander, 67
Simeon the New Theologian, 30
Smith, David, 243
Smith, Gordon T., 58–59, 67
Stark, Rodney, 18
Stedman, Ray, 60–61
Stern, Karl, 197
Stewart, James S., 55n9
Stott, John, 101

Taylor, Charles, 281

Taylor, Jeremy, 102
Taylor, John V., 267
Temple, William, 77, 86–87
Tennyson, Alfred Lord, 51, 54, 69
Thompson, James, 34
Tilby, Angela, 121
Tomlin, Graham, 76, 84

Wainwright, Geoffrey, 64
Wesley, John, 4, 9, 212, 213, 214, 230
Wells, Sam, 153
Wojtyla, Karol (John Paul II), 65
Worden, J.W., 208
Wright, Nigel, 229
Wright, N.T., 34, 153

Yancey, Philip, 249n32
Yung, Hwa, 226, 227

Zell, Katarina Schutz, 26

Subject Index

"actualization", 54
addictive behaviour, 177
Alpha Course, 257
Anglican Consultative Council, 254
Anglicanism
    as one expression among many of the one, holy catholic and apostolic church, 111–12
Anglican Methodist Commission for Unity (AMICUM), 97
Anglican ministry
    essentials of, 73
    understanding of the pastoral task of, 74–77
    the minister as exemplar to the flock in, 104–5
    as inherently hierarchical, 139
Anglican Ordinal, 92–113, 114, 277
Apostolicae curae, 112
Archbishops' Council, 254
A Secular Age, 281
Attachment Theory, 157–59, 203–4
authenticity, 163–64

bands (Methodist), 215
bereavement
    the impact of bereavement, 202–3, 204–5
    and attachment, 203–4
    and pastoral response to grief, 205–6
    and role of ritual, 207–9
    and post-bereavement care,

Berkeley Statement of the International Anglican Liturgical Commission, 101
Bible
    as truth, 77
    and reason, 80–82
    and tradition, 82–85
    as Scripture, 85–87
    new world of the, 87–88
bishops, 92, 95, 96, 103, 104, 107
Book of Common Prayer, 75, 92, 93, 155, 156
"buffered self" (the), 281
burnout, 120–22
busyness, 277–78

calling, 76–77, 97–98, 99–101, 227–28, 281
Chicago-Lambeth Quadrilateral, 112
Christoformity, 38–39, 40, 49, 274
Christ's ministry
    as Shepherd, 129–30
    as Servant, 88, 112–13, 130–31
    as Steward, Sentinel and Messenger, 132–33
    as Alpha and Omega, 132
churchwardens, 126
Clinical Pastoral Education (CPE), 190
Christendom, 218–19
church decline, 218–19
Church of England, 263
collegial ministry, 40, 118
COVID 19 pandemic, 117, 205–6

community formation, 34, 35, 56–57
collaborative leadership, 125, 225–27
collaborative ministry, 212, 221–25
confession (the), 155
coping strategies, 122–23
"Creation and Fall", 274
cross (the), 87–91, 233–34
cure of souls (*cura animarum*), 20, 24, 31, 87, 97

dangers of the teaching ministry, 110–11
deacons, 92, 93, 97, 99–100, 104–5, 109
definition of pastoral care, 15–16
Didache, 18, 19
Dignitas infinitas, 191–92
discipleship, 1, 18, 84, 118–19
discipline within the church, 106–8, 125
Dominion, 273
Dublin Central Misssion, 232
Durham Essays, 73

emotional intelligence, 127
episcopal role, 135–38
eternal salvation, 103
Ethiopian eunuch, 82
evangelism, 25, 109–10
every member ministry, 50

forgiveness, 60
female pastoral ministry, 26, 50
Fourth Lateran Council, 21, 23

Gaudium et spes, 191
General Confession, 51–52
giving, 43–44, 62–63
goal of pastoral ministry, 24, 25, 38–39, 40, 47, 48, 52, 54, 68
Good Friday Peace Agreement, 156

hatred of enemies, 59
healthcare ministry
    and the experience of a chaplain, 188
    and "seeing as Jesus wants us to see," 189
    and the patient as a unique and unrepeatable human being, 190
    and community, 194–96
Hebridean Revival, 57
home visitation, 26
house blessing, 159
human dignity, 187, 189, 190, 191, 192–94

Ignatian spirituality 161–62
image of Christ (*imago Dei*), 53, 58, 78, 192, 274–75, 279
immigration, 232–33, 239–40, 245–47
improvisation, 153–54, 164–65
integration of diverse communities, 279
interpretive guides, 186
Irish Hospice Foundation, 204

Jesus
    as Divine Healer, 187
    as Savior, 188
    as Physician, 189
joy, 67–68, 124–25

kavod, 192

lay ministry, 280
"laying on of hands", 95, 98–99
Lay Reader, 253
leadership, 140–41, 228–29
Liber Regulae Pastoralis, 20
Litany, 104
"little Christs", 52–53
loneliness (in episcopal ministry), 143–45
loving God and neighbour, 1, 44–47, 59–60, 229–30

marriage
    and impediment to ordination, 99
    as covenant, 168, 169
    cultural influence on, 168
    as a contract, 169

SUBJECT INDEX

marriage
    alternative patterns to, 169, 170
    intercultural marriages, 169–70
    and the development of healthy habits, 173
    care for children, 174–75
    and church commitments, 174
    and preventative care, 176
    general principles for pastoral care in, 172–77, 180–82
    breakdown, 177–79
marriage preparation, 175–76, 278–79
maturity, 53–58
Melchizedek, 90
mentoring/coaching
    definition of, 252
    in the workplace, 255–56
    in a Christian context, 256–59
    and volunteers, 262–63
    and inappropriate behaviour, 265–67
    and the Holy Spirit, 267–71
    and the importance of a mentor figure, 278
messianic eschatology, 35–37, 41, 42, 43, 47–48
metaphors of pastoral ministry, 117–18
Methodism in Ireland, 213–17, 221–25
Mind Matters, 126
monasticism, 19
Moravians, 214

narrative of Nathan and King David, 151–52

ordination, 97–99

pastoralia, 74
pastor as shepherd, 1–2, 11, 16–17, 88, 94–95, 96
pastoral care
    of the dying in the early church, 23
    via the church community, 28–29, 50
    as a ministry of presence, 106
    as a ministry of prayer, 108
    as a ministry of seeking the weak and vulnerable, 109
    and culture, 163
    in a multi-cultural context, 247–51
    as a secular value, 273
    and modern psychology, 278
pastoral competence, 3–5
pastor pastorum, 137–47
pastoral visiting, 26, 151–67
pastor-teacher
    loves of the, 77–79
    challenges to the ministry of the, 79–85, 90
    always a combined ministry, 101–4
    the centrality of the, 103, 275–76
people of God, 56, 96
post-Christian West, 273, 281
pre-Constantinian church, 18
priests/presbyters, 92, 93, 94, 95, 96, 100, 106

Quakers, 214

racism, 235
reason, 80–82
rediscovery of Paul as "pastor," 32–34
Reformed expressions of pastoral care, 24–28
Reformed Pastor (The), 27–28
resilience in pastoral ministry, 117–26
RCN (Royal College of Nursing), 193
Rule of Benedict, 20

sacerdotal priesthood, 93
sacramental healing, 22
safety in a pastoral setting, 163
Scylla and Charybdis, 74
sensus plenior interpretation of Scripture, 57
self-care, 114, 119–20

service/servanthood, 62–63, 112–13, 186
sexual ethics in Paul, 41, 49
SMART analysis, 184
social holiness, 66-67
solitude, 55
Spirit of God (Holy Spirit), 54–55, 86, 87, 100, 267–71
spiritual discipline/s, 55, 56, 118–19
St Beuno's, 55
suffering, 21–22, 24, 25

"Tasks of Mourning," 208
The Marriage Course, 175
The Lord's Supper, 279
theological reflection, 74, 127–28, 182–83
The Ruthless Elimination of Hurry, 277
Thirty-Nine Articles, 83
tradition, 82–85
training, 81–82, 127–28
Trinity (the), 57, 58, 61

union with Christ, 56, 60
unity within the Church, 63–65, 233
utilitarian view of the human person, 274

valley of Baka, 166
violent behaviour, 177

workload, 114–17, 142–43

www.ingramcontent.com/pod-product-compliance
Lightning Source LLC
Chambersburg PA
CBHW061429300426
44114CB00014B/1609